SUCCESSFUL PACKAGED SOFTWARE IMPLEMENTATION

SUCCESSFUL PACKAGED SOFTWARE IMPLEMENTATION

Christine B. Tayntor

Auerbach Publications
Taylor & Francis Group
Boca Raton   New York

Published in 2006 by
Auerbach Publications
Taylor & Francis Group
6000 Broken Sound Parkway NW, Suite 300
Boca Raton, FL 33487-2742

International Standard Book Number-10: 0-8493-3410-1 (Hardcover)
International Standard Book Number-13: 978-0-8493-3410-8 (Hardcover)
Library of Congress Card Number 2005048304

Library of Congress Cataloging-in-Publication Data

Tayntor, Christine B.
  Successful packaged software implementation / by Christine B. Tayntor.
      p. cm.
  Includes bibliographical references and index.
  ISBN 0-8493-3410-1 (alk. paper)
  1. Computer software--Development. 2. Information technology. I. Title.

QA76.76.D47T396 2005
005.1--dc22   2005048304

Dedication

For my brother, William A. Bailey, Sr., a man of many talents.

Contents

SECTION II: The Selection Process

SECTION III: Legal Issues — Contracts and Software Licenses

Section V: Implementation

List of Exhibits

The Author

With over 30 years of experience in information technology (IT), **Christine B. Tayntor** has worked in the life insurance, banking, and manufacturing industries as well as having worked as a consultant. Her experience includes implementing and maintaining packaged software, negotiating IT contracts, and outsourcing both software development and support. The author of Auerbach's *Six Sigma Software Development*, she is also a frequent contributor to technical publications and a speaker at various conferences.

PLANNING

1

Concerned by the high cost (in terms of both dollars and time) of developing systems in-house and the even greater cost of having to maintain those systems, many companies have come to rely on packaged software. Unfortunately, some packaged software implementation projects are undertaken with unrealistic expectations and minimal understanding of the tasks needed to make them successful. Despite the fact that many implementations are less successful than originally anticipated, the trend toward buying rather than building software shows no signs of abating. This book is designed to help companies increase their chances of success and prevent the enthusiasm that normally accompanies a major project's initiation from turning into disillusionment.

Careful planning is the first step toward achieving success. Chapter 1 helps companies assess whether or not packaged software is the correct solution to their problems, and Chapter 2 outlines the first steps that they should take once they have decided to proceed.

Chapter 1

Getting Started

The Packaged Software Dilemma

Whether it is called shrink-wrapped software or given an acronym like COTS (commercial off the shelf), there is no doubt that the use of packaged software is an important part of most information technology (IT) departments' application development strategy. Companies have embraced the concept of vendor-supplied software, promising senior management that a COTS solution will prevent the problems frequently associated with custom development and give them a better product cheaper and faster.

Companies enter into the project with high expectations, and in many cases those expectations are met — at least partially. In other cases, the projects are such spectacular failures that careers are destroyed and a company's credibility is reduced. The purpose of this book is to help guide the IT department through the selection and implementation of packaged software, pointing out potential pitfalls and ways to avoid them. Although there is no way to guarantee successful implementation, following proven procedures will increase the probability of success.

Expectations

It is important to understand why companies embark on packaged software implementation projects. Although there may be ancillary reasons, the primary expectations are normally the following:

- *Reduced cost.* It is typically less expensive to license packaged software than to develop a system in-house. Not only does the initial outlay cost less than custom system development, but the ongoing support costs, what have been described as the portion of the iceberg beneath the surface, are lower than for in-house systems. It should be noted that the cost of actually developing the packaged software is normally greater than a single custom development project. However, because the vendor expects to license the software to many companies, it need recoup only a portion of its development costs from any one customer. Similarly, the costs of support and upgrades, commonly classified as "maintenance," are spread among many customers.
- *Shorter implementation schedule.* Because substantial portions of the software development life cycle (SDLC) have been completed by the vendor, the time to implement software is normally less than for custom development. Exhibit 1-1 shows a traditional SDLC model, sometimes referred to as the "waterfall" model. With the use of a COTS solution, system design, construction, and large portions of system analysis, testing and quality assurance become the vendor's responsibility. Exhibit 1-2 illustrates the changes to the SDLC phases in a COTS project.
- *Lower risk.* Custom development is rife with risks, among them schedule and budget overruns and delivery of incomplete or inaccurate functionality. Use of packaged software that is a proven commodity helps reduce those risks because the majority of the development is complete and the functionality that is included has been defined, allowing the company to understand exactly what will be — and what will not be — delivered.

The Horror Stories

Unfortunately, although a COTS solution can — and in many cases does — achieve those expectations, there are numerous examples of failed software implementation. In some cases, the software is referred to as "shelfware" because it remains on someone's bookshelf rather than being installed and used. In other cases, major cost and schedule overruns caused the project to be aborted. In still others, although the software is installed and in use, the cost savings that drove the project were never realized.

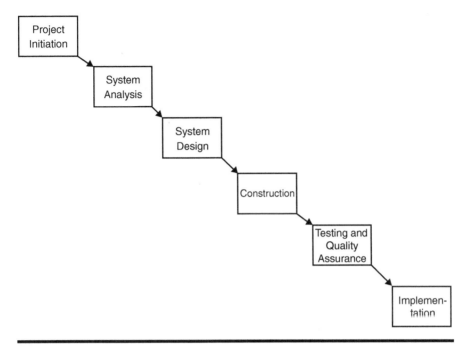

Exhibit 1-1   Traditional System Development Life Cycle (Waterfall)

Exhibit 1-2   Changes to SDLC Phases during a COTS Implementation

Standard Waterfall SDLC Phase	COTS Implementation
Project initiation	Very few changes; issuing an RFI or RFP may occur during this stage.
System analysis	Very few changes; detailed requirements are still needed.
System design	Streamlined, because design documents will be needed only for configuration, interfaces, data conversion modules, and any customizations.
Construction	Streamlined, because only interfaces, data conversion modules, and customizations will be constructed.
Testing and quality assurance	Streamlined, because unit and system testing can be eliminated for the majority of the system. Integration, stress, and acceptance testing are still required.
Implementation	Slightly streamlined, because vendor may provide basic training materials and customer documentation.

The problems companies experience with packaged software implementation include the following:

- *Increased cost.* In some cases, cost overruns are caused by unrealistic budgets. Dimitris Chorafas states, "Studies that have focused on the cost effectiveness of ERP [enterprise resource planning] implementation suggest that to make the system work in their applications environment, user organizations spend 200 to 800 percent more than they paid for their off-the-shelf software."[1] If the project budget includes only the software license, it is obvious that there will be cost overruns. In other cases, the software costs more than in-house development because it includes functionality that will never be used. This is analogous to car buyers selecting a Mercedes because they were impressed with the global positioning system (GPS), when the reality is that the car will be driven only within the small town that the driver knows very well. In this case, a Hyundai would have met the buyer's true needs at a substantially lower cost.
- *Longer implementation schedule.* Schedule overruns may be the result of unrealistic schedules; that is, the failure to include all tasks (similar to the unrealistic budgets described above) or failure to include contingencies. Problems do occur in projects. Overruns may also be the result of selecting the wrong product, either one that was not completely tested or one that does not meet all the end user's requirements.
- *Unused software.* Even after the software is installed, end users may refuse to use it. Although there may be a number of reasons for this end-user rebellion, the most likely is that requirements were not understood.

The Decision

Faced with these apparent contradictions, what should a company do? The answer is, approach packaged software implementation carefully, understanding that it is neither a panacea nor an opportunity to abdicate responsibility to the vendor. This book is designed to assist in the decision-making process. But first, a few definitions and explanations.

Types of Software

IT departments typically acquire three classes of packaged software:

- *System software*, the tools that make servers and PCs work, including operating systems and software distribution tools
- *Applications software*, the systems that perform business functions such as accounting, payroll, and human resources as well as enterprisewide software such as ERP
- *Productivity tools*, which are often called "shrink-wrapped software." This last category includes word processing, spreadsheets, presentation software, and personal databases, as well as Internet browsers and e-mail clients.

Although this book focuses primarily on the issues associated with acquiring, installing, and implementing applications software, because that is the most complex category of software from an IT manager's view, it also has applicability to shrink-wrapped and system software.

Target Audience

Although the primary audience for this book is the IT department, with chapters that will be helpful for everyone from the department manager who needs to sell the solution to senior management to the project manager whose career depends on successfully implementing the package, this book will also be of assistance to those individuals within the procurement department who are responsible for negotiating license agreements and ensuring that the company obtains the greatest value for its software dollars.

Implementation versus Installation

This book makes a distinction between installing software and implementing it. It is relatively easy to install packaged software. Open the box, insert the compact disk (CD), run the installation program, test the results. Although that is obviously an oversimplification, throughout this book installing software is defined as the process of loading vanilla software onto a computer. Implementation, on the other hand, encompasses the entire project, from determining requirements to selecting the correct software to modifying it, if needed; training end users; and ensuring that the results meet expectations. The entire SDLC is included, as well as several steps that are not always included in a development life cycle.

Is Packaged Software the Answer?

The first step in ensuring successful project software is to make an honest assessment of whether packaged software is the correct solution. As noted above, packaged software, although a powerful tool in the IT manager's arsenal, is not a panacea. There are problems a COTS package cannot solve and situations where packaged software is the wrong choice for one company, whereas it may be the ideal solution for another.

The following questions should be answered before initiating a COTS-based project. If the answer to any one of them is a resounding "no," the project's chances of success are diminished. Exhibit 1-3 provides a checklist, summarizing these questions.

1. *Is the business application to be automated a standard one that is used across one or more industries?* Software vendors are not philanthropic institutions; they want to make a profit. As a result, the software that they develop is designed to meet the needs of many companies. Although most vendors provide for individual company customization, the COTS applications that they develop address business functions that are common across more than one company. This allows them to spread the cost of developing the software among multiple customers and results, at least in theory, in a lower cost for each company than custom development. Payroll, human resource-related applications such as benefits calculations and vacation tracking, general ledger and other financial applications, and ERP are examples of applications for which a number of COTS packages exist. On the other hand, if the application is unique to a specific company, either because the functionality provides a competitive advantage to the company or because past practices have resulted in nonstandard processes, it is not a good candidate for packaged software. An example of a competitive advantage application is project tracking that includes

Exhibit 1-3   Initial Assessment Checklist

✓	Criteria
	Standard business application
	Champion
	Funding/budget
	Documented business processes
	Willingness to change
	Packaged implementation experience

proprietary tools. Nonstandard processes include pension calculations for a company that has several dozen plans, each with exceptions. In these cases, acquiring a COTS package and attempting to tailor it to the company may be more costly and time-consuming than developing a custom application.

2. *Does the project have a champion?* Whether it is called a sponsor or a champion, it is essential to have someone at the senior management level who not only is in favor of the project, but who also will break down the barriers that inevitably occur. Ideally this person should be the head of the end-user department for which the system is being developed because that person has the most to gain from the project's success. The role and characteristics of champions are discussed in more detail in Chapter 11.

3. *Is the project funded?* Although it may seem obvious, there is little point in initiating a project that is not funded. Final funding typically occurs after the software package is selected and the final project plan is developed, but it is important to secure a budget commitment before beginning the software selection process. It is also important to ensure that the budget can be carried from one fiscal year to the next should the project extend into future years or should the schedule slip.

4. *Are the business processes that will be automated clearly understood and documented?* An adage says, "If you don't know where you're going, any road will take you there." The software equivalent is less positive: "If you don't know what it is you're automating, no system will help." One of the major causes of failure in custom software development is incomplete or incorrect requirements. This is also true for packaged software implementation. Understanding in detail the processes that the system is expected to automate is critical to selecting the correct package and ensuring that end users will be satisfied with the result. As noted above, although most vendors provide for some customization of their software, substantial modifications are costly in terms of both budget and time and may, in some cases, be impossible.

5. *Is the end-user department willing to change?* A COTS solution, by definition, is designed to meet common needs. Although systems are typically designed in consultation with a number of different companies and will reflect functionality that is common across many companies, the processes for using that functionality may not match those of an individual company. If the end-user department is so wedded to its existing processes that it will not consider changing them, packaged software may not be the correct solution.

Modifying software to match a process can be expensive and, as noted above, sometimes impossible.

6. *Does IT have experience implementing packaged software, or is it willing to hire that expertise?* Although there is some commonality with custom software development, implementing packaged software — particularly an enterprisewide system — presents different challenges. Many of those are described in this book along with solutions to the challenges. For large, multiyear projects, it is, however, important to recognize that specialized assistance may be required. Options for acquiring that assistance are discussed in Chapter 11.

Criteria for Success

Every IT project has critical success factors (CSFs), and the majority of them apply to packaged software implementation. In addition, however, there are two overriding criteria that must be present if the implementation of a COTS solution is to be successful: realistic expectations and organizational flexibility.

Realistic Expectations

It is essential that everyone associated with the project, from the champion and the members of senior management who approve the budget to the members of the IT department who will be developing interfaces and conversion programs to the end users whose jobs will be impacted by the new system, understand what is involved, what the system will do, what it will not do, how long it will take to implement, and what the costs and expected benefits are.

As noted above, implementing a COTS solution is more complex than simply installing software. At the simplest level, that means that the project will require funding beyond the cost of licensing and a longer schedule than that shown in many vendors' sales presentations. Chapter 12 discusses methods for calculating the total cost of the project and developing realistic schedules. Once those are complete, the first task is to sell the complete project plan to senior management. Suggestions for developing a winning presentation are also included in Chapter 12. But gaining senior management approval is only the first step. It is also essential to gain, if not the approval, at least the understanding of everyone who will be impacted by the project. Chapter 13 outlines techniques for effectively communicating project plans and objectives to all affected parties and for understanding and dealing with the potentially negative effects that may accompany change.

Organizational Flexibility

As noted above, the implementation of COTS solutions frequently requires organizations to change their underlying business processes. If a company is not willing to do this, it should anticipate a more difficult, more expensive, and longer project and should consider alternative approaches.

Even when the company as a whole embraces change, it is possible that some employees will not do so and may attempt to sabotage the project to avoid having to change their way of working. Chapter 13 discusses the psychology of change and suggests ways to gain end-user buy-in.

When asked what made their projects successful, some managers quote the five Ps: Prior Planning Prevents Poor Performance. There is no doubt that planning is essential, because it forms the foundation for the project. But successful execution of that plan is also needed. The remainder of this book is designed to assist in developing the plan as well as to provide suggestions for techniques that will help ensure successful execution.

Reference

1. Chorafas, Dimitris N., *Integrating ERP, CRM, Supply Chain Management and Smart Materials.* Auerbach Publications, Boca Raton, FL, 2001, p. 10.

Chapter 2

The First Steps

Once the company has completed its initial assessment and determined that the problem to be solved appears to be a good candidate for a commercial off-the-shelf (COTS) solution, the project is ready for its kickoff. At this point, there should be a champion and at least a verbal commitment for funding. The company is now prepared to begin the product selection process.

The Need for a Formal Selection Process

Although it is possible to select packaged software based on (1) a sales presentation, (2) another company's experience with the system, or (3) the fact that the company already uses other products from that vendor, a formal selection process, outlining specific requirements and evaluating the ability of a number of products to meet those requirements, will increase the probability of project success. It should be noted that although this process is used most frequently for application software, it can also be applied to the selection of system software and productivity tools.

There are five major steps in the selection process:

1. Form the selection team.
2. Identify and prioritize requirements.
3. Identify potential products.
4. Evaluate the products.
5. Evaluate the vendors.

Each of these steps consists of a series of substeps or tasks. It should be noted that although the first three steps are normally performed sequentially, it is possible — and frequently desirable — to conduct the product and vendor evaluations (Steps 4 and 5) in parallel.

Because it is part of the initial planning stages, Step 1 is described in this chapter. Steps 2 and 3 are reviewed in Chapter 3, and Steps 4 and 5 are outlined in Chapter 5.

Step 1: Form the Selection Team

Although team formation is listed as the first major task, there is actually a step that should precede it, namely project definition. It is important that both the team and those individuals who will approve the project understand what is being undertaken and why. Although the format will vary, project definition should include what journalists refer to as the five Ws: who, what, where, when, and why. These elements of any good news story apply equally to a project definition.

The Project Charter

As part of the project definition process, some companies establish formal project charters similar to the one shown in Exhibit 2-1. The purpose of the charter, which is created when the project is initiated and updated periodically throughout the project's life cycle, is to provide a summary of the project, including the problem to be resolved, the high-level schedule, and estimated benefits. In addition to periodic updates of milestones met, the charter will be updated at the conclusion of the project with the actual benefits achieved. Appendix B provides step-by-step instructions for completing a project charter.

In some cases, a project charter is developed for an entire packaged software implementation project, beginning with product selection and continuing through implementation. In other cases, product selection is treated as a separate project. The format and purpose are the same, regardless of the scope of the project.

Whether it is called a project summary or charter, the information is important to the company, and there are multiple benefits to having that information captured in a formal document. Among these benefits are the three Cs: clarity, commitment, and conciseness.

Clarity

The simple act of putting thoughts into writing encourages the author to clarify those thoughts. Although all sections of the charter require clarity, the description of the project, which includes a definition of the problem to be resolved, is the most critical at this point of the project. It is essential that the team, when it is formed, understand what they are expected to accomplish. The team is not simply selecting a software package. They are selecting a software package that is expected to accomplish very specific goals or resolve specific problems. For some companies, this definition is referred to as a problem statement.

Recognizing the importance of clarity, some companies use the Specific, Measurable, Attainable, Relevant, and Timebound (SMART) criteria to evaluate whether or not the problem statement is clear. Because SMART criteria are relevant at various stages of the project, they are explained in some detail here, using as an example the proposed problem statement, "Revenues are decreasing. It is necessary to increase them." Although the problem and solution may appear to be clear as written, it will be difficult to determine whether or not the project has met its objectives because the statement is not SMART. Exhibit 2-2 uses this problem statement to provide a further definition of SMART.

Commitment

Motivational speakers frequently tell their audiences that the first step in turning a dream into reality is to put it in writing, changing the words "I want to" into "I will." Together, the act of writing and the positive verb transform a wish into a goal. The second step toward achieving a goal is to post the sheet of paper where it will be seen regularly, focusing attention on the goal and making it more difficult to ignore. Writing and focusing are the first steps toward commitment.

The written format of the project charter encourages commitment in three areas: planned benefits, schedule, and team membership. At this point in the project, benefits may not be fully quantified and the schedule may be rudimentary. The "Team Membership" section, however, can and should be completed.

Selection of team members is discussed below. The charter simply documents the decisions. The "Name" and "Department" columns are self-explanatory. "Role" refers not to team members' day-to-day responsibilities in their home departments but to the functions they will perform on this team. Typical roles are shown in Exhibit 2-3. It is important that roles be clearly understood so that there is no vying for power between the designated team leader and other team members and so that members understand that their roles are participatory, that they are not serving as advisors.

Exhibit 2-1 Project Charter

Summary

Project description (problem to be solved)			
Start date		Target completion date	
Departments impacted		Processes impacted	
Estimated cost		Estimated ROI	
Team leader		Champion	

Benefits

	Units	Current	Goal	Projected date for achievement/Actual achievement date	Actual achieved
Cost reduction					
Cost avoidance					
Improved customer satisfaction					
Other end-user benefits					

Team Membership

Name	Role	Department	Percent time

Schedule

Milestone/ Deliverable	Target date/Actual completion date	Owner	Estimated cost	Comments

Support Required

Training required	
Other support required	
Critical success factors and risks	
Factors	
Risks	

Approvals

Role/Title	Name	Date

Authors	Date

Revision history

Revision number	

Exhibit 2-2   The SMART Criteria

Original problem statement: Revenues are decreasing. It is necessary to increase them.

Characteristic	Explanation
Specific	*The problem must be quantified.* "Decreasing revenues" is not specific and does not provide any context for the proposed improvement. Were revenues decreasing in all regions? By how much? Were specific products' revenues increasing while others were decreasing? Similarly, the proposed resolution must be quantified.
Measurable	*The problem and its proposed resolution must be able to be measured.* In this example, it is possible to determine whether or not revenues have increased, so this portion of SMART has been met with the original problem statement.
Attainable	*The goal must be realistic.* In the original problem statement, the goal was not specific and, thus, was not truly attainable. It is important both to quantify the goal and to ensure that it can be met. Establishing an overly optimistic goal, one that everyone knows cannot be met, has the effect of discouraging the project team. If failure is guaranteed, why try?
Relevant	*The problem and proposed resolution must be of importance to the end user.* Airlines report on-time departure, defined as the moment that the cabin door is closed. Frequent flyers will tell you that that measure has little relation to what matters to them: on-time arrival. They would argue that the on-time departure metric has little relevance to them. In the original problem statement, it is likely that increased revenues are relevant to at least some of the end users of the proposed system. This portion of SMART was met.
Timebound	*The timeframe for resolution must be specified.* When will revenues be increased? This year or in 20 years? The original problem statement was open-ended, which meant that the results could not be measured, and it was impossible to determine whether the goal was relevant. Increased revenues in the distant future might be of no importance to the end user, because it could be argued that if revenues continued to decline for a substantial period, the company might no longer be in existence.

(continued)

Exhibit 2-2 (continued)   The SMART Criteria

A SMARTer problem statement: To increase clarity and to meet all SMART criteria, the problem statement could be rewritten as, "Nonseasonal item revenues in Region 1 have decreased by three percent for each of the last four years. The objective of the project is to have level revenues in Year 1, with increases of two percent in each of the next four years."

Characteristic	How Satisfied
Specific	The problem and goal are defined in enough detail that there is no ambiguity. Only nonseasonal sales in Region 1 are the target of the project.
Measurable	Because there is a baseline and clearly stated goals, it is possible to measure achievements.
Attainable	The percentage improvement goals appear reasonable and attainable.
Relevant	Sales are relevant to the company.
Timebound	The inclusion of timeframes for the improvement make this statement timebound.

Exhibit 2-3   Team Members

Role	Explanation
Team leader	Has overall responsibility for the success of the project team's efforts; typically serves as spokesperson for the team. Each project should have only one team leader.
Team member	An active participant in all team activities. Team members may have specific responsibilities, such as serving as scribes or timekeepers at meetings. These are in addition to their overall responsibilities as members of the team.
Advisor (optional)	Provides expertise in one or more areas; is not normally a voting member of the team.
Facilitator (optional)	May lead meetings and requirements-gathering sessions; like the advisor, is not normally a voting member of the team.

Next to role, time commitment (the "Percent time" column) is the most important element of the "Team Member" section. It is critical that each team member understand the expectations. Although some members may be fully dedicated to the project, others may be part-time participants. As part of the commitment-gathering step, the person who forms the team — normally the champion or team leader — should obtain the approval of each proposed team member's supervisor that the person can spend that percentage of time on the project. This should be done prior to inviting members to join the team. At the point that team members are invited, they should be informed of the time commitment expectation and the fact that their managers have approved this level of participation.

Conciseness

The simple tabular form of the project charter encourages the author to be concise. Because it is likely that a large COTS implementation project will span multiple years and generate reams of paper, having a summary document that can be easily referenced and understood by all levels of the organization helps keep everyone focused and adds to the probability of success.

Team Selection

There are two steps to selecting a team. The first is to determine its overall characteristics. The second is to choose the individuals who will comprise the team. The first step is discussed below. Exhibit 2-4 provides guidance for the selection of individual team members.

When defining a team's characteristics, there are three primary considerations: composition, size, and continuity.

Composition

Although some companies perform software selection using only members of an information technology (IT) department, if the project is to succeed, it is essential to include representatives of the end-user departments that will be affected. The reasons are twofold. First, the two groups provide different perspectives, both of which are required if the COTS solution is to meet the company's needs.

- *Functional.* The primary concern of end users is functionality. Their presence on the team helps ensure that the software selected

Exhibit 2-4   Characteristics of Effective Team Members

- *Objectivity.* Although personal preferences are a fact of life, it is essential that team members be able to evaluate software products based on their ability to meet the company's requirements.
- *Commitment.* The individual must believe in the project and be willing to do "whatever it takes" to make it successful. A member of the IT department who feels strongly that all software development should be done in-house or an end user who does not want to change the status quo may try to undermine the project. Neither is a good choice for the selection team.
- *Bias for action.* The team member must have a sense of urgency and feel compelled to finish the project successfully.
- *Flexibility.* Because implementation of packaged software frequently requires process changes, each team member must not only be able to adapt to change, but must also embrace the concept of change.
- *Personal influence.* Because the team will become agents of change and will serve as their departments' representatives on the project, it is highly desirable for all members to be well respected within their own communities so that their decisions have credibility and are supported by the department.
- *Teamwork.* No matter how creative and committed individuals may be, unless they can work successfully as part of a team, they should not be part of the core team. Key "individual contributors" who lack cooperative and collaborative skills may be called on to provide expertise at various stages of the project but should not be part of the core team.
- *Available time.* Individuals who are close to burnout because of a too-heavy workload should not be chosen for the team. Not only will they not be effective, but they may also create dissension within the team by missing meetings or failing to deliver on commitments.

will satisfy their requirements. Although the IT department may understand the basic needs, only the people who are actually doing the job can fully describe the problems they encounter.

- *Technical.* Even the most functionally complete software is of no value if it cannot run on the company's infrastructure or if the company is incapable of supporting it after it is installed. One of the key reasons for including the IT department on the team is to ensure that technical requirements are considered and met.

Just as important as their functional knowledge, end users need to be part of the solution to provide credibility to everyone who will ultimately use the system. Inclusion of end users promotes acceptance of the solution and helps break down "us versus them" barriers. Working together, the two groups will provide a balanced evaluation.

It should be noted that for both IT and end-user departments, it is helpful to include members at different levels in the organization. Although it is typical to include an IT program manager and the manager of the end-user department, it is important to also include "workers," that is, at least one individual from the end-user department who will use the proposed software on a daily basis and the technician from the IT department who will be responsible for installation and support. These people provide different and needed perspectives.

In the case of an enterprisewide system that affects more than one department, the selection team should include members of all departments and key functions.

Depending on the company's procedures for approving expenditures for software, the team may benefit by including representatives from the procurement or finance departments. If the company expects either (or both) of these functions to perform a detailed review of the selected software prior to approving the project, it may be helpful to have them participate on the team during the selection process.

Size

Group dynamics indicate that the optimum size for a working team is between six and ten individuals. A larger team becomes unwieldy, and it is difficult to reach consensus. A smaller team runs the risk of being dominated by one person. In the case of large enterprisewide systems where a dozen or more departments may be affected and should be represented on the team, it is helpful to create subteams, each of which is responsible for identifying the functional requirements for that department.

Continuity

As noted above, some companies treat software selection as a separate project from implementation. Although from a budgeting viewpoint the two phases may be separate projects, from a team standpoint it is important that they be considered part of a single initiative.

Not all team members from the selection phase may continue onto implementation, but key players should. At a minimum, one of the end-user representatives and an IT team member should be part of both projects. The reason for this is simple. Even with extensive documentation and formal handoffs, things are invariably "lost in the translation." Furthermore, although major decisions are typically documented, smaller ones are not always committed to writing, nor is the reasoning behind those decisions. At later stages in the project, it is helpful — sometimes essential — to understand the reason why certain decisions were made. Having key team members remain on the team helps ensure that that "tribal knowledge" is retained.

The Team Leader

It can be argued that selecting the correct team leader is one of the critical success factors for the project, because this is the individual responsible for keeping the project on schedule and ensuring that the overall objectives are met. When selecting this person, there are several factors to be considered.

Key Characteristics

In addition to the general characteristics of team members shown in Exhibit 2-4, the team leader should possess the following:

- *Project management experience.* This is one of the key differentiators between a successful and an unsuccessful project leader. The team leader must understand the fundamentals of managing projects, from team dynamics to project schedules. Although formal training is important, there is no substitute for experience, and on a large or critical project, only team leaders with prior experience on successful projects should be considered.
- *Ability to gain consensus.* Moreso than for any other member of the team, it is the leader's responsibility to resolve differences of opinion. Team leaders should allow all members to express their opinions and then work with them to reach a resolution that is satisfactory to everyone. Chapter 13 provides techniques for conflict resolution.
- *Ability to conduct meetings.* Because meetings are typically the forum for accomplishing much of the team's work, the leader needs to run effective meetings. This includes establishing and publishing an agenda prior to the meeting and ensuring that the meeting stays on schedule and that the correct players are invited and attend. Although some of the responsibilities may be delegated — for example, a timekeeper may be appointed to ensure adherence to the agenda — the leader has overall accountability and is normally the person who conducts meetings.
- *Verbal and written communication skills.* The team leader is normally the spokesperson for the project. As such, it is important

that team leaders be effective communicators. They may be called upon to present the project to senior management or to workers on the assembly line and should be comfortable in either situation. They must also ensure that all decisions are fully documented. Note that this responsibility may be delegated to a team member, typically called a scribe or recorder, but that the team leader is still accountable.

■ *Respect.* Although "personal influence" is a key characteristic of all team members, it is particularly important that the team leader be well regarded throughout the company. As the project's spokesperson, the team leader must be recognized as an employee whose opinion is valued and whose skills are unquestioned.

End User versus IT

In an ideal world, the team leader would be a member of the end-user department. The rationale behind this is that the end-user department is the one that will be most affected by the project. End users are the people who have the most at stake, and so they are — or should be — the most committed to the project's success. In the real world, it is possible that no one in the end-user department possesses all of the key characteristics, especially previous project management experience. Although IT is a project-oriented function, many other departments within the typical company are task oriented. The difference is critical. Without a team leader who is experienced in managing projects, the software selection and implementation process is less likely to succeed.

One versus Two

Although it would appear that one solution to the problem of inexperienced end users would be to have two team leaders, one from IT and the other from the end-user department, coleadership creates more problems than it resolves. Even in the most collaborative organizations, it is important to have a single person with ultimate accountability. Team members need a single decision maker and a single person to provide overall direction. As noted in Exhibit 2-3, there should be only one team leader.

Choosing the team leader is the project champion's responsibility. The decision should be made and the leader appointed before any of the other team members are invited.

Facilitators

Although the team leader should possess all of the characteristics shown above, there are times when a company may want to use a facilitator to conduct meetings and gain consensus. Facilitators are normally individuals who have received specialized training in group and meeting dynamics. They may be other employees of the company or consultants from outside firms. The advantages that a facilitator brings are twofold: specific skills and objectivity. Because facilitators are not full-fledged members of the team and, ideally, are not members of either IT or the end-user department, they should have no bias. Their responsibility is to help the team articulate needs and concerns, sort facts from opinions, and make decisions based on those facts.

In highly charged and emotional situations in which two groups appear to be unable to compromise or even to understand each other's position, it is helpful to have a facilitator. In these cases, the facilitator can be viewed as a referee.

Outside Advisors

Some companies employ research services and outside advisors to assist with the product selection process. As discussed in subsequent chapters, both of these groups can be valuable in software selection, particularly in Step 3, identifying potential products. They may also be useful during contract negotiations because some advisory firms have had prior experience with specific vendors and know what flexibility there is in pricing and terms andconditions. Chapter 6 provides more information about the use of advisors during contract negotiations.

Like facilitators, outside advisors are optional, and the success of the project does not depend on their being used. Indeed, it can be argued that the use of the wrong advisor can have a negative effect on the project. Because of this, it is important to ensure that the right advisor is chosen.

The advantages of including advisors in the selection process are similar to those for facilitators, although instead of providing specific skills, an outside advisor provides access to specific knowledge. In both cases, the company should expect objectivity. Exhibit 2-5 provides a list of criteria that help determine whether or not the advisor has the desired background and objectivity.

If an advisor is used, as shown in Exhibit 2-3, it should be clear that the advisor provides guidance and expertise but is not a voting member of the team. Decisions should be made only by the team members.

Once the project has been defined and the team assembled, the first steps are complete. The team can now begin the actual selection process.

Exhibit 2-5   Outside Advisor Selection Questionnaire

Question	Explanation
How long have you been providing these services?	A company that is new to the business may not have the needed experience. One exception may be when experienced individuals leave another firm and form their own company.
Who are your prior clients?	It is important to check references. Particularly for enterprisewide systems which have industry-specific modules, at least some references should be from the same industry. It is also important to note the date of the reference. Old dates may indicate that the advisor is no longer well regarded. Other questions to be asked of the references include: How satisfied were the references with the services they received? What did they like best? What is one thing they would have changed?
Are you a partner with any software vendor?	If the advisor provides implementation or other services for one of the vendors being considered, his or her objectivity is questionable. The ideal advisor will have no ties to any vendor.
Do you provide implementation services?	An advisor who also provides implementation services has a bias, whether or not it is admitted. Because the revenues from implementation are normally greater than from the selection process, the advisor has a vested interest in guiding the company to select a packaged solution, perhaps even the one that is the most difficult to implement, whether or not it is the best solution for the company, because the advisor's firm will hope to provide at least part of the implementation services. Although it may not be a clear conflict of interest, the objectivity of an advisor who also performs implementation is questionable.
What is your fee structure?	There is no such thing as a free lunch. When advisors provide assistance at no fee, they expect to recoup those costs later, probably during implementation.

THE SELECTION PROCESS

One of the most critical steps toward ensuring a successful packaged software implementation project is selection of the correct product. Although that may appear intuitive, some companies wind up selecting a package for the wrong reasons. In some cases, the software is more powerful than they need, a "solution looking for a problem." In others, although the software appeared to meet the company's needs, much of what the vendor demonstrated was future-ware. A formal selection process can help avoid those mistakes.

The first step is to understand exactly what it is that the software must accomplish. Chapter 3 outlines a process for identifying those requirements. Communicating the requirements to various vendors and evaluating their products' ability to meet the requirements are the subjects of Chapters 4 and 5. Chapter 4 discusses the creation of a request for proposal, and Chapter 5 addresses the evaluation process.

Chapter 3

Identifying Requirements and Potential Products

Chapter 2 outlined five steps in the packaged software product selection process. This chapter discusses the second and third of those steps, namely, defining what the system is expected to do and performing a preliminary identification of software products that appear to meet those requirements.

The Selection Process — Step 2: Identify and Prioritize Requirements

One of the common mistakes in packaged software implementation is choosing the wrong system. This happens when the team does not fully understand what the system must do or is influenced by extraneous factors such as the example in Chapter 1 of buying a car because of its global positioning system when there is no need for that feature. Selecting packaged software is one situation where *caveat emptor* is particularly appropriate. It is the buyers' responsibility to ensure that they have chosen wisely. Vendors are skilled at marketing. Glossy brochures and glib presentations can make even a poorly designed product look appealing and can mask the fact that desirable features are "future ware." The team must sort through marketing hype and select the commercial off-the-shelf (COTS) system that will meet their requirements. It should be evident that the only way to ensure that requirements will be satisfied by a particular software product is to have those requirements clearly identified and documented. The importance of this step cannot be overemphasized. To make a fact-based decision, it is essential to understand not only the problem that is to be solved, but also all the aspects of the existing functionality that must be included in the solution.

Identifying Requirements

Requirements for packaged software can be grouped into three categories: functional, technical, and vendor related.

- *Functional* requirements are those that end users develop, and they answer the question, "What must the system do?"
- *Technical* requirements are developed by an information technology (IT) department and relate to the operating environment. They answer the question, "How does the system run?"
- *Vendor-related* requirements are normally developed by the IT department and answer the question, "Is this the right vendor?"

Functional Requirements

As discussed in Chapter 1, it is essential to understand exactly what the COTS solution is expected to do. Although there are a number of ways to identify requirements, including interviews with end users and focus group discussions, the result should be detailed, documented answers to the following four questions:

1. What is the current process?
2. What is missing from the current process, and what in it does not work properly?
3. Which of the items identified in the previous question must be corrected by the new system?
4. What criteria will be used to prove that the proposed system satisfies the requirements? When developing the answers to these questions, it is important to consider all groups of end users. In some cases, such as an enterprise resource planning system, the end-user community may extend outside the company to include suppliers and customers. Although they may not be active participants in the project, these groups' needs should be considered.

Question 1: What Is the Current Process?

Although it is to be expected that the end-user team members understand the current process, there are benefits to documenting it. Not only is clarity improved, but the act of explaining the current process frequently identifies nuances that were not common knowledge and occasionally reveals hidden steps. There are three components to the overall process: inputs, the process itself, and outputs. When collecting inputs, whether paper forms or screen layouts, it is useful to identify each field, indicating how that field is completed, by whom, and what entries are valid. This information will be helpful in answering the fourth question. Similar documentation should occur for output. Outputs should include all reports and printed forms as well as any electronic outputs (e.g., Web pages). The majority of the effort is normally spent documenting the process itself. Many companies create verbal descriptions of their processes. Some, however, prefer pictures or what some call process maps. There are a variety of different process map formats. Some list all steps in the sequence in which they are performed but make no indication of who performs each step. These detailed process maps are easy to understand and are particularly applicable when responsibility for all steps is confined to a single department. Exhibit 3-1 is an example of a detailed process map for an employee's vacation planning.

In other cases, when responsibility for the process spans departments and when it is important to understand who performs each step, a functional process map is a better choice. Exhibit 3-2 is a functional process map of the software selection process described in this and the following chapters. In addition to showing the steps and their order, the functional process map shows the function or department responsible for each step.

The challenge is ensuring that all the steps are identified. One technique that some companies have found useful for creating process maps is to have brainstorming sessions where team members and subject matter experts (SMEs) from the end-user departments write steps on small self-adhesive notes, then arrange them on a flip chart. Using the self-adhesive notes allows steps to be reordered and additional steps to be added. Only when the team is satisfied with the order are the steps transcribed into a final format.

Question 2: What Is Missing from the Current Process, and What in It Does Not Work Properly?

While the team is documenting the current process, they should be determining what could be improved. After all, if the current process is

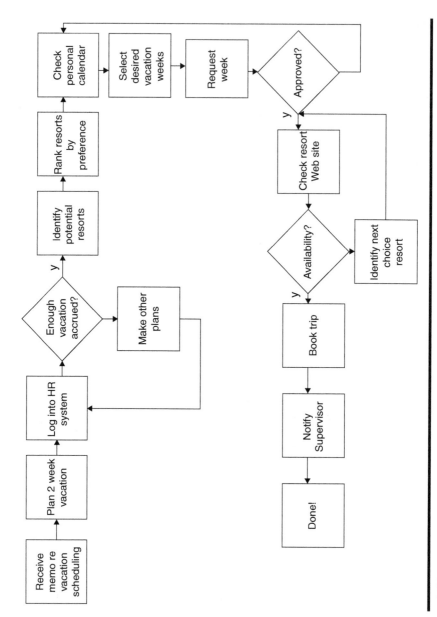

Exhibit 3-1   Detailed Process Map

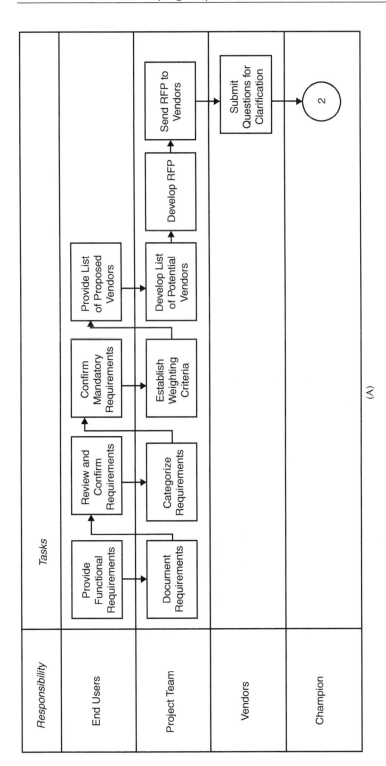

(A)

Exhibit 3-2   Functional Process Map: Software Selection Process

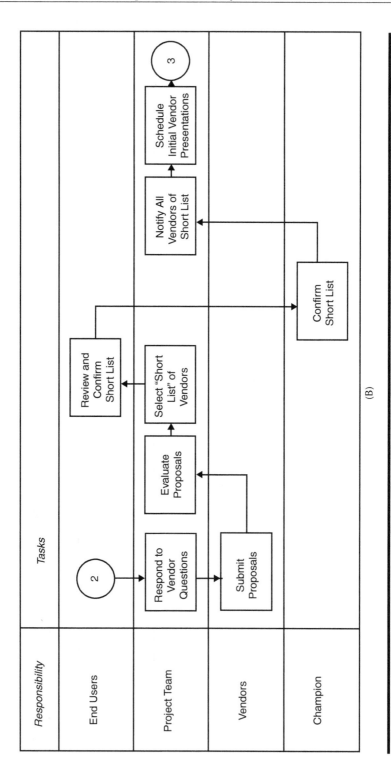

Exhibit 3-2 (continued)

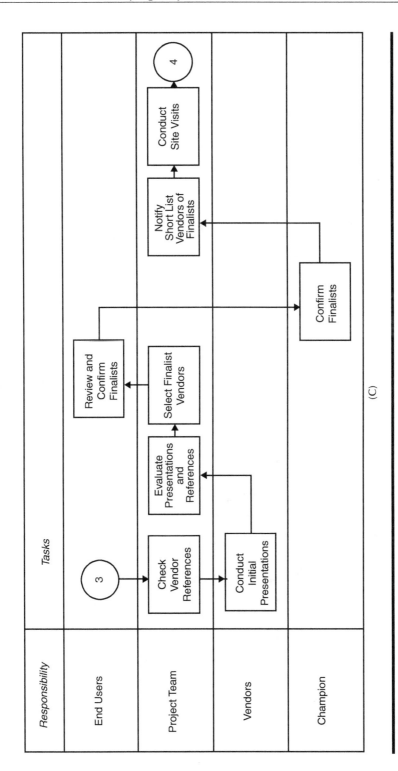

(C)

Exhibit 3-2 (continued)

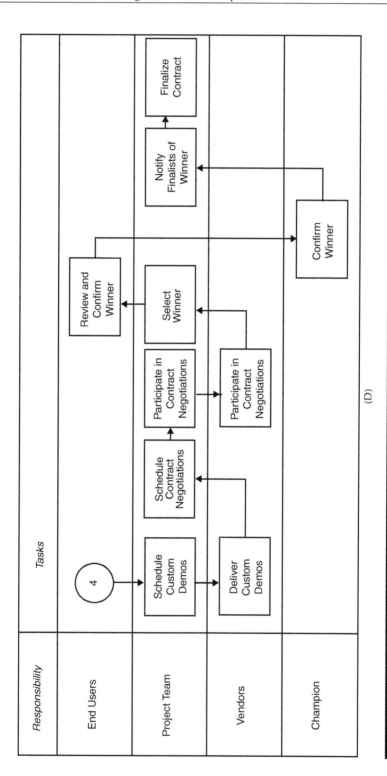

Exhibit 3-2 (continued)

working perfectly, there is little impetus for a new system. Some deficiencies may be apparent when the current process is defined. For example, if one of the steps includes manual lookups of codes or a manual calculation, efficiencies would be gained by automating those steps. In other cases, potential improvements can be identified by asking the SMEs defining the process what aspects of the process irritate them the most and what new functionality would make their jobs easier. In all cases, it is useful to quantify the proposed improvement. For example, if one of the objectives of the new system is to reduce the time required for the process, it is helpful to identify the time involved in each step currently. This will enable the team to establish some goals and then to measure whether or not those objectives are met.

Question 3: Which of the Items Identified in the Previous Question Must Be Corrected by the New System?

Asking end users what they would like improved is sometimes like opening Pandora's box; it unleashes unexpected forces. It is possible that the responses to the previous question will create such a long list of desired improvements that either no system will be able to satisfy them or the desired system will be excessively expensive. To avoid these problems, end users should be asked to prioritize the items once they have identified their "wish list."

Prioritization can take several forms. The first is to group all items into three categories: mandatory, important, and nice-to-have. If this approach is taken, the end users should understand that all mandatory items will be included in the solution and that some of the important ones will probably be included, but that nice-to-have items may not be satisfied until future releases of the software or may never be implemented.

A second approach is to give each item a ranking based on a score of one to ten. If this approach is used, it is important that there be a limit to the number of items that can be given a ranking of ten.

A third approach is to give each person ranking the items a total of some arbitrary number of points — typically either 100 or 1000, depending on the number of items on the list — and ask for the points to be divided among the various items. Although each approach has advantages, the third frequently provides the greatest differentiation among items, because it forces the rankers to weigh each potential improvement against the others. Regardless of the approach used to prioritize them, only those items that receive consistently high rankings should be considered requirements for the new system.

Question 4: What Criteria Will Be Used to Prove That the Proposed System Satisfies the Requirements?

As was true of the project's overall goals, it is important to be able to clearly demonstrate that the proposed solution will in fact meet the end users' needs. Before the team can answer the question of how they will validate the solution, they must ensure that the requirements that were identified adhere to the Specific, Measurable, Attainable, Relevant, and Timebound (SMART) criteria. For example, if "response time must be reduced" were a requirement, it would be impossible to determine whether a proposed COTS solution fully met that requirement, because the requirement is not SMART (e.g., would a reduction of one nanosecond be sufficient?). Once the team has rewritten requirements if needed to make them SMART, the team is ready to develop acceptance criteria for each of the requirements. Although some teams object to the effort involved in creating acceptance criteria, the criteria are useful in evaluating vendor packages and form the foundation of the test plan. Test plans are described in more detail in Chapter 15. A sample of acceptance criteria is shown as Exhibit 3-3.

Exhibit 3-3 Requirements Acceptance Criteria

Requirement	Acceptance Criteria
Department code must be numeric and a valid entry from the chart of accounts.	Valid entries are accepted. Invalid numeric entries are rejected. Blank entries are rejected. Alphanumeric entries are rejected. Purely alpha entries are rejected.
Response time for error messages will not exceed one second during normal working hours (8 AM to 5 PM, Eastern time, Monday through Friday, excluding company holidays).	Response time for one workstation in Manhattan does not exceed one second. Response time for two workstations in Manhattan pressing the <Enter> key at the same time does not exceed one second. Response time for one workstation in Los Angeles does not exceed one second. Response time for two workstations in Los Angeles pressing the <Enter> key at the same time does not exceed one second. Response time for one workstation in Manhattan pressing the <Enter> key and one in Los Angeles pressing the <Enter> key at the same time does not exceed one second.

Technical Requirements

Functional requirements are important, but they are only one part of the equation. The solution that is ultimately chosen must not only meet the end users' requirements for functionality, but it must also be able to be run on the company's infrastructure, and it must be able to be supported effectively. Developing technical requirements and including them in the evaluation process helps ensure that the correct solution is selected. Technical requirements are normally developed by an IT department and include the hardware, operating software, and network resources that can be supported. If, for example, company standards indicate that only a specific version of a Web browser will be used and a proposed solution requires a different browser or a more current version, the company may not be willing or able to implement that product. Similarly, if one product requires a database that is not a company standard, the cost associated with supporting that database may make that solution less attractive than another.

Vendor-Related Requirements

The final category of requirements deals with the vendor rather than a specific product. The objective of vendor-related requirements is to ensure that the vendor of the product the team selects is one with which the company wants to do business. This is critical. Although it may appear that buying software is a one-time event, the reality is that the relationship with the vendor is normally an ongoing one. As such, the company will want to choose a vendor who is both competent and cooperative.

Because most packaged software is designed to be used for a number of years and updates may be required or desired, it is important to ensure that the vendor will be in business for the life of the software. It is also important to understand early in the selection process what services the vendor will and will not provide and how easy they are to work with. Exhibit 3-4 provides a list of questions that can help assess vendors. These questions are designed for initial screening and should not be considered a comprehensive list of vendor-related requirements.

Prioritizing Requirements

Although SMEs were asked to prioritize potential process improvements as part of the development of functional requirements, that is only the beginning of the prioritization process. It is normal at this point to have literally hundreds of requirements, all of which the team would like to

Exhibit 3-4   COTS Vendor Assessment Questionnaire

Question	Reason for Asking
How long have you been in business?	Younger companies may not have a proven track record.
How long have you been in the software development business?	This may be a new line of business, even though the company itself is established. In that case, the track record of the software division is unproven.
What version of the software are you currently selling?	Version 1.0, although theoretically a production version, may be close to beta and, therefore, riskier.
When was the initial version of this package first implemented? ("Implemented" means installed in production mode, not beta.)	Although no guarantee of quality, an older product may be more stable.
When was the current version of this package first implemented?	If the current version involved major changes or additions to functionality, it may be desirable to wait until it has been in production for several months. This is similar to the Version 1.0 concern.
How many developers are working on this package?	A small staff means a higher dependence on individuals and greater risk if key staff should leave.
How many customers have this package installed and in full production?	A small installed base may be an indication that the product is either new or somehow inadequate. It is important to distinguish between the number of companies and the total number of installed "seats." One large company may distort the statistics.
How often do you release new versions of the software?	Frequent releases will require more support; no regular schedule of releases could mean that the company has no future plans for the package.
What is the warranty period for the software?	It is important that the warranty be long enough to cover all normal processing. For example, a financial system that has separate quarter- and year-end processing should be warranted through the first time that all logic is exercised in production.

(continued)

Exhibit 3-4 (continued)   COTS Vendor Assessment Questionnaire

Question	Reason for Asking
What support is included in the purchase price?	Although there is no right answer to this question, it is important to understand what services the vendor supplies.
What other services do you provide?	Vendor-supplied training or conversion services may shorten the project schedule.
What hours or days is help desk support available?	If the system is used 24 hours a day, 7 days a week, a fully staffed help desk may be important.

have satisfied by a COTS solution. The reality is that some of these requirements are more important than others, and some are so critical that if a vendor's software cannot meet them, the company will not consider that solution. Prioritization is essential. It should be noted that some companies perform this task after they have begun investigating packages. The fallacy in that approach is that team members may be impressed with elements of a specific product demo and may rank those elements higher than they would have if the requirements had been ranked in an ivory tower environment. As noted above, companies should beware of being influenced by marketing hype. Some packages have features that appear to be useful but are "solutions looking for a problem." If the company does not have that problem, there is no point in buying the solution. The team's objective is to select the package that meets the company's requirements. Although the presence of additional functionality that may be used in the future may be used in the final decision, elements that do not directly satisfy the company's needs should not drive the selection.

Prioritizing requirements is a three-step process:

1. Categorize each requirement.
2. Assign importance rankings.
3. Document the desired response.

Although there are similarities to the prioritization approaches discussed above, this process is more formal and incorporates the first two approaches rather than making them mutually exclusive. The results of the full prioritization process will be used when evaluating vendors' responses to a request for proposal (RFP) and their product demonstrations.

Categorize Each Requirement

The first step in prioritizing requirements is to divide the requirements into three categories: mandatory, critical, and nice-to-have. The distinctions among the categories are the following:

- *Mandatory.* As the name suggests, when all potential solutions are evaluated, if a vendor or package does not satisfy one of these requirements, it is eliminated from further consideration. These are the "show stoppers." Missing a single mandatory requirement disqualifies the vendor.
- *Critical.* These requirements are the ones that the company believes are important to the success of a project. Once a potential solution has passed the preliminary screening and has met all mandatory requirements, the critical requirements are used to determine how closely each solution meets the company's needs. Unlike mandatory requirements, scoring is not binary, and potential solutions are not eliminated if one of these requirements is not met. In Step 2, the team will give each of these requirements an importance ranking and then score the proposed solutions by comparing the vendor's response to what the team has established as an ideal response in Step 3.
- *Nice-to-have.* These are discretionary requirements. Although they are given importance rankings and scored similarly to critical requirements, the resulting scores are of lesser importance than those for critical requirements. Nice-to-have requirements can be considered tiebreakers. If at the end of the full evaluation two products have close scores for critical requirements, the nice-to-have scores can be used to determine the winner.

Assign Importance Rankings

After requirements have been categorized, the next step is to assign an importance ranking to each requirement in the critical and nice-to-have groups. Normally a scale of 1 to 10 is used. Although it is possible to rank using all ten numbers, there are two disadvantages to that approach.

1. The ranking process is more difficult and requires more time because it is necessary to establish scoring criteria for each number within the range (see Step 3).
2. Resulting scoring may not provide clear differentiation among various products.

Exhibit 3-5   Ranking and Scoring Criteria

Number	Ranking	Scoring
0	Used only for scoring, not for ranking.	**Missing.** The vendor did not respond to the question, or the product does not satisfy the requirement at all.
1	This requirement is of low importance. The solution will be successful even if it is not met.	**Unacceptable.** The response provides minimal information, or the product appears to satisfy only a small portion of the requirement.
4	This requirement is of moderate importance.	**Barely acceptable.** The responseor product meets less than half of the requirement.
7	This requirement is important. Having it will satisfy key needs and will add to the project's overall success.	**Acceptable.** The response or product meets the majority of the requirement, but there are still gaps between it and the ideal response.
10	This requirement is very important. Without it, the project may not be successful.	**Excellent.** The requirement is fully met.

Because the objective of the ranking and subsequent scoring is to distinguish one product from another, it is helpful to use a ranking scheme that facilitates those distinctions. One recommended approach is to use only the numbers 1, 4, 7, and 10 both when ranking and scoring. An explanation of the ranking and scoring criteria associated with each of the numbers is shown in Exhibit 3-5.

It should be noted that some companies use 2, 5, 8, and 10 rather than 1, 4, 7, and 10. The disadvantages of the 2, 5, 8, 10 ranking are twofold:

1. Five is the middle of the range, allowing team members to classify items as being of average importance or being satisfied to an average degree. Statisticians warn against the normal tendency to rank things as average and suggest using scales that avoid a middle-of-the-road score.

2. There is less difference between 8 and 10 than between 7 and 10. Because the objective is to select the best product, it is important to clearly distinguish between "acceptable" and "excellent."

Document the Desired Response

Once the requirements have been categorized and importance rankings determined, the team should establish an ideal response for each of the requirements and, whenever possible, identify the criteria that will be used to assign scores. The purpose of this is to reduce subjectivity in the evaluation process by ensuring that when responses and products are reviewed, everyone is using the same criteria to score them. Exhibit 3-6 shows a ranking spreadsheet with sample functional, technical, and vendor-related requirements after this step.

Exhibit 3-6   Initial Ranking Spreadsheet

Requirement/Question	Mandatory, Critical, or Nice-to-Have	Importance Ranking	Desired Response
System includes tax calculations for all 50 states.	M	N/A	System includes tax calculations for all 50 states.
How frequently are tax updates provided?	C	10	Tax updates are guaranteed to be provided no less than 48 hours before the changes are effective.
The database is SQL Server or Oracle.	C	7	Preference is for SQL Server. SQL Server = 10; Oracle = 7; any other response = 0.
How long has the company been in business?	M	N/A	Must have been in business for a minimum of five years.
How long is the initial warranty period (included in base license price)?	N	4	Ideal is greater than five years. Warranty period of five years or greater = 10; greater than two years but less than five years = 7; greater than one year but less than two years = 4; one year = 1; less than one year = 0.

The Selection Process — Step 3: Identify Potential Products

The team's next task is to develop a list of potential vendors and products. The first question teams frequently ask is how many products they should consider. Other than the time required to evaluate additional products, there are no disadvantages to having an extensive list of potential vendors. The advantage to considering a wide variety of solutions is that the probability of meeting the company's requirements is increased. The next question, and one of the most critical, is how to develop the list of vendors and products. Although the most obvious answer is to include vendors with whom the company already has a relationship, other sources of vendor names include research services, Internet searches, networking, industry group publications, vendor advertisements in IT journals, and presentations and exhibits at conferences and expos. The pros and cons of each one are the following:

- *Current vendors.* Because the company already has a relationship with these vendors, there is less risk of selecting a vendor whose product appears good but who fails to deliver on promises. Current vendors are proven quantities. The potential disadvantage is that the company may be using Vendor X for one system where they excel, but their offering for the software that is needed for this project is either immature or mediocre. As a result, it is important to evaluate current vendors as carefully as new ones.
- *Research services.* The primary disadvantage is that research services' recommendations are not normally free; however, these firms have the advantage of being objective. As such, they can help cull a long list of vendors to a more manageable size by providing information about previous companies' experiences with them.
- *Internet searches.* Although the Internet search engines provide an inexpensive way to obtain a list of possible vendors, substantial time may be required to sift through the responses. A Google search for "ERP vendors" generated close to 600,000 hits.
- *Networking.* Learning about other companies' experiences is an important part of the evaluation process (see the section on reference checking in Chapter 5). At this stage, although no decisions should be made simply because Company A uses Vendor X, knowing that a company in the same industry has had successful experiences with Vendor X is a good reason for putting Vendor X on the list to be evaluated.
- *Industry group and IT publications.* Both established and newly formed software companies advertise in industry and IT trade

journals, hoping to gain new customers. Ads and articles discussing customers' experiences with various products are good ways to obtain names of vendors and products.

■ *Conferences and expos.* Both software and industry conferences attract vendors as speakers and exhibitors, making this a source of information about vendors and their products. The team should be aware that in some cases, vendors "sponsor" conferences. Translation: they underwrite some of the costs. As a result, their products may be hyped more than they deserve, and other vendors with equally good products may not be present. Because of this, conferences should not be the only source of vendor names.

One additional source of potential vendor names is for team members to ask each vendor they contact, "Who do you consider your primary competitors?" Although some vendors may not answer, many will. Their responses can be cross-referenced to the list that the team developed from other sources, and if new products are mentioned, they can be added.

The next step in the evaluation process is to develop an RFP. Although identifying potential vendors and developing the RFP are presented as sequential steps, it is possible to continue adding vendors to the list while the RFP is being drafted. Chapter 4 describes the RFP process.

Chapter 4

RFPs and RFIs

Once the team has identified the requirements that the software is expected to meet and has identified potential vendors and products, it is ready to obtain detailed information about each of those vendors and their products so that team members can evaluate how well the products satisfy the company's requirements. Although this can be done in a variety of ways, the most common is to issue either a request for information (RFI) or a request for proposal (RFP). The RFP can be considered preparation for Steps 4 and 5 in the selection process, that is, the evaluation of products and vendors.

RFI versus RFP — What Is the Difference?

There are more similarities than differences between an RFI and an RFP. In both cases, the company issues to all potential vendors a formal document that explains what it is trying to accomplish, the projected timeframe, and the scope of the project, along with the location and expected size of the user base. In other words, the company addresses the five Ws. In both cases, it asks the vendors to respond in writing to a series of questions that are designed to help the company evaluate each vendor's ability to meet its requirements. In both cases, the company expects the vendors to be bound by their responses, although the expectation is that the responses will provide the starting point for negotiations rather than being accepted verbatim. The primary difference between an RFI and an RFP is that an RFP asks the vendors to provide a proposal, normally including cost and schedule, of how they would accomplish the requirements that are set forth in the document, whereas an RFI simply asks for information about products and approaches but does not require the vendor to commit to cost or a schedule. It is assumed that the stage after the evaluation of an RFI will include cost and schedule proposals but that only those vendors who reach the short list will participate in that stage and be required to provide cost and schedule information. For simplicity, from this point on, the document will be referred to as an RFP, although the points discussed, with the exception of cost and schedule, apply equally to an RFP and an RFI.

What Is the Value of an RFP?

There are three primary reasons why a project team would issue an RFP.

To Increase the Objectivity of the Evaluation

It is a fact of life that people have biases and that those biases can affect evaluations of vendors and products. By establishing a written list of requirements, categorizing them, and assigning importance rankings as discussed in Chapter 3, the team helps reduce the effect of those biases. Issuing an RFP and rating the vendor's responses to those requirements helps make the decisions fact based rather than being emotional or subjective.

To Ensure That All Key Requirements Are Included in the Evaluation

If vendor and product evaluations are based on seat-of-the-pants criteria, it is likely that the team will use a somewhat different set of criteria for each vendor, simply because they have forgotten one or because the vendor's presentation steered them in another direction. Although the omissions are not deliberate, this informal approach introduces variation into the process. This has the effect of reducing objectivity and may result in the wrong product being selected. Even with a written list of requirements, it is possible that when the team is evaluating a product, they may miss a few requirements or weigh their importance differently. An RFP provides consistency across vendors and products, ensuring that each vendor receives exactly the same list of requirements. It also ensures that all products are ranked according to the same set of criteria.

To Separate Facts from Vendor Marketing Hype

The RFP requires vendors to respond in writing to all questions. The advantages of this are twofold. First, having written responses increases clarity, because there is no question of the team hearing something different from what the vendor said. Second, putting responses in writing decreases the probability that vendors will exaggerate their products' capabilities, because it would be relatively simple for the team to verify the accuracy of statements.

What Are the Disadvantages?

There are two reasons why a company would not want to issue an RFP: the effort required to draft the document and evaluate the responses, and the elapsed time required for the process.

Effort

The amount of effort to draft the RFP is dependent on several factors, including the number of requirements that were identified in the previous step and that therefore need to be incorporated into the document, as well as the experience level of the team members writing the RFP.

Because the RFP is a key component in the selection process, some companies enlist outside assistance in drafting it. Although the outside advisors or law firms cannot identify the requirements, they can normally provide the framework, including standard clauses and legalese, and can assist in rewording requirements to make the document consistent and easy to understand.

Even if outside advisors are used to draft the RFP, the company's legal counsel should always be engaged when issuing an RFP. The attorneys may not draft the RFP, but they should review it.

Timeframe

The RFP process does take time, and, as a result, some companies choose not to issue one. Exhibit 4-1 presents a three-month timeframe for RFP creation, response, and evaluation. It should be noted that this is a best case scenario. Although it is possible to shorten the first two steps if the company has an RFP template that includes all the boilerplate text, companies may find that the schedule shown in Exhibit 4-1 is aggressive. It is possible that vendors will request extensions to the "response due" date, because three weeks may not be adequate for a comprehensive

Exhibit 4-1   Basic RFP Timeframe

Event	Weeks
Team drafts RFP from completed requirements	1 and 2
Attorney reviews and revises RFP	3 and 4
Team leader issues RFP to all vendors	5
Vendors respond to RFP	8
Team leader reviews responses for mandatory items and forwards to the rest of the team all responses that successfully answered the mandatory questions	9
Team members review all responses, ranking each question	10 and 11
Team leader compiles individual rankings and creates overall scoring spreadsheet	12
Team meets to review results and resolve discrepancies, selecting "short list" vendors	
Champion and key users review and approve "short list"	12
Team leader notifies all vendors of status and schedules next steps for "short list" vendors	

response. Furthermore, if the team members are assigned to the project only on a part-time basis, review of the responses may require more than two weeks.

There is no doubt that issuing an RFP requires time and effort; however, when the project is large, complex, and expensive, the advantages to be derived from the RFP process outweigh the costs and time expended.

When Is an RFP Needed?

Although there are no rules about when to use an RFP, certain categories of projects for packaged software implementation warrant the time and costs associated with an RFP. Those projects can be classified as large, complex, or expensive. It should be noted that each company's definition of those three adjectives will vary. An organization accustomed to projects that cost less than $10,000 each will consider a $100,000 effort to be expensive, whereas a company whose typical software initiatives have minimum budgets of $500,000 will have a higher threshold. In general, though, multiyear projects that require budget approval at a level higher than the head of the IT department and that affect more than one department are candidates for an RFP.

Some software implementation projects rarely have RFPs in their life cycle. Those projects include the licensing and installation of shrink-wrapped productivity software where there are only a few dominant

Exhibit 4-2   RFP Table of Contents

1. Introduction and background
2. General information
3. Vendor profile
4. Term
5. Termination
6. Specific project requirements
7. Program management
8. Vendor staffing
9. Work space and other vendor requirements
10. Vendor tools
11. Cost proposal
12. Proposed schedule
13. Payment terms
14. Vendor nonperformance
15. Changes in scope

vendors and where the products' capabilities can be evaluated without requiring written responses from the vendors. Although formal evaluations occur in these cases and pricing negotiations may require multiple vendors to submit written proposals, many companies forgo a full RFP.

Other software implementation projects that may not use an RFP are those where only a few products are under consideration and all of them are from vendors with which the company already has a successful relationship. In these cases, the portions of the RFP that relate to the company, its stability, and its references are not needed, and the company may choose a less formal evaluation. In these cases, the scripted presentation described in Chapter 5 may be adequate for product evaluation.

Contents of an RFP

Although the contents of an RFP can and will vary from company to company and between projects within a company, there are certain elements that should always be included and others that are needed for specific types of projects. Exhibit 4-2 presents the table of contents of a sample RFP. Explanations of each section (1 through 15) are given below.

1. Introduction and Background

This section presents the five Ws, explaining to the vendors why the company is issuing an RFP, what it expects to accomplish through the project, its projected timeframe, and any constraints that may impact the vendor's responses. Typical subsections include a brief description of the company itself, the reasons why the company believes a COTS solution is needed, and a general scope of the project. Sections 1 and 2, unlike the rest of the RFP, present information to the vendors but do not expect responses. As noted later, with one exception, the items in these sections are not categorized and ranked because there are no responses to them.

2. General Information

A subtitle for this section could be "legalese and other disclaimers," although those are not the only items included. The purpose of this section is to outline the process that will be followed by both the vendors and the company and to ensure that the vendors understand their responsibilities. Critical subsections are outlined below.

Instructions for Responses

This subsection establishes the due date (and time, including time zone) when responses are due and specifies the format of the response. Because it is typical to require vendors to provide an electronic copy of their response along with a specified number of paper copies, the format (e.g., word processing software version) to be used is critical.

This section typically indicates that vendors are expected to respond to each item, even those that are statements, indicating their approval of the item or any changes they propose. For example, the company may state that the only reason a vendor may terminate an agreement is for the company's failure to pay invoices within 180 days. Each vendor would be expected to either agree with this statement or propose a different time period.

It is also important to require vendors to follow the numbering scheme used in the RFP when preparing their responses because that facilitates the review and evaluation of the response. This item (formatting) is the exception to the statement that Sections 1 and 2 are not ranked. Although it may seem trivial on the surface, in addition to making the response more difficult to review and score, failure to follow instructions for numbering responses may be indicative of other problems with that vendor. If, for example, a vendor has his own format for responding to an RFP and refuses to use the company's numbering scheme, that vendor may also be less flexible in other dealings with the company. Compliance with formatting should not be a mandatory item, but it is typically given a fairly highly importance ranking as a "critical" item.

Exhibit 4-3   Schedule for RFP Process

Event	Start Date	End Date
Company issues RFP	N/A	xx/xx/xxxx
Company accepts vendor questions	xx/xx/xxxx	xx/xx/xxxx
Company responds to vendor questions	Each Friday, beginning xx/xx/xxxx	(5 PM eastern standard time, the Friday following the end date for the previous event)
Vendor proposals received by company	N/A	9 AM eastern standard time, xx/xx/xxxx
Company evaluates vendor proposals	xx/xx/xxxx	xx/xx/xxxx
Company announces short list (maximum of five)	N/A	xx/xx/xxxx
Company schedules vendor in-person presentations	N/A	xx/xx/xxxx
Company checks short list vendor references	xx/xx/xxxx	xx/xx/xxxx
Short list vendors present their products	xx/xx/xxxx	xx/xx/xxxx
Company evaluates presentations	xx/xx/xxxx	xx/xx/xxxx
Company announces finalists (two)	N/A	xx/xx/xxxx
Company conducts site visits to finalists' references	xx/xx/xxxx	xx/xx/xxxx
Company schedules custom demos	xx/xx/xxxx	xx/xx/xxxx
Finalist vendors conduct custom demos	xx/xx/xxxx	xx/xx/xxxx
Company and finalist vendors negotiate contracts	xx/xx/xxxx	xx/xx/xxxx
Company signs contract with one vendor	N/A	xx/xx/xxxx

Schedule

As the name implies, this subsection presents the schedule for the entire RFP and vendor-product selection process. Exhibit 4-3 lists the items that are typically included in the schedule. As noted by the "N/A" designation, some events have only an end date, although others span multiple days or weeks. In addition to setting expectations about the overall timeframe for product selection, the schedule gives vendors advance warning of when key personnel may be needed to provide demos or participate in presentations.

Inquiries and Contacts

Because it is inevitable that vendors will have questions about the RFP, the team should establish a process for responding to them. This includes specifying how questions must be submitted, the name of the person to whom they should be directed, and the schedule for response.

It is important to designate a single point of contact for vendor questions to ensure consistency of responses and to minimize vendor "end runs." Particularly in the case of current vendors who have relationships established within the company, it is not uncommon for those vendors to approach members of senior management, hoping to influence the team's decision. Although these "end runs" cannot be prevented, champions should use their influence to minimize them. If the team anticipates that this will be a problem, this section of the RFP may also include a statement that inquiries outside the designated process may be grounds for disqualifying a vendor from future consideration.

As has been noted several times, having everything in writing is beneficial to both the company and the vendors. This is also true of questions about the RFP. One approach that some companies have found useful is to require that all vendor questions be submitted in writing (typically via e-mail). Those questions and the company's responses to them are then circulated to all vendors so that no vendor has an advantage over another. It should be noted that, although all questions are included in the response document, there is no indication of which vendor submitted each one.

This subsection should also set forth the time period during which questions will be accepted and the frequency of responses. Although questions may be submitted daily, the company's responses are normally not provided more often than weekly. This allows time for legal review of responses, if required, and does not place an undue burden on the team.

Vendor Selection Criteria

This subsection indicates to the vendors the general categories of items that the company will use to select vendors. It does not list them in order of importance. Typically, these criteria are generic and include such items as cost, ability to meet functional requirements, vendor stability and reputation, and flexibility of contract terms and conditions. The actual scoring criteria that the company intends to use should never be disclosed to the vendors.

The "legalese and disclaimers" portions of Section 2 include the following:

- *Vendor expense.* It is important to specify that the company will not reimburse the vendor for any expenses incurred in the preparation of the RFP and subsequent negotiations.
- *Company rights reserved.* This subsection is designed to protect the company and typically includes statements that the company:
  - May discontinue the RFP process without selecting a vendor
  - Is not obligated to select the lowest cost proposal
  - May negotiate with more than one vendor concurrently
  - May request additional information from any vendor
  - May negotiate a contract based on terms and conditions other than those proposed by the vendor
  - Will not provide reasons for rejection of any vendor
    The last point is an important one, because vendors will typically ask for a debriefing session that explains why they were not selected. Although the company may choose to provide this information, particularly to current vendors with whom it wants to maintain a good relationship, having this disclaimer gives the company the ability to refuse.
- *Nondisclosure and publicity.* This subsection states that the vendor may not disclose any company information that it receives during the RFP process, nor may it publicize the fact that it has received an RFP from the company. Among other benefits, this wording is designed to prevent a flood of calls to the company from other vendors who want to be included in the selection process.
- *Limitations of company liability.* This subsection reiterates that the company has no financial liability to the vendor and that issuing the RFP does not in any way obligate the company to select a vendor or sign a contract.

3. Vendor Profile

The purpose of this section is to obtain general information about the vendors. (Section 6 addresses technical and functional product-related information.) Because this is the first section that will be categorized, ranked, and scored, it is important that each key point be written as a separate subsection to facilitate that process. Subsections typically include questions relating to vendor's financial stability, the percentage of the vendor's total revenues that are related to software, the size of development and support staff, and the length of time the vendor has been engaged in the software business. The questions shown in the COTS Vendor Assessment Questionnaire (Chapter 3, Exhibit 3-4) are normally part of Section 3.

Other subsections should include a request for customer references and for an indication of the vendor's market share in the company's industry as well as the methods by which the vendor assesses customer satisfaction and the results of those assessments.

In addition, the RFP may ask for the vendor's prior experience with the company. For small companies or those that are highly centralized, that question may not be necessary, but large or decentralized companies may find that vendors who they thought were new to the company are currently doing business with one of their divisions.

If the project is multinational, the company may include questions about the vendor's presence in specific countries, total staff in those countries, and the number of employees that would be available to work on the company's account. The distinction between total and available staff is a key one. One vendor may have 1000 employees in a country but only 10 available, whereas another vendor may have only 250 total employees in that country, but 100 of them would be available to the company. In this case, the second vendor may be a better choice. This subsection is important if the company anticipates using the vendor's staff for implementation and ongoing support.

The final question is normally an open-ended one, asking each vendor to indicate what he believes differentiates his company from other software vendors. Although this is one that is difficult for the team to score objectively because there is no ideal response for it, the answers can be useful in understanding the vendor's philosophy and corporate culture.

4. Term

Although the term for a software license agreement is typically perpetual, the company may want to specify a term for support or professional services. Alternatively, it may ask the vendors to propose a term.

5. Termination

The company may want to specify the conditions under which it or the vendor may terminate the agreement. Typically these include "cause," which means that one of the parties has breached the agreement, and "convenience." The latter can be likened to a no-fault divorce, because the party that is terminating for convenience does not need to list any reason or prove any breach of contract. In either case, there is normally a notice period and, in the case of termination for cause, a period during which the breaching party is allowed to resolve the breach.

Exhibit 4-4 Detailed Requirements Matrix

Requirement	Included in Base Software	Not Included; Available at Extra Cost (Specify Cost)	Not Included in Current Version; Will be Available in Future Release (Specify Date)	Not Included; Not Planned for Future Releases

The RFP may either state the company's preferred conditions for termination or may ask the vendors to propose them.

6. Specific Project Requirements

This should be the longest section of the RFP because it is here that the company lists the functions it expects the software to perform. This is also the section where technical requirements are identified. Because this is a lengthy section, the company may wish to list detailed requirements in an appendix to the RFP. One approach that facilitates review of the response to specific requirements is to create the appendix in tabular form as shown on Exhibit 4-4.

7. Program Management

If the vendor is going to provide implementation services, it is important to understand how those services will be staffed and managed. Sections 7 through 9 address these issues. Section 7 deals specifically with the management of the project and should ask the vendors to explain the number of levels of management they propose, how frequently they intend to rotate these key individuals, the communication structure and frequency, and how they would address dispute resolution. Responses to this section help the team determine whether a vendor's approach to project management is compatible with their own. If, for example, a vendor is unwilling to guarantee that the program manager will not be rotated off the account during the initial implementation, the company may want to either consider another source of implementation support or establish a contingency plan.

8. Vendor Staffing

If the vendor will provide services as well as a product, it is important that the company understands how staff will be assigned to their account, how often they will be rotated off the account, and what qualifications that staff will have. This section refers to all staff, although the restrictions on reassignment may be less stringent for general staff than for program managers.

If vendor staff will work at a company site, the company's security and other requirements such as background checks and drug testing may apply to them. If this is the case, those requirements should be included in this section of the RFP.

This section should also ask vendors about their proposed use of subcontractors and should include a statement that the company will hold the vendor responsible for all acts and omissions of subcontractors as if they were employees of the vendor. Although this provides protection for the company, the team should be aware that vendors have less control over subcontractors than they do over permanent staff and that, under some circumstances, it may be undesirable to have subcontractors on the account.

9. Work Space and Other Vendor Requirements

This section applies if vendor staff will work at a company site and should ask vendors to indicate the type of office space they will require, along with any administrative support or office equipment they will need. The purpose of this section is to ensure that there are no surprises in the form of unexpected costs.

10. Vendor Tools

If the vendors will provide services, it is possible that they may use proprietary tools to provide those services. This section should require them to indicate whether or not they will use such tools, and — if the tools will be embedded in the final work product — to specify what rights the company will have to the tools. Normally the company will ask for a royalty-free license to use any embedded tools.

11. Cost Proposal

This is one of the key sections because it is here that the vendors provide their cost proposal for the software license, along with any assumptions they made in developing it. If there are additional software modules that are not needed for the initial implementation but that might be required for subsequent deployments, their costs should be shown separately, as should ongoing maintenance costs. If the vendors will provide implementation services, the associated costs and the method used to calculate those costs should be shown separately from the software license. In all cases, there should be a clear indication of who pays taxes, if applicable.

12. Proposed Schedule

If the vendors are expected to provide implementation services, this section should require a detailed schedule of that implementation along with the assumptions that were used to develop it. Even if the vendors are providing only the software, the RFP should ask them to indicate the normal timeframe for implementation of their software for projects of a similar size and complexity. Although the team may have established a high-level implementation schedule prior to issuing the RFP, vendor responses are useful in determining whether that schedule is feasible.

13. Payment Terms

This section addresses how and when payments are made. Because vendors will typically want to be paid more quickly than the company wishes to pay them, it may be advantageous to set forth aggressive payment terms that are favorable to the company and ask vendors to agree with them rather than simply asking vendors to propose their normal terms.

14. Vendor Nonperformance

This section outlines the criteria that will be used to determine whether or not vendors have met the company's expectations and the process that will be followed if they do not. Although this applies primarily when services are being provided in addition to software, the company may want to include penalties for such nonperformance as late delivery of software or failure of the software to perform as indicated in vendor literature.

15. Changes in Scope

Because it is possible that the project may change in scope, either because the company may decide to implement greater or lesser functionality than originally planned or because of changes in the location and size of the user base, it is important to provide for those contingencies. This section typically indicates the types of changes in scope that may occur, the process by which the company will notify the vendor of a change in scope, and the pricing adjustments that are expected. In addition to establishing a formal process, the goal of this section is to understand all potential costs.

Ranking RFP Sections

The team should review all sections of the RFP and decide whether or not they will be ranked or simply read. This is a continuation of the categorization and ranking of requirements that was discussed in Chapter 3. Some subsections, such as the differentiating comments in the vendor profile (RFP Section 3) may not be ranked. All those that will be scored should be divided into the three categories established above (mandatory, critical, and nice-to-have), with all critical and nice-to-have items given an importance ranking. All sections should include the ideal response as well as scoring criteria, when possible.

For ease of review, the ranking spreadsheet that was established for requirements (Chapter 3, Exhibit 3-6) should be updated to include RFP section numbers and then be sorted by those sections. Exhibit 4-5 shows how the initial ranking spreadsheet was updated after the creation of the RFP. Note that in addition to including the RFP sections, the wording was changed to reflect that of the actual RFP.

The team is now ready for the next step, evaluating the responses.

Exhibit 4-5 RFP Ranking Spreadsheet

RFP Section	Requirement/Question	Mandatory, Critical, or Nice-to-Have	Importance Ranking	Desired Response
3.11	Please indicate how long your company has been in business.	M	N/A	Must have been in business for a minimum of five years
3.55	Please indicate the factors that you believe differentiate your company from your competitors.	Not rated	None	Must provide some response; team will discuss relevance during short-list discussions.
6.04	Please indicate the frequency with which tax updates are provided.	C	10	Tax updates are guaranteed to be provided no less than 48 hours before the changes are effective.

(continued)

Exhibit 4-5 (continued)   RFP Ranking Spreadsheet

RFP Section	Requirement/Question	Mandatory, Critical, or Nice-to-Have	Importance Ranking	Desired Response
6.21	The company has offices in many U.S. states and three Canadian provinces. Please indicate the tax jurisdictions for which calculations are included in the base package.	M	N/A	System includes tax calculations for all 50 states.
6.95	The company has technology standards that dictate which database managers can be employed. Please indicate the underlying database structure for your product.	C	7	Preference is for SQL Server. SQL Server = 10; Oracle = 7; any other response = 0.
10.2	Please indicate your policy regarding access to vendor-specific tools upon termination of the agreement.	N	7	Ideal is no cost to company.
11.4	Please include in your cost proposal an indication of the length of the base warranty period.	N	4	Ideal is greater than five years. Warranty period of five years or greater = 10; warranty greater than two years but less than five years = 7; warranty greater than one year but less than two years = 4; warranty of one year = 1; warranty less than one year = 0.
11.5	Please provide a cost proposal for ongoing maintenance (updates and enhancements) of the system.	C	7	Less than seven percent of the base cost = 10; between seven and ten percent = 7; between ten and fifteen percent = 4; fifteen percent = 1; >fifteen percent = 0.

Chapter 5

Product and Vendor Evaluation

Once the company has issued a request for proposal (RFP) and received the responses, the next step is to evaluate those responses, selecting the vendor and product that most closely meet the company's requirements. This evaluation comprises Steps 4 and 5 of the overall selection process, steps that lead directly to contract negotiation. As is true of most processes, product and vendor evaluation can be divided into a series of smaller steps. These are shown in graphical format in Chapter 3, Exhibit 3-2.

- Step 1: Team evaluates responses and creates short list of vendors.
- Step 2: Team schedules vendor presentations.
- Step 3: Team checks vendor references.
- Step 4: Short-list vendors present their products (standard demo) and capabilities.
- Step 5: Team evaluates presentations and creates finalist list of vendors.
- Step 6: Team conducts site visits to key customers of finalist vendors.
- Step 7: Finalist vendors present customized demos of products.
- Step 8: Team determines whether to negotiate with all finalists.

The objective of the various steps is to perform ever more detailed evaluations of vendors and products at the same time that the number of vendors being evaluated is reduced. Although it is possible to include all vendors in all steps, the reality is that teams rarely have sufficient time to perform a comprehensive evaluation of every possible product. The process outlined above can be viewed as a series of increasingly finer filters, designed to let only the best product pass through the final one.

As noted in Chapter 4, even if the team does not believe it necessary to issue an RFP, there should always be multiple products under consideration, and a formal evaluation should still occur. In this case, Step 1 shown above would be eliminated and Step 4 would become a scripted presentation. Scripted presentations are discussed at the end of the current chapter.

Step 1: Team Evaluates Responses and Creates Short List of Vendors

There are four substeps in response evaluation:

1. One person reads all responses, checking that all mandatory requirements are met and eliminating any vendor whose response failed to meet even one mandatory requirement.
2. Multiple members of the team read those responses that met all mandatory criteria, scoring the critical and nice-to-have items.
3. The team leader creates a comprehensive ranking spreadsheet, showing the individual rankings as well as the composite.
4. The entire team meets to review the ranking spreadsheet and to select the short list of vendors.

Review of Mandatory Items

As soon as the responses are received, one member of the team — typically the team leader — should read those sections of each response that relate to mandatory items to determine whether or not the vendors satisfied those requirements. Although reading all responses may appear to be a burden for one person, it is important that a single member of the team perform this step to ensure consistency. It is important to note that the reviewer is not reading entire responses but only the mandatory sections. Because these sections are typically spread throughout the response, the importance of vendor adherence to the RFP numbering scheme is obvious.

To facilitate the review process, it is helpful to create a subset of the RFP ranking spreadsheet, sorting first on the mandatory, critical, nice-to-have columns; then on the RFP section column; then creating a separate spreadsheet with only the mandatory items in it. This spreadsheet is then used to record all vendors' responses to the mandatory requirements. Exhibit 5-1 shows a sample mandatory items spreadsheet after all responses were received and reviewed. Note that because Vendor 2 did not meet the first mandatory requirement, the review of that response ended at that point. A single "miss" of a mandatory requirement disqualifies the vendor immediately.

Evaluation of All Critical and Nice-to-Have Items

Once the review of mandatory items is complete, the team leader should distribute all responses that passed the initial screening to the team members who will evaluate them. Along with the responses, each evaluator should be given an RFP scoring spreadsheet similar to that shown in Exhibit 5-2. Note that the mandatory items have been removed from this spreadsheet and that it is sorted in RFP section order, because the reviewers will read responses sequentially.

There should be a separate spreadsheet for each vendor's response, with calculations of the degree satisfied done automatically. All columns except "Score" should be locked to prevent inadvertent miskeying. Typically these spreadsheets are part of a workbook that has a summary sheet showing the degree satisfied totals for each vendor rated. Like the individual row calculations, the summary sheets are created automatically from the total rows on each vendor's sheet.

Several procedures help ensure consistent, fair evaluation of the proposals.

- *At least two people should evaluate each proposal.* It is likely that the entire project team will not be able to evaluate the proposals; however, it is important that more than one person be involved in the evaluation to minimize personal bias in the selection process.
- *Evaluations should be done independently rather than as a team.* Because it is possible for strong-willed individuals to sway a group, this is a corollary to the preceding point. Again, the objective is to ensure as fair an evaluation as possible.
- *All evaluators should evaluate all proposals.* The logic for this is the same as for having a single person read all responses to verify the mandatory requirements: it increases consistency.
- *All evaluators should use the same scoring scale.* Although any scale can be used, it is helpful to use the same scale that was used to

Exhibit 5-1 Mandatory Items Spreadsheet

RFP Section	Requirement/Question	Mandatory, Critical, or Nice-to-Have	Desired Response	Vendor 1	Vendor 2	Vendor 3	Vendor 4	Vendor 5	Vendor 6	Vendor 7
3.11	Please indicate how long your company has been in business.	M	Must have been in business for a minimum of five years.	Y	N	Y	Y	Y	Y	Y
6.21	The company has offices in many U.S. states and three Canadian provinces. Please indicate the tax jurisdictions for which calculations are included in the base package.	M	System includes tax calculations for all 50 states.	Y		N	Y	Y	Y	Y

indicate the importance, and as noted previously, a 1, 4, 7, 10 scale with zero reserved for responses that are either missing or totally wrong helps differentiate among responses. Having clear scoring criteria as shown in the "Desired Response" column in Chapter 4, Exhibit 4-5 facilitates the review process and helps remove bias.

Creation of Composite Ranking Spreadsheet

When the team leader has received the completed scoring spreadsheets from each of the evaluators, the next step is to aggregate the scores and create an initial ranking of the vendors. A spreadsheet similar to the one shown as Exhibit 5-3 is useful in this process. Note that the spreadsheet sums individual reviewers' scores for critical items separately from those categorized as nice-to-have and creates a separate ranking for each category. Summing the two total scores ***should not be done***, because the two categories have different significance. As discussed in Chapter 3, the nice-to-have scores are designed to be used as tiebreakers, if needed.

If the number of vendors being scored exceeds ten, it may be helpful to create a ranking column for each team member as shown in Exhibit 5-4. The purpose of the individual rankings is to highlight major discrepancies and to serve as input for the final step.

Selection of Short-List Vendors

Because the next steps in the selection process are time intensive, it is important to limit the short list to a manageable number of vendors. Although this will vary by company and project, a rule of thumb is that no more than one third of the respondents to the RFP should be included in the short list. And, if the RFP was sent to a large number of vendors, it may be desirable to limit the short list to an arbitrary number such as five.

Although all team members may not have reviewed the responses to the RFP, they should all be involved in the selection of the short-list vendors. Normally the selection would be done as part of a meeting once the ranking spreadsheet (Exhibit 5-3 or 5-4) is created. It should be noted that the overall ranking shown on the spreadsheet *is the starting point* for the selection. Although this ranking may be the final one, it is important that the whole team review the results, understand them, and concur with the relative ranking that was established by the evaluators.

It is also possible, as shown in Exhibit 5-4, that there may be wide discrepancies among the reviewers' ratings. If the objective were to create a short list of three vendors from the five shown on this exhibit, selecting

Exhibit 5-2   RFP Scoring Spreadsheet

RFP Section	Requirement/ Question	Mandatory, Critical, or Nice-to-Have	Importance Ranking	Desired Response	Score	Degree Satisfied — Critical	Degree Satisfied — Nice-to-Have
				Vendor 1			
6.04	Please indicate the frequency with which tax updates are provided.	C	10	Tax updates are guaranteed to be provided no less than 48 hours before the changes are effective.	4	40	
6.95	The company has technology standards that dictate which database managers can be employed. Please indicate the underlying database structure for your product.	C	7	Preference is for SQL Server. SQL Server = 10; Oracle = 7; any other response = 0.	7	49	

10.2	N	7	Ideal is no cost to company.	7	49
11.4	N	4	Ideal is greater than five years. Warranty period of five years or greater = 10; warranty greater than two years but less than five years = 7; warranty greater than one year but less than two years = 4; warranty of one year = 1; warranty less than one year = 0.	1	4
11.5	C	7	Less than seven percent of the base cost = 10; between seven and ten percent = 7; between ten and fifteen percent = 4; fifteen percent = 1; greater than fifteen percent = 0.	4	28
Totals				117	53

Exhibit 5-3 Initial Vendor Ranking Spreadsheet

Vendor	Critical						Nice-to-Have					
	Ranking	Total Score	Susan	Bill	Joe	Donna	Ranking	Total Score	Susan	Bill	Joe	Donna
Vendor 1	2	609	117	156	147	189	3	239	53	32	65	89
Vendor 4	1	744	240	168	117	219	2	271	110	7	56	98
Vendor 5	4	405	96	96	96	117	4	193	44	40	77	32
Vendor 6	3	584	168	38	168	210	1	275	77	98	44	56
Vendor 7	5	337	24	77	168	68	5	173	11	65	65	32

Exhibit 5-4 Initial Vendor Ranking Spreadsheet with Individual Evaluators' Rankings

Critical

Vendor	Overall Ranking	Total Score	Susan Rank	Bill Rank	Joe Rank	Donna Rank	Susan Score	Bill Score	Joe Score	Donna Score
Vendor 1	2	609	3	2	3	3	117	156	147	189
Vendor 4	1	744	1	1	4	1	240	168	117	219
Vendor 5	4	405	4	3	5	4	96	96	96	117
Vendor 6	3	584	2	5	1 (tie)	2	168	38	168	210
Vendor 7	5	337	5	4	1 (tie)	5	24	77	168	68

Nice-to-Have

Vendor	Ranking	Total Score	Susan	Bill	Joe	Donna
Vendor 1	3	239	53	32	65	89
Vendor 4	2	271	110	7	56	98
Vendor 5	4	193	44	40	77	32
Vendor 6	1	275	77	98	44	56
Vendor 7	5	173	11	65	65	32

the top three from the overall ranking would make Bill's lowest-ranked vendor one of the short list. Similarly, Joe's fourth-ranked vendor received the highest overall ranking.

Prior to the meeting, the team leader should review the individual evaluators' scores to see whether there are any outliers, that is, any scores that differ widely from the others. In this case, the team leader might want to call Bill and Joe individually and ask why Bill scored Vendor 6 so poorly, when the other evaluators ranked that vendor fairly highly, and why Joe's score for Vendor 7 was so much higher than those of the other evaluators. It is possible that personal biases were involved, perhaps because of previous experience with those vendors. If that is the case, either the questionable scores should be "neutralized" by replacing them with the average of the other evaluators' scores, or another team member should evaluate all the responses. The latter option is unlikely to be employed, simply because of time constraints.

When the team meets, they should review the results of the scoring, ensuring that everyone on the team agrees with the final ranking. Prior to announcing the short list, the team leader should present the results of the evaluation to the project's champion, ensuring that that person — and the steering committee, should one exist — is comfortable with the team's decision.

It is important to have senior management approval before making the short list public. Although undesirable, there may be times when a vendor is placed on the short list for political reasons, even if that vendor did not score as well as other vendors. The circumstances under which that may occur include the following scenarios:

- The company is negotiating other contracts with that vendor and wants the leverage of more potential work to aid in the other negotiations.
- The vendor already has a large presence at the company, and the company fears that service may suffer if the vendor is eliminated this early in the selection process.

Once the decision has been made and ratified by senior management, the team leader should call the short-list vendors, notifying them of their status. When that is complete, the team leader should issue an e-mail to all other vendors, thanking them for their responses and indicating that, unfortunately, they are not on the short list. Depending on company policy, this e-mail may also include the names of the vendors who were placed on the short list. Exhibit 5-5 provides a sample notification letter.

Exhibit 5-5   Sample Letter to Non–Short-List Vendors

On behalf of The Company, I would like to thank you for responding to our RFP for (fill in the blanks with the name of the project). The team was impressed with the caliber of the proposals we received and the quality of the products being proposed. Unfortunately, not every company could be on the short list, and you are not. Although I know that you are disappointed in not being selected and may want to understand specific reasons why your product was not rated as highly as others, Section 2.08 of the RFP specifies that The Company will not provide reasons for any vendor's failure to be selected.

Again, thank you for participating in this project. We appreciate the time and effort that went into the preparation of your response to our RFP.

Step 2: Team Schedules Vendor Presentations

Scheduling

Once the short list has been developed, the team leader should invite those vendors to demonstrate their products to the project team. At this stage, the demos are the vendors' standard marketing presentations rather than being customized for the company. Although vendors will normally present an overview of their corporate history, sales growth, and list of key customers in addition to demonstrating the products themselves, from the project team's view, the objective of these presentations is to evaluate the products' ease of use and to confirm that the functionality the vendors claimed was present is indeed included in their software. Because these two objectives may be mutually exclusive, the onus is on the company to ensure that its needs are met. This can be accomplished in several ways, the first of which is effective scheduling.

The presentations should be scheduled within a tight timeframe, ideally all the same week. Although this requires a significant time commitment from the team members, it improves the quality of the evaluation, because the team's memories of Vendor 1 are still fresh when they see Vendor 2's presentation. Typically, half-day presentations are adequate at this point, making it possible to schedule two presentations each day. It should be noted that this is an aggressive schedule and that companies may prefer to schedule only one presentation per day. This is one reason why a maximum of five short-list vendors is desirable.

Exhibit 5-6   Sample Vendor Presentation Agenda

Time	Activity
9:00–9:15	Vendor's corporate overview
9:15–10:30	Product demonstration
10:30–10:45	Break
10:45–11:30	Question and answer period

Agenda

Although some companies allow the vendors to establish the agenda for these presentations, it is advantageous for the company to develop an agenda and require all vendors to adhere to it because the team's goal is to provide an objective, fact-based evaluation of the various products. This helps ensure consistency. It also indicates to the vendors the relative importance of the various agenda items. A sample agenda is shown in Exhibit 5-6. It should be noted that the question and answer period is sometimes nicknamed "Stump the Stars." The team should use this period to ask difficult questions that will help differentiate one vendor from another. One question that can elicit valuable information is, "Why should we buy your product rather than Vendor X's?"

The agenda should be given to the vendors at the time the presentations are scheduled so that they can prepare appropriately. During the actual presentations, the team should take note of whether or not each vendor adheres to the times established in the agenda. Failure to respect the company's wishes may be a harbinger of future problems with that vendor.

Evaluation

As was true of the RFP, the team should develop a set of criteria by which they will evaluate each of the presentations and should create a scoring spreadsheet that will be used during the presentations. Although these criteria may not always have weighting factors as the RFP sections did, the team should use a consistent scoring scale, ideally the same one that was used for the RFP responses. Exhibit 5-7 presents a simple evaluation form. It is also possible to use the requirements shown in the project-specific portion of the RFP as detailed evaluation criteria, although this normally happens in Step 7, the custom demos.

Exhibit 5-7 Simple Evaluation of Vendor Presentation

Item	Score (0, 1, 4, 7, 10)
Functionality matched product literature	
All needed functionality was demonstrated	
Screen navigation was intuitive	
System appears to meet company's requirements	
Vendor responses to company questions were satisfactory	
Total Score	

Exhibit 5-8 Short List and Finalist Vendor Evaluation

	Vendor 1	Vendor 4	Vendor 5	Vendor 6
Reference checks	100	74	96	48
Initial presentation	88	74	94	96
Total	188	148	190	144
Finalist vendor?	Y	N	Y	N
Site visits	96		88	
Custom demo	100		100	
Gap analysis	88		100	
Total	284		288	
Continue to negotiations?	Y		Y	

Although the agenda shows the meeting ending at 11:30, that is only when the vendor's portion ends. Once the vendor staff have left, it is important that the team have a debriefing session to discuss what was presented and to score that vendor. Ideally, all team members should participate in all demos to provide consistency, and scoring should be done individually prior to having a group discussion. As is true throughout the process, results of the demos and the team's evaluation should be documented. Exhibit 5-8 provides an example of a short list and finalist vendor evaluation spreadsheet.

It is also important to note that although the short-list vendors had a relative ranking at the end of the RFP response evaluation, they should enter into this round of evaluation as equals. Teams frequently find that although some vendors may excel at responding to RFPs and, as a result, score very highly at that stage, the actual product may not be as robust as the written response.

Step 3: Team Checks Vendor References

Normally there is a period of several weeks between scheduling of the vendor presentations and the actual presentations. This allows the vendors time to prepare. It also gives the team a chance to conduct reference checks. This is an important step and should not be skipped or short-changed.

When selecting software, it is important to distinguish between marketing hype and reality. One way to accomplish that is to ask customers who are currently using the software how satisfied they are with both the product and the vendor. This is typically done through phone calls rather than site visits. (Site visits occur in Step 6.)

Although it is expected that a vendor will supply the names of only satisfied customers, it is still possible to distinguish among vendors by asking open-ended questions of the references. Questions that frequently elicit valuable answers are, "If you could change one thing about your experience with this vendor, what would it be?" and "What do you like most and least about the software?"

To ensure consistency, it is important to develop the list of questions prior to conducting the reference checks. Exhibit 5-9 shows a sample questionnaire. It is also important to have a single person make all the calls, again for consistency reasons. That team member should take notes during the phone calls and provide written copies of the responses to the entire team. When all reference checks are complete, the team leader should schedule a meeting so that the entire team can review the results and award scores to each vendor based on its references. Exhibit 5-8 should be updated with the team's evaluation.

Exhibit 5-9   Vendor Reference Check Questionnaire

Vendor:

Reference company:

Person interviewed:

Phone number:

Title:

Years with company:

Reference date:

1. When did you first install the software?
2. Which version of the software do you have installed?
3. Do you have multiple instances of the software?
4. If yes, how many?

(continued)

Exhibit 5-9 (continued)   **Vendor Reference Check Questionnaire**

5.   How many locations are using the software?
6.   Are any outside of the United States?
7.   If yes, where are they?
8.   How many users do you have in total?
9.   Are you fully implemented?
10.   If not, how many users do you expect when the system is fully implemented?
11.   Which other vendors and products did you consider?
12.   Why did you select Vendor X rather than the others?
13.   What were your objectives for the project (cost savings, etc.)?
14.   Were they met?
15.   If not, why not?
16.   Did you implement full functionality as part of the initial project?
17.   If not, which functions were included?
18.   How long did the initial implementation take?
19.   What problems did you encounter?
20.   If the vendor was involved in resolving the problems, how would you rate the speed with which they resolved the problems, on a scale of 1 to 10?
21.   Were problems resolved correctly the first time?
22.   If not, how long did it take for full resolution?
23.   If you could change one thing about your implementation, what would it be?
24.   On a scale of 1 to 10, how would you rate the product's functionality (does it do what you need done)?
25.   Is there any functionality that you have found missing?
26.   If yes, how did you address that gap?
27.   Do you use the vendor for ongoing support?
28.   If not, how do you support the product?
29.   If yes, on a scale of 1 to 10, how would you rate the vendor's ongoing support?
30.   What do you like best about the product?
31.   What do you like least?
32.   What do you like best about the vendor?
33.   What do you like least?
34.   What advice do you have for us?

Step 4: Short-List Vendors Present Their Products (Standard Demo) and Capabilities

This is the step in which all the planning that occurred during Step 2 is turned into action. Guidelines for the presentations were discussed in Step 2. Although it is likely that vendors will ask for feedback on their presentations following the individual meetings, the team should not provide any at that point because the evaluation is not complete.

Step 5: Team Evaluates Presentations and Creates Finalist List of Vendors

Although the team evaluates each presentation as it is given, team members should have a separate meeting following the final presentation to review all the vendors' performances and to rank them. The objective is to identify a limited number of vendors — ideally two — whose products would meet the company's needs. The team will then continue evaluating only those vendors' products. The selection of these finalist vendors is typically based on the scoring that occurred during the individual presentations as well as the team members' responses to the more subjective question, "Do I want to do business with this vendor?"

It is possible that, if the short list consisted of four or five products, three products may be chosen as finalists, because the team believes that those products are equally viable. It is also possible that at this point only one product appears to meet the company's needs. In this case, although it may be tempting to skip the last three steps and enter into contract negotiations with that vendor, the company will have greater negotiating leverage if there appear to be two finalists, either of which the company will consider. Even though additional time is required to continue evaluating two vendors, as is discussed in Chapter 6, it is important to do everything possible to improve the company's position during contract negotiations. Apparent competition helps.

Step 6: Team Conducts Site Visits to Key Customers of Finalist Vendors

For each of the finalist vendors, the team should visit at least one customer who is currently using the software. Ideally this would be a customer who is in the same industry as the company and who has an implementation similar to the one that is being proposed by the team's project. If that is not possible, the team should ask to visit a customer whose implementation is on the same scale as the company's. Visiting a customer with only a few modules installed at one site will be of minimal value to a project team that is planning a multinational implementation of all modules.

The site visit can be viewed as an extended reference check. As such, the team should develop a number of questions that members would like answered, in addition to seeing the software in live operation at the customer site. These questions typically include ease of implementation, problems encountered, and an evaluation of end-user acceptance.

Site visits should be conducted without the vendor being present because that may provide more candid answers. Although vendors are typically uncomfortable with this approach, the team should insist on it. Even though the vendor may accompany them to the site and be present during the product demonstration, there should be a period during which the team meets with the customer without the vendor.

As was true of all preceding steps, results of the site visits should be evaluated and documented because the team's goal is to provide as objective a selection as possible. Exhibit 5-8 can be used for summary documentation.

Step 7: Finalist Vendors Present Customized Demos of Products

In Step 4, the short-list vendors demonstrated their products, using their standard data and scripts. Although this was an important step in evaluating the products and shortening the list of potential vendors, it should not be the only demo of the products. Each of the finalist vendors should be required to demonstrate that his software will meet the company's requirements by using company-supplied data, because there may be idiosyncrasies in the company data that are incompatible with the software. During these customer demonstrations, the team will evaluate both ease of use and functionality, that is, how easily the company's data can be entered into the system and whether the resulting output meets their expectations.

It is at this point that the team typically uses the requirements from the product-specific section of the RFP to evaluate vendor performance. If the team created detailed requirements and acceptance criteria as shown in Chapter 3, Exhibit 3-3, those requirements can be translated into input data for the demo.

Although the ideal situation would be to not give the vendor the test data prior to the demo and to have a member of the team enter the data, those may not be realistic expectations. Because team members are not familiar with the system navigation, it might take too long for them to enter the data. Companies typically allow the vendors to enter the data and provide it to them prior to the demo; however, all team members should have a checklist of the requirements that are going to be tested and should evaluate how well the software met them. An evaluation form similar to that in Exhibit 5-7 can be used. Alternatively, if the team is using the requirements established in the RFP, a subset of the RFP Ranking Spreadsheet (Chapter 4, Exhibit 4-5) that includes only those items from Section 6 can be used. Because this includes the weighting factors that were established before the RFP was issued, the scoring that results will reflect the team's assessment of each requirement's relative importance as well as how well each vendor's product met that requirement.

When all of the customized demos are concluded, the team should meet to review them and again rank the vendors' performances.

Step 8: Team Determines Whether to Negotiate with All Finalists

It is possible that a clear winner will be apparent at the conclusion of Step 7. Even if that is the case, it is important to perform a functional gap analysis. In that, the team identifies any gaps that exist between the requirements that the team established and the proposed software's functionality and evaluates the ease with which those gaps can be bridged. If customization of the software will be required, the team should estimate the cost and time to make the modifications. A chart similar to that in Exhibit 5-10 is helpful in identifying the gaps and quantifying the impact of those gaps. A large number of high/high/high gaps may indicate that packaged software is not the correct solution for this project and that the company should either expand its search for alternative software products or consider custom development.

Exhibit 5-10   Functionality Gap Analysis

Gap	Cost to Bridge	Time to Bridge	Impact If Not Bridged
No validation of department code against chart of accounts	Low	Medium	High
Allows a maximum of 3000 accounts	High	High	Low
Allows alphanumeric department codes	Medium	High	Low

If gaps appear to be either easy to bridge or of minimal impact to the end users, the team should make its recommendations to senior management to proceed with contract negotiations. As noted above in Step 5, although one product may appear to be the best, the company should seriously consider having two vendors involved in contract negotiations because that improves the company's position. Contract negotiations are discussed in detail in Chapter 6.

Scripted Presentations

There are times when the team will not want to issue an RFP but still needs to evaluate several competing products. This can be done through a scripted presentation, which asks vendors to respond to some of the points that would normally be included in an RFP in addition to demonstrating their product.

Typically, vendors are sent written invitations to participate in the selection process. The reasons for putting the invitation in writing are the same as for a formal RFP: to improve clarity and ensure that all legal considerations are included. Although an RFP may be 100 or more pages long, the "invitation to present" will typically be fewer than ten pages. Items to be included in the invitation are the following:

■ Brief explanation of the reason for the invitation, that is, what the company expects to accomplish through the project
■ Timeframe for the presentation and selection process
■ Legal disclaimers similar to those included in Section 2 of the RFP
■ List of all points the company wishes the vendor to address during the presentation

The last item is what makes this a "scripted" presentation. Exhibit 5-11 shows a portion of the "script."

The team should create a scoring sheet, similar to that in Exhibit 5-7, that includes each of the items in the script and use that to rate each vendor's presentation. After the final presentation, the team should select a list of finalist vendors, check references (Step 3), and continue with Steps 6 through 8.

Whether the team follows the traditional RFP evaluation process or the more streamlined scripted presentation, the objective of these final steps in the selection process is to identify two or more products that will meet the company's needs and to have clearly documented reasons for eliminating the other products.

Exhibit 5-11   Scripted Presentation

General

The Company expects you to address each of the points that are raised below. In addition, please bring:

- Three references of companies currently using the version of the product that you are recommending to us
- Three references of companies for which you provided implementation support, if you propose to assist us with the implementation of this product

The Company has employees in most European and Asian countries. Although many speak English, a multilingual support staff is desirable. Please indicate the number of your staff members who are multilingual, including the languages in which they are fluent. Please count only those individuals who would be available for assignment to the Company account.

Product

1. Please describe and demonstrate the functionality that is included in your product.
2. Describe any functionality that is specific to the industry in which The Company operates.
3. Describe the technical environment in which your product runs.
4. What do you believe are the greatest strengths of your product?

Product Implementation

1. Please describe the typical timeframe that other companies of our size have required for full implementation of your product.
2. Describe the size and composition of the staff you would propose to assist us with product implementation.
3. What role would you expect The Company to play during product implementation?

Product Support

1. How often do you provide updates to the software?
2. We believe that this system will require 24/7 help-desk support. Please describe your process for providing such support.
3. Where is your help desk located?
4. Please describe the process you use to select, train, and retain staff for the help desk.
5. Please indicate what you believe to be your greatest strengths in the support arena.

LEGAL ISSUES — CONTRACTS AND SOFTWARE LICENSES

III

Although many project teams consider software license negotiations to be more painful than a root canal, the reality is that they are a necessary part of packaged software implementation, and the team should be involved in them. This section attempts to take some of the mystery (and the pain) out of contracts.

Recognizing that vendors are normally more experienced in negotiating contracts than the company, Chapter 6 proposes a process negotiation that is designed to improve the company's position and help it obtain favorable terms.

Unfortunately for those who dislike contracts, there are different types of contracts associated with packaged software implementation. Chapters 7 through 9 outline the clauses that are normally included in the three primary types of software-related contracts, explaining why the clauses are important. Chapter 7 deals with software licenses, and Chapter 8 is devoted to professional services agreements. Chapter 9 concludes the section with a discussion of service contracts and statements of work.

Chapter 6

The Negotiation Process

There is a natural tendency to want to start the actual implementation of software as soon as an apparent winner has been identified. "Let's get to the 'real work' while the lawyers hash out the details" is a familiar refrain. Although understandable, beginning to work with any vendor before a contract is signed is a major mistake. Not only does it undermine the company's position by signaling that this vendor has won the business, but also there is the possibility that the work may need to be redone if the company and the vendor are unable to agree on the contract terms. Although not common, in some cases companies do walk away from a deal because of contract terms.

A contract is not simply a legal document. It also forms the foundation for the relationship between the company and the vendor. As a result, it is important that key members of the project team understand the terms of the contract and participate in the negotiating process. While this is occurring, other team members can begin the "real work" by establishing the project road map. Chapter 10 provides information about the road map.

Because contracts are more than just pieces of paper designed to keep attorneys employed and then gather dust throughout the rest of the project life cycle, the team should understand not just the terms and conditions (Ts and Cs) of the contract itself, but also the psychology and strategy of negotiations.

Types of Contracts

A contract is a contract is a contract. Unfortunately for those who dislike the entire negotiating process, that is not true. Although there will be at least one contract included in the implementation of a commercial off-the-shelf (COTS) package, typically there is more than one, and each will have unique Ts and Cs. Exhibit 6-1 shows the variety of contracts that may be part of a packaged software implementation project and the parties to those contracts. Although each type of contract has different Ts and Cs, which will be reviewed in Chapters 7 through 9, the negotiation process for all software-related contracts is similar, and there are common precepts that should be understood and followed.

Exhibit 6-1 Possible Types of Contracts for Packaged Software Implementation

Contract	Purpose	Number to Be Signed	Other Party
Software license	Gives the company the right to use the software.	One	Vendor
Software maintenance agreement	Provides ongoing support (bug fixes) or periodic updates to the base software.	Zero to one	Vendor
Professional services	Provides custom services to the company, typically during the implementation of the software. Services may include assistance with contract negotiations, installation of the software, customization of the software, and development of conversion programs and interfaces.	Zero to many	Vendor or a third-party supplier
Support services	Provides ongoing support of the software, including all customizations. This is typically in addition to the Software Maintenance Agreement and is a service that is tailored to the company's needs.	Zero to one	Vendor or a third-party supplier

Some companies use the term *master services agreement* (MSA) interchangeably with contract. For the purpose of this book an MSA will be considered to be a contract that is negotiated at a corporate level and encompasses multiple locations or projects, rather than being a "one-shot" agreement.

MSAs are particularly useful for companies with multiple divisions, each of which may be a separate legal entity, because they establish consistent Ts and Cs across the corporation as well as eliminate the need for multiple negotiations. It should also be noted that companies are normally able to gain more favorable pricing terms when negotiating for the entire corporation rather than a single division.

Project Team Involvement in Negotiations

Many project teams consider contracts a necessary evil and delegate their review and negotiation to the law and procurement or purchasing departments. This can be a mistake. There is no doubt that contracts are necessary, but the reality is that, far from being evil, they provide substantial benefits to the company, including clarifying and protecting the company's rights. To increase the likelihood of overall success in the implementation of a COTS package, it is important to have key members from the project team participate in the negotiation of each contract.

The reasons for this are the following:

- *The team members represent the business aspects of the contract.* Contracts consist of a number of sections, which can be classified as financial, protective, legalese, and business related. The last section addresses at least four of the five Ws. It defines the functions that will be included ("what"), company and vendor responsibilities ("who"), locations where the software will run or the work will be performed ("where"), and the overall schedule ("when"). Although other members of the negotiating team have expertise in their own areas, they are not as well qualified to discuss these items as the project team.
- *The team members understand the request for proposal (RFP).* The purpose of the whole RFP process is to clearly identify the company's requirements and to determine how well each vendor's product meet those requirements. Many of the sections of the RFP relate to items that will be part of the contract. Although it is possible for other members of the negotiating team to review the responses to the RFP and the team's ranking of vendors, team members have a greater depth of knowledge of the selection

process. They understand why each section was given its importance ranking and which sections they considered essential to the
project's overall success. Even with detailed documentation, some
nuances are lost. Having team members participate in the negotiations helps ensure that "tribal knowledge" is retained and that all
key issues are considered.

■ *Continuity is increased.* As noted above, the contract is the foundation for the relationship with the vendor. That relationship does
not end when the contract is signed and the software delivered.
Instead, it is ongoing. Having project team members as part of the
negotiating team helps ensure that they understand the logic behind
any changes that were made to the contract and both parties'
positions on key points. This becomes part of the "tribal knowledge" and is helpful during actual implementation.

Other Team Members

There are some project teams that believe they can negotiate contracts
without outside assistance. Just as declining to participate is a mistake, so
too is failing to involve other departments.

A contract is a legal document. No matter how simple it appears to be
— and software licensing agreements rarely appear simple — it is important
to understand every single clause and the reason each was included. No
project team should consider entering into contract negotiations without
having an attorney as a part of the team. Most companies have a law
department with attorneys who specialize in contract law. If not, it is
advisable to engage outside counsel, particularly for large contracts.

The other department that should be included is procurement or
purchasing. Although the name may vary, the function is consistent:
ensuring the best pricing.

Some companies may wish to engage outside advisory firms to help
them with contract negotiations. The services provided by these firms
vary. Some will be active participants at all stages of contract negotiations,
including sitting at the negotiating table. Others will serve as behind-the-
scene advisors, working with the project team before and after negotiating
sessions but not actually participating in them.

The value that outside advisors can bring includes:

■ *Prior experience.* Although the company may negotiate a large
software license agreement only occasionally, some advisors' entire
business may be based on those contracts. If they have experience
with the specific vendors under consideration, they should be able

to provide suggestions on which Ts and Cs are most likely to be sticking points as well as make recommendations on how to obtain the most favorable terms.

■ *Pricing information.* This is a corollary to the previous point. If the advisors have negotiated multiple contracts with the vendors, they should be able to provide information about the pricing deals that were included in other contracts. It should be noted that advisors will typically be bound by confidentiality agreements and will be unable to provide specific pricing from other clients' contracts, but they will be able to tell the project team whether the proposed pricing structure is the best they can expect, and if not, what range they should insist on.

■ *Impartiality.* Contract negotiations can become contentious, with each side viewing the other as an adversary. Because advisors are one step removed from the negotiation, they can help the project team maintain a balanced view.

As discussed in Chapter 2, if an advisor is to be engaged, it is essential to select the correct one. Chapter 2, Exhibit 2-5 provides a list of questions that may help evaluate advisors' capabilities. In addition to those questions, the team should clearly understand both the services that the advisor proposes to provide, including whether or not the advisor will be an active participant in the actual negotiations, as well as how often (and how recently) the advisor has negotiated contracts with the vendors under consideration. As noted in Exhibit 2-5, outdated experience may be of little value and may be indicative of a problem with the advisor.

For companies with little prior experience negotiating large-scale contracts, the right advisor can be a valuable addition to the team. Companies with extensive contract negotiation experience may find them of less value. In all cases, it is important to choose an advisor whose background matches the project team's needs.

Basic Precepts

Prior planning prevents poor performance. Because the contract is such an important component of packaged software implementation, it is vital that the company employ the five Ps and plan its negotiating strategy as carefully as it would an advertising campaign or a new product rollout.

No matter what type of contract is being negotiated, there are four concepts that are common to any contract and that should be considered when developing a negotiating strategy.

1. Contracts Are Drafted to the Author's Advantage

It is a basic precept of writing contracts that the party that drafts the contract does it to its advantage. Although there may be clauses that protect both parties, the majority of the contract is written with the drafting party's interests in mind. This is a critical point, because most software licenses are written by the vendor. Typically, the vendor will give the company its standard contract and ask the company to sign it with no changes. Some companies do exactly that; however, that approach can be dangerous because the vendor's contract may not provide the level of protection the company needs, and the Ts and Cs may be unacceptable to the company.

The ideal situation is for the company to draft its own contract and ask the vendor to sign it. Unfortunately, this is not always possible for one or more of the following reasons:

- *Lack of expertise.* The company's law department may not be experienced in drafting this type of agreement. In this case, outside counsel would be required. That, however, introduces the second potential problem.
- *Lack of budget.* The cost of drafting a contract, whether with internal legal staff or outside counsel, may exceed some companies' budgets.
- *Vendor refusal.* Some vendors will refuse to consider a contract that they did not draft. Although this is less common when they are negotiating with major corporations, it is still a possible impediment.

Because it is likely that the company will have to work with the vendor's contract, it is important to read each clause skeptically, realizing that even the most innocuous clause has a reason for being there and that that reason is to protect the vendor.

2. Vendors Have More Expertise in Contract Negotiations Than the Company

Although companies may have experience in negotiating many types of contracts, this is what the vendors do for a living. Their attorneys and contracts staff have one goal: getting the very best deal for their company on every contract, whether or not they have drafted it. They are specialists in their contracts, and because they negotiate more often than most companies' staff do, they are the experts. In many cases they have finely honed negotiating tactics that are designed to make the company concede key points.

Vendor staff also have a different motivation than that of the project team. Those negotiating for the vendor need the revenue generated by the sale to keep their company solvent and themselves employed, whereas no matter how committed they are to the project's goals, few on the project team risk unemployment if the contract is not signed.

Vendors are the experts. To mitigate the risks caused by this expertise, the company should do everything it can to improve its negotiating position. Techniques are discussed below.

3. It Is Essential to Understand Every Clause in the Contract

This point cannot be overemphasized. Particularly when the contract has been drafted by the vendor, it is important that the project team understand everything that is in it. This is one of the reasons why it is critical to have an attorney who is experienced in contract law as part of the company's negotiating team. If this is the first time the team has reviewed a contract, it is helpful to have the company's attorney walk through the entire contract with the team, explaining the significance of each clause.

4. Everything Is Negotiable

Although the vendor may present the contract as a document that cannot be changed, the reality is that almost everything is negotiable, from license fees to ownership of custom code to protection of the company's data. The savvy negotiating team will recognize that and will tailor their demands accordingly.

Improving the Company's Negotiating Position

As discussed above, the single most important thing a company can do to improve its negotiating position with a vendor is to draft the contract and require that the vendor sign it, rather than start with the vendor's standard agreement. Although this is highly desirable, it may not be feasible. In that case, the points discussed below take on additional importance.

Whether or not the company drafts the contract, it should consider the following strategies prior to commencing contract negotiations:

1. Negotiate with More Vendors Than Needed

As discussed in Chapter 5, if the vendor knows that the company has selected him, the company's negotiating position is diminished, because vendors know that few companies will be willing to reopen the selection process if contract negotiations become contentious. As a result, vendors will be less willing to compromise than if they believe that winning the deal is contingent on their being flexible with contract terms.

To obtain the best pricing as well as favorable Ts and Cs, it is important that the company keep the vendor in a competitive situation until the contract is actually signed. In the case of a software license, this normally means negotiating with two vendors, because the company will use only one product. In the case of service contracts, particularly during implementation, it is possible that the company will want to engage two or more firms. In that case, it is important to keep a "spare" on the list of finalists. The result of this competitive environment is that the company will normally obtain better Ts and Cs and a lower overall cost.

2. Consider Timing

Most vendors are publicly held corporations and, as such, are sensitive to quarterly reports to Wall Street. If possible, the team should enter into negotiations close to the vendor's quarter end, because vendors are typically highly motivated to sign contracts and book revenue at that time and may agree to more favorable terms than they would have without the pressure of quarter end.

3. Establish the Ground Rules

Regardless of when contract negotiations occur, the company should determine how those negotiations will be conducted. Remembering that the vendor has greater experience, it is important to do everything possible to give the company an advantage. This includes the following:

Determine the Type of Negotiating Session

Although traditionally contract negotiations are done in person, with all members of the two teams in the same room, it is possible to conduct successful negotiations via teleconference. The advantages of telecons are reduced travel costs, greater flexibility in scheduling, and increased comfort levels for those participants who shun confrontation. (It is easier to say no to a voice on the other end of the phone line than to the person sitting across the table.) The primary disadvantage is the inability to read the other team's "body language."

The company's negotiating team should meet early in the selection process to determine which type of session they prefer.

Determine the Length of Negotiating Sessions

Most contracts require a number of hours — sometimes days or weeks — to finalize. Although vendors frequently prefer all-day sessions, these may not be advantageous to the company. Not only is fatigue a factor in lengthy sessions, sometimes leading the team to agree to points simply to have them resolved, but there can be competing priorities. Unlike the vendor's negotiating team whose sole assignment is normally this particular contract, company team members typically have work assignments outside the contract negotiations. If they are worried about the backlog of e-mail and phone calls, they will not be as effective in their negotiations. Scheduling shorter sessions — ideally no more than half a day each — mitigates these problems and has the added advantage of giving both parties time to resolve issues between negotiating sessions.

Determine the Timing of Negotiating Sessions

This is a corollary to the previous point. If the company has decided on half-day sessions, the negotiating team should decide whether those will be morning or afternoon meetings. The decision should be made based on when the company believes its team members will be the most effective.

Limit the Number of Negotiators

It is not uncommon for vendors to bring a large number of their staff to a contract negotiation. In some cases, the vendor's corporate bureaucracy requires this because no one person can agree to all aspects of a contract. In others, it is done as a negotiating technique, designed to intimidate the company. To avoid this problem, the company should determine how many negotiators it will have and require that the vendor have no greater number. This "levels the playing ground."

4. Do Not Begin Work without a Signed Contract

This point is critical enough to be repeated. Even when one vendor is the clear winner, it is a mistake to begin work until the contract is signed.

Giving any work to a vendor indicates that he has been selected and will typically reduce his incentive to agree to more competitive prices and terms. This is a major mistake, and one that should be avoided.

The Negotiation Process

Although many project teams think of contract negotiations in terms of the meetings that are held with the vendor, the actual process is more extensive, begins before any meetings are held, and extends outside those meetings.

Prior to the first meeting, the company's negotiating team should do the following:

1. Review the Contract

The first step in the process is for the company to review the vendor's proposed contract. If the basic contract was drafted by the vendor, this will be the vendor's standard contract. If the company drafted the contract, what will be reviewed are the changes that the vendor proposed to the company's draft. In either case, it is desirable to have the contract in electronic format both for review and for eventual revisions, and the company should insist on receiving the contract electronically.

When the company receives the contract from the vendor, the entire negotiating team should review it and comment on it. As noted above, if many of the negotiating team are unfamiliar with contracts, it may be advantageous to have the company's attorney walk through each clause with the team.

If team members are familiar with the contract, it is possible to conduct the initial review electronically. A round-robin approach, with one member of the team beginning the review process and passing the annotated document to the next member, avoids the problem of juggling multiple copies of the document. For clarity, it is helpful if each team member prefaces comments with his or her name or initials.

2. Determine Company's Position on Each Point

Once the round-robin review is complete, the team leader should schedule a meeting to discuss the comments, questions, and suggested changes. The objective of this meeting is to determine the ideal resolution for each point. This is similar to establishing the optimal response to each item in the RFP. Although team members may disagree at this stage, it is important that they present a united front when dealing with the vendor. To help accomplish this, it is useful to annotate the marked-up contract with the team's decision for each point of contention.

3. Categorize Required Changes

It is likely that there will be a number of changes that the company feels are important. For ease of negotiating, these should be grouped into categories, such as "ownership of data" and "payment terms," because the individual points may be scattered throughout the document. When negotiating, it is helpful to address all related clauses together. At the same time, the team should prioritize the changes because some will be of great importance, although others may be conceded in trade for a concession from the vendor. Again, it is important that the team be in agreement on these points.

Meetings and discussions with the vendors should not begin until the company's team is fully prepared. This means that they understand the contract and the changes they believe are needed. During the actual negotiating sessions, the team should do the following:

Determine Who Will Lead the Sessions

Although the vendor will typically offer to lead the negotiations, it is to the company's advantage to have one of its team members in this role because that person can control the order of points being discussed and can end sessions prematurely if the two sides reach an impasse.

In many cases, the project team leader is not the leader for contract negotiations. The reasons for this are twofold:

1. *Other members may have greater negotiating experience.* It is likely that the representatives from the law and procurement departments have negotiated more contracts than the project team leader. As a result, they may be better qualified to lead the discussions.
2. *Future relations with the vendor may be improved.* The majority of contract negotiations involve some arguments. Because the project team leader will have an ongoing relationship with the vendor, which the representatives from the law and procurement departments will not, it can be advantageous for the project team leader to take a secondary role during negotiations to avoid being perceived as a difficult negotiator.

Establish Ownership of the Document

Either party can "own" the document, that is, make all agreed-upon changes and circulate it to the full negotiating team. The advantage to company ownership is one of perception. The party that owns the document may be perceived as the one that is in control. The disadvantage to ownership is the time required to keep the document updated.

Provide for Breakout or Offline Discussions

Even though the company has developed its internal position on each point, there will be times when it is necessary to discuss one of the vendor's proposals before agreeing to it. If meetings are being conducted in person, there should be two breakout rooms, one for each group. If the negotiations are done via teleconference and all team members from each team are in the same room, simply pushing the mute button will have the same result. When team members are not located together, instant messaging or a separate conference line that is available only to the company can be used. Although it is possible to table internal discussions until after the official meetings, being able to come to agreement on some points during the meetings helps maintain the momentum.

Keep Accurate Records of Discussions and Open Items

Regardless of which party owns the document, it is important for the company to keep notes related to each point and to establish a list of open items, along with an indication of who is responsible for resolving the open item and a projected timeframe. Although the person who is leading the negotiations can perform this function, it is easier if the team establishes a separate scribe.

Actual review of the contract and negotiation of each point can occur in two different orders: page-turning and priority. Page-turning, which is the review of each point in the order that it occurs in the contract, is used when there are very few points of discussion. The disadvantages of using page-turning when there are numerous points are the following:

Related Issues Will Be Discussed Multiple Times

As noted above, disputed items typically fall into a few categories, each of which may appear anywhere in the contract. By reviewing the contract sequentially, the team will be forced to refer back to points that were resolved previously.

Negotiations May Be Bogged Down in Lower-Priority Items

Just as the team leader evaluated the mandatory sections of the responses to the RFP first to determine whether or not a vendor was suitable rather than reading the entire response, it is important to resolve high-priority contract items before expending energy on others. If the company has points that are nonnegotiable and the vendor is not willing to concede those points, there is no reason to continue negotiations.

Categorizing points and addressing the high-priority or big-ticket ones first allows the team to focus its attention on the key points at the beginning. Once those are resolved, the remaining issues are normally resolved relatively easily.

It should be noted that the final step in contract negotiations should be a full page-turner, where the two teams walk through the entire contract, confirming that the changes that were made are the ones they both agreed to.

Once the contract is signed, what many teams consider the "real work" of packaged software implementation can begin.

Chapter 7

Key Elements of Software Licenses

There are two primary components to obtaining a successful contract: knowing *how* to negotiate and knowing *what* to negotiate. Chapter 6 outlined the fundamentals of the negotiation process, the "how." Chapters 7, 8, and 9 review the contents, that is, the "what." Although these chapters make no attempt to include the actual wording that will be used in a contract, they provide suggested contents and can be used as a checklist for proposed contracts.

The software license is the single most important contract that the company will sign in a packaged software implementation project and is the one contract that will be included in every project. Quite simply, this is the agreement that gives the company the right to use the commercial off-the-shelf (COTS) package it has so carefully selected.

It is important to understand that in many contracts, including some of the professional services agreements and service contracts discussed in Chapters 8 and 9, the company buys a product or service and obtains ownership of it. This is not the case for software licenses. In them, the vendor retains ownership and grants only the right of use. It should be noted that that usage is normally restricted by various terms and conditions within the license.

As discussed in Chapter 6 and shown in Exhibit 6-1, the company may sign two different software licenses: one for the basic software and one for ongoing maintenance of that software. In the ideal situation, these

Exhibit 7-1   Software License Table of Contents

1. Introduction
2. Definitions
3. Term
4. Termination
5. License
6. Deliverables
7. Schedule for Deliverables
8. Maintenance (If Contained in the Base Software License)
9. Fees and Payment Terms
10. Confidentiality and Protection of Data
11. Representations and Warranties
12. Indemnification
13. Limitation of Liability
14. Miscellaneous Provisions

would be separate contracts; however, because they are sometimes combined into a single agreement, the components of both are discussed in this chapter. When they are separate, many of the items included in the basic software license agreement are repeated in the maintenance contract.

Exhibit 7-1 presents a sample table of contents for a software license. Although the order of sections will vary, depending on who drafted the agreement, the key points discussed below should be included in all software licenses.

Introduction

This section identifies the parties to the agreement, including each party's address, type of entity (corporation, etc.), and state of incorporation. It may also include references to the request for proposal (RFP) and the vendor's response and may state that the vendor's response forms a part of the agreement, although that stipulation is uncommon.

Although this section may appear to be no more than a perfunctory recital of facts, the identity of the parties is critical to the company. This is one of the clauses that determines whether the contract is a master services agreement (MSA), providing the rights negotiated within it to the entire corporation, or whether the license applies to only a single division or location.

Definitions

This section lists the important terms that are used in the contract and provides a definition for each. When these terms are used in subsequent sections of the agreement, they are capitalized. Although frequently a large number of terms are defined, certain ones are of greater importance. These include, in alphabetical order:

- *Correction.* If the company is willing to accept a workaround in lieu of correction of a bug or defect, that should be indicated in the definition. Note that "Correction" and "Defect" apply to the basic software license as well as the maintenance agreement because all software should have a warranty period during which the vendor is required to correct any defects the company uncovers.
- *Defect.* Because the company wants to ensure that the software functions as promised, it may include the words "or apparent failure" in addition to "failure of the Software to perform" and may insist on conformance with functionality described in the vendor's response to the RFP as well as the official documentation.
- *Documentation.* Documentation typically includes user manuals and installation instructions. If the response to the RFP included descriptions of the software's functionality that were part of the company's decision to select this vendor, the definition for Documentation should also include a reference to that response.
- *Licensed software.* The definition should include all Upgrades and Updates (see the definitions below) as well as the software that was delivered initially. Although it is unlikely that a dispute would occur over this point, the company will want to ensure that it has the right to use all versions of the software that the vendor provides.
- *Licensee.* If the company has multiple divisions or affiliates, they should be included in the definition of Licensee. Failure to include them may mean that if a second division chose to use the software, it would be necessary to negotiate a new agreement and pay additional licensing fees.
- *Maintenance.* If maintenance is included in the agreement, the services to be provided should be defined.
- *Release.* The definition should specify that releases include all updates and upgrades as well as new functionality that is normally included in a scheduled release. Like the definition of Licensed Software, the reason for this stipulation is to ensure that there are no disputes over what software the company is entitled to use.

- *Updates.* "Updates" typically refers to bug fixes, whereas "Upgrades" include new functionality. The distinction should be made clear in this section.
- *Upgrades.* All changes in functionality should be included in this definition.
- *Warranty period.* The period during which the vendor will provide free bug fixes and support should be clearly defined.

The primary purpose of the definitions section is to remove ambiguity and ensure that both the company and the vendor have a common understanding of key terms.

Term

Although the preceding section dealt with terminology, a different kind of term is addressed in this section. In addition to listing the effective date of the agreement, this section should specify the length of the agreement. Typically, software licenses are "perpetual," meaning that the company pays the licensing fee once and can use the software for as long as it chooses. Maintenance agreements are normally one year in length with automatic renewals. The difference in term length is one reason why maintenance agreements and license agreements are often separate contracts.

Termination

Termination clauses should be viewed as prenuptial agreements, providing a way to end the relationship without major disputes. This is one section for which contents will vary, depending on whether the contract is for the base software license or for maintenance. There are two primary types of termination clauses.

Termination for Breach of Contract

In both software licenses and maintenance agreements, each party normally reserves the right to terminate the agreement if the other breaches the contract and does not remedy the breach within a specified period following written notification. The key variable is the effect of such a termination. In the case of a software license, if the agreement is terminated for either party's breach, normally the company must return materials and cease using the software. The question is, if the company terminated because of the vendor's breach of contract, what are the financial consequences? An aggressive negotiating position is to require that the vendor return all license fees that have been paid. It is, however, unlikely that the vendor will agree to this because the software may have been in use for several years before the termination occurred. A more likely scenario is a *pro rata* refund, based on the expected life of the software (five or more years) and the time it has been fully implemented. As is true of all contract clauses, the calculation should be clearly specified.

It can be argued that termination of a maintenance agreement is less serious than termination of the base license because the company can still continue to use the software, even though it will no longer receive support, updates, and upgrades. If the company terminates for the vendor's breach of contract, it should require a refund of fees paid for the current year, possibly amortized for the period that the agreement was in effect and not breached.

If the maintenance agreement is combined with the base software license, it is important to stipulate that termination of the maintenance portion does not affect the base software. Termination of the base software license will by definition also terminate the maintenance portion.

Termination for Convenience

Using the marriage analogy, termination for convenience is a no-fault divorce. The party terminating the agreement does not need to prove that the other party breached the contract; all it needs to do is provide written notice of its intent to terminate the agreement. Software licenses rarely have this clause because the license is perpetual. Maintenance agreements, however, should allow the company to terminate the agreement if it no longer wishes to receive maintenance services.

In some maintenance contracts, there is no formal termination section. Instead, failure to pay the annual maintenance fee constitutes termination for convenience. Because payments could be delayed by corporate bureaucracy rather than a decision to discontinue maintenance, it is preferable to insist that termination for convenience will occur only upon written notice.

It is also important to note that although the company may want the right to terminate for convenience, vendors should not be given the opportunity to terminate a maintenance agreement for convenience. One of the reasons the company has chosen a packaged software solution is the expectation of ongoing support and upgrades, and allowing the vendor to cease providing that service negates a key advantage of a COTS solution.

License

This is one of the key sections of the agreement because it is here that the terms of the license are described. The ideal license from the company's view is one that is unrestricted, meaning that there are no limitations on locations where the software can be installed or used, or on the number of users, seats, or computers. In an unrestricted license, the company is given the explicit right to reproduce and use both the software and the documentation.

Some license agreements are limited to a specific number of end users or seats and may be further restricted to the computers on which the software may be installed. In these cases, it is essential that there be a clear definition of both User and Seat and that there are provisions for transferring the software from one computer to another. It is also important that there be provisions for revising the number of Users or Seats and adjusting the license fees accordingly. In some cases, the vendor will require the right to audit the number of Users or Seats. Although this is typically specified in a separate clause, the company will want to limit the frequency of such audits and to include wording that indicates that the vendor cannot disrupt normal operation of the software during an audit.

The license section should not only allow the company's employees to use the software, but also extend those rights to third parties. Typically this includes "agents," which might be consultants, outsourcers, or other service providers. (If the term Agent is used, it should be defined in Section 2.)

Extension of rights to agents is an important provision because the company may at some point outsource support of the software or use contractors and consultants to apply upgrades. Without the "agent" clause, the company could be in breach of contract. At a minimum, it would need to petition the vendor for consent to allow those agents access to the software. In some cases, the vendor will grant such consents only upon payment of a substantial sum.

There are other groups that may be included in the license. Depending on the company's business and the type of software being licensed, this section may also give the right to use the software to customers and suppliers because they may be end users, particularly of enterprise resource planning (ERP) systems.

If the company has a number of divisions or affiliates, this section may also include the right for divested entities to continue using the software for a specified period following their divestiture. In the case of essential operational software such as ERP and payroll, this clause may become critical because it provides the acquiring company time to integrate the acquisition into its own computer systems.

Deliverables

This section, which may refer to an appendix, lists everything that the vendor is to deliver to the company. This includes software, documentation, and — if the agreement includes maintenance — upgrades and updates. If the software is modular, all modules that are included should be listed. Specific versions and releases should be specified along with the deliverable. It is in this section that the company may also want to list all functionality that is to be included in the software.

The company may also require an evaluation period for the software, with licensing fees due only if the software meets its needs and is in conformance with the documentation. The evaluation period and criteria for acceptance should be specified in this section.

Schedule for Deliverables

If an appendix is used to list the deliverables, the schedule for delivery of each item can be included in it. If not, the delivery dates should be specified in this section.

Maintenance (If Contained in the Base Software License)

If there is a separate maintenance agreement, the elements contained in this section would be specified in various sections of that contract, including the Deliverables section. For a combined software license or maintenance agreement, the following items should be included:

- *General statement of services to be provided.* This may be as simple as "provide all assistance required to ensure that the Software performs in accordance with the Documentation." It may also include references to upgrades and response to user questions about the software's functionality. The key here is to specify what the vendor will do.
- *Hours when service will be provided.* When services will be provided is almost as important as what is included. For mission-critical systems, hours of service should be twenty-four hours a

day, seven days a week. If lesser coverage is acceptable, this section should clearly indicate the time zones associated with the hours of service and — if holidays are excluded — a list of the specific holidays the company observes because these may differ from the vendor's. The company may also use this section to specify that the vendor will provide a toll-free hotline for reporting defects.

■ *Expected response time.* Because the hotline may need to forward calls to a second-level support group, this clause specifies the time in which that second level will respond to the bug report. If services are not being provided twenty-four hours a day, seven days a week, the section should define response time for calls that occur outside normal working hours or close to the end of the workday.

■ *Definition of severity levels.* Defects are normally assigned severity levels, depending on their impact to the company, and speed of resolution typically varies based on the severity. A clear definition of each severity level should be included. This section should also indicate who assigns the severity (normally the company).

■ *Expected resolution time.* This clause specifies the time in which a defect will be resolved, based on its severity. It is important to note that even when services are provided twenty-four hours a day, seven days a week, the vendor may work on low-severity items only during normal business hours. If that is the case, this section should indicate whether or not problem resolution requires staff to work outside of normal hours, based on severity and, like Expected Response Time, should provide for calls placed outside normal business hours.

Fees and Payment Terms

As the title indicates, this section lists the fees that will be paid to license the software or ongoing maintenance. If the software is modular, fees are typically shown by module and may be included in an appendix. When fees are based on the number of users or seats, the per-user or per-seat costs and quantity discounts, if applicable, should be indicated.

This section should also specify when the vendor will invoice the company and when payment is due. Because the company's standard payment terms may be longer than the vendor's ideal situation, this is a clause that is frequently the subject of negotiation. So, too, are the consequences of late payment. If penalties are to be incurred for late payment, the calculation of those penalties and the date on which they will be assessed (which is normally 15 to 30 days after the due date of the payment) should be clearly identified. Responsibility for payment of taxes should also be included in this section.

Although maintenance is sometimes priced at "x percent of the then-current license fee," it is to the company's advantage to put a cap on fee increases by either specifying that the maintenance fee is based on the license fee the company actually paid, not the one in effect each year, or by insisting that fees cannot increase by more than the lesser of y percent or some price index that is relevant to the company.

Because maintenance involves providing services as well as concrete deliverables, the company may want to give the vendor an incentive to meet the response and resolution times established in Section 8. This can be done by including a clause specifying that if the vendor fails to meet the agreed-upon response and resolution times, the vendor will give the company credits against its next invoice. The calculation of these credits can be based on the amount of time the defect was unresolved and is normally a percentage of the overall fee. Without such a clause, the company's only resort should the vendor fail to meet its problem resolution commitments is to terminate the contract for breach. In most cases, that is not the desired remedy for poor service.

Confidentiality and Protection of Data

Because it is possible that the vendor will gain access to some company confidential information or may have copies of company data, whether or not classified as confidential, it is important to include a section indicating the responsibilities for protecting that data and confidential information.

This section is normally made bidirectional because the company may also have access to vendor data or confidential information.

Representations and Warranties

Representations and warranties can be viewed as promises that each party to a contract makes to the other. Although this section falls into the "legalese" category and is of interest primarily to the attorneys, there are several clauses that are particularly important to the company.

- *Noninfringement.* The vendor states that the software does not violate or infringe on any other party's patents, trademarks, copyrights, or other forms of intellectual property (IP). This is critical because software that violates another company's IP rights can be the subject of lawsuits, and the vendor may, as a result of that litigation, be prohibited from licensing the software to anyone. Such a decision would leave the company without an operational system.

■ *Conformance.* The vendor agrees that for a specified period the software will operate as specified in the documentation. Because the functionality described in the documentation is one of the reasons the company selected this product, this is an important clause.

■ *Viruses.* The code as delivered by the vendor is virus free. The importance of this warranty should be self-evident.

■ *Disabling code.* There is nothing in the software that will cause it to cease to function either totally or partially on a specific date or when a specific number of users access it. Although it is understandable that the vendor will want to be paid for the number of users or seats actually used if pricing is by user or seat, shutting down the system if the agreed-upon number is exceeded places the company at high risk and should be prohibited.

■ *Compliance with laws.* If the software is designed to comply with state, local, or federal laws (e.g., a payroll system), the vendor agrees that the software is indeed in compliance and that it will provide updates on a timely basis to ensure that the software remains in compliance. Like Conformance, this is one of the reasons the company selected packaged software.

Indemnification

Although the vendor has warranted that its software does not infringe on anyone's IP, there is always the possibility of a claim. This section states that should the company be sued for trademark infringement or other intellectual property claims as a result of using the software, the vendor will assume financial responsibility for those claims. This section also outlines the company's rights should such a suit occur. These typically include as a last resort the ability to terminate the agreement and receive a refund of fees if the vendor is unable to resolve the suit or provide a satisfactory workaround.

Limitation of Liability

Because most companies and vendors are risk averse, it is normal for contracts to include a limitation of liability section. This puts a cap on the amount of damages (punitive or actual) either party can receive from the other. It also lists the exclusions to that cap. Exclusions typically include breach of the confidentiality and representations and warranties sections. The reason for these exclusions is that the responsibilities outlined in those sections are critical to the company and the vendor, and failure of one party to live up to those obligations could have serious negative effects on the other party.

Miscellaneous Provisions

Although a catchall section, there are several critical clauses in it:

- *Source code escrow.* This clause is designed to protect the company. If the vendor does not provide source code as part of its deliverables, source code and documentation should be placed in escrow and made available to the company in the event the vendor breaches the contract, files for bankruptcy, or ceases doing business. Having source code may enable the company to continue running and enhancing the system if the vendor is no longer willing or able to do so.
- *Force majeure.* This clause indicates that neither party is responsible for delays if caused by an event beyond their control. The events that qualify as *Force Majeure* should be clearly defined. Typically, they include natural disasters such as hurricanes and earthquakes as well as general strikes and acts of terrorism.
- *Dispute resolution.* Unfortunately, disputes do occur, and it is important to provide a method for dealing with them. If the individuals who raised the dispute cannot resolve it, there should be a clear multilevel escalation path along with a timeframe for the various escalations. Because it is possible that the company and the vendor will not be able to resolve the dispute even at the highest escalation level, this clause should also specify whether or not disputes will be resolved by a court of law or arbitration.
- *Assignment.* Because mergers and acquisitions occur, it is to the company's advantage to retain the right to assign the contract to another party, including a successor company, should the company be acquired by or merge with another firm. This helps guarantee that the software will continue to run even during a period of transition.
- *Nonsolicitation.* Employees are valuable assets. As a result, a nonsolicitation clause is normally included in any contract where the company and vendor employees will interact. This clause prevents

either party from hiring the other's staff without prior approval during the term of the contract and for some period afterward. Although this is standard, the company may want to reserve the right to hire the vendor's staff if the agreement is terminated for breach of contract by the vendor. Hiring vendor staff could improve the company's ability to continue running and enhancing the software if it no longer does business with the vendor.

- *Audit.* If the license fee is based on a specified number of seats or users, the vendor may want the right to audit the company's compliance. As noted above, this clause should include a maximum number of audits per year as well a maximum duration for each audit.

- *Other.* The Miscellaneous Provisions section normally also includes the state law under which the contract will be governed, the names and titles of the persons who should receive notices related to the contract, and provisions for amending the agreement.

Whether or not the company chooses to sign the vendor's standard license agreement without modifications, it is important that the project team understand the contents of the contract and that the company's attorney approve the wording. The contract is, after all, the foundation for the relationship between the vendor and the company, and it is in both parties' interest to have that foundation be a strong one.

Chapter 8

Professional Services Agreements

All contracts are not created equal. As discussed in previous chapters, there are significant differences among the various types of contracts. For the purposes of this book, contracts are divided into three categories: software licenses, professional services agreements, and service contracts. Software licenses, as Chapter 7 explains, grant the company the right to use a standard product, whereas professional services agreements and service contracts provide more customized services.

Professional services agreements and service contracts can be classified as service-based agreements and have more similarities than differences. The primary distinction between them is that professional services agreements are typically for a one-time effort, whereas service contracts provide for ongoing support. Professional services agreements are reviewed in this chapter, service contracts in Chapter 9.

As shown in Exhibit 8-1, the differences between software licenses and service-based agreements (both Professional Services Agreements and Service Contracts) are more significant than those between the two types of service-based agreements. The fundamental difference is that when a company signs a software license agreement, it is buying the right to use a product. That same product is offered to a number of companies without any modification. This is, of course, the essence of packaged software. Regardless of the cost, risk to the company is reduced, because the product is standard and, presumably, already in use and of proven quality.

Exhibit 8-1   Differences between Software Licenses and Service Agreements

Element	Software License	Service-Based Agreement
Deliverable	Product	Service
Ownership of deliverable	Vendor	Normally company
Deliverables unique to company?	No	Yes
Risk to company of erroneous deliverable	Low	Medium to high
Importance of individual vendor staff	Medium to low	High

The deliverables in service-based agreements, on the other hand, are unique to each company. Whether it is advice about negotiating with a specific vendor, guidance and support during implementation, or the development of reports, interfaces, conversions, and extensions (RICE), the work is customized for each company. Although the supplier of these services may have guided many companies through contract negotiations, provided implementation support for a dozen different instances of the software, or developed hundreds of reports, the services it provides to each company — although similar to those it has provided to others — will differ in some respects. Those differences increase the risk to the company.

Similarly, because the work is customized and will be provided by specific individuals, the qualifications of those individuals are important to the company. The company is no longer dealing with a product that was developed by a faceless team. Instead, the success of the work is contingent on the staff's abilities, just as it would be if the work were being performed by the company's own employees.

Services are fundamentally different from products. As a result, service-based agreements normally contain a number of sections in addition to those that are included in a software license. In terms of the journalist's five Ws, the majority of the sections relate to who, what, and where. Other clauses can be classified as fee related and miscellaneous.

Who?

Because the work being performed is so dependent on the individuals assigned to the engagement, there are a number of clauses that the company needs to consider including.

Qualifications

If the company expects the consultants, advisors, and staff (which will be referred to as "consultants" for simplicity) to have specific expertise, the contract should be explicit in defining that expertise. At a minimum, it should include a phrase similar to "Vendor shall assign employees that it has determined are qualified to perform all necessary tasks." Assignment of staff who are clearly lacking the necessary qualifications is a violation of the contract and would give the company reason to request their replacement.

Interviewing

One way of determining whether or not consultants have the needed expertise is for the company to review resumes and interview each proposed consultant. Although this approach has its merits, some companies choose not to interview consultants because they fear coemployment suits.

In a coemployment suit, consultants allege that although they were paid by the vendor, their work was directed by the company and because they were treated like the company's employees, they should be entitled to company benefits such as pensions and profit sharing. Although such suits are most common in long-term engagements, some companies have established polices that prohibit interviewing and day-to-day direction of consultants, even on short projects. Whether the company plans to interview proposed consultants or not, the contract should leave no doubt about its position.

Dismissal

The company should reserve the right to require the vendor to remove any consultant for any reason. This may become a point of contention during contract negotiations, with the vendor insisting that consultants be removed only "for cause." Because "cause" requires egregious violations of the contract, dismissal for "cause" is normally too limiting to the company and should be avoided. Personality conflicts, which could interfere with the successful completion of the project, are not "cause" but should be a reason for replacement of a consultant.

Replacement Policy

If consultants need to be replaced, either because the company found them lacking or because of vendor-planned rotation or their leaving the vendor, there should be a clearly defined policy of who bears the cost of training the replacement staff. Normally, the company will specify that replacement is done at no cost to it and that there is a predetermined overlap or transition period.

Management

If the engagement will be large or lengthy, the company will typically want to specify that the vendor will provide a program or project manager. Because the manager is a key player and the company wants to ensure continuity, this section should include a guarantee that the manager will remain on the account for a specified time. It may also indicate that the manager will be assigned to the account full time.

Solicitation Policy

Because the company and vendor staff will be interacting more often on a professional services agreement than would occur with a simple software license, it is important to have a clear policy about solicitation of each other's staff. Although this clause is typically included in a software license, the terms may vary for a service-based agreement. The company will normally seek to prohibit the vendor's solicitation of its employees but may want the right to hire consultants, particularly if the contract is terminated for cause. It may also grant the vendor the right to hire its staff if that staff will be laid off as a result of this project.

Noncompete

Because the vendor's consultants may have access to company confidential information and may, as a result of their work with the company, learn of processes that the company considers part of its competitive advantage, it is not uncommon for the company to insist on a clause prohibiting the vendor from assigning consultants to one of the company's competitors for a specified timeframe. This is in addition to the standard confidentiality clauses and is designed to provide additional protection for the company.

Subcontractors

Some vendors use subcontractors as well as their own employees to perform services. To some extent, this increases the company's risk, because although the contract should clearly specify that the vendor is responsible for any subcontractors as if they were its own employees, the vendor has less leverage over subcontractors than it does over employees.

If the company wants to allow the vendor to use subcontractors, the contract should include clauses that allow it to reject subcontractors, as if they were vendor staff. This rejection may encompass entire subcontracting firms as well as individuals and is particularly useful if the company has had poor experiences with specific firms that might be used as subcontractors.

Background Checks

If consultants will be working on the company's site, the company may want to ensure that the vendor has performed background checks, drug testing, and any other screening that the company would perform on its own employees. The purpose of this clause is to reduce the company's risk by ensuring that all on-site staff meet its minimum standards. Although less common, this clause may be extended to the vendor's off-site staff.

On-Site Considerations

As part of the company's risk reduction plan, the contract should include clauses that ensure that any consultants who are working at a company site will follow the company's code of conduct and adhere to security, safety, and other policies. Because the company has some liability for on-site consultants, this is an important stipulation. It protects the company's own employees as well as the contractors.

Nondisclosure Agreement

When consultants will be used, in addition to the standard nondisclosure and confidentially clauses in the contract, the company may want to attach its own nondisclosure agreement (NDA) and require that each of the consultants sign it or an equivalent agreement. Although consultants are bound by the standard clauses, this provision ensures that they are aware of their responsibility.

The NDA restricts disclosure of company confidential information and, for simplicity's sake, may also include noncompete clauses. When software will be developed or processes reengineered, the NDA may also address intellectual property (IP) rights. It is common for the company to insist that it owns anything that the consultant develops while working on the account and to require assignment of those rights to the company.

What?

Although a software license includes sections related to deliverables, a service-based agreement typically has additional clauses.

Acceptance of Deliverables

This provision is similar to the evaluation clause for a software package in that it specifies how long the company has to review deliverables and what happens if the company rejects them. There are, however, additional considerations. Although the company will terminate a license agreement and pay nothing if the package does not meet its requirements or does not conform to the documentation, the issue is more complex for service-based work. Because the work is customized for the company, there is a greater likelihood that the deliverables may not meet the company's expectations when first produced. It is in neither party's best interests to terminate the agreement over minor discrepancies.

- *Acceptance criteria.* To avoid contention over whether or not a deliverable meets the company's requirements, there should be clearly defined written criteria for evaluating and accepting each deliverable. These acceptance criteria may include format as well as content and functionality. For example, if a deliverable is the project plan, acceptance criteria might be, "A detailed project plan delivered in MS Project 2003. Responsibility for each task will be shown, and no task will exceed 40 hours." If there are a number of deliverables, they and the related acceptance criteria may be shown in an appendix.
- *Rework period.* Normally if the company rejects a deliverable, it will give the vendor a specified period of time to correct the problem and provide a reworked product. Although this timeframe should be specified in the contract, it is helpful to add "or unless otherwise mutually agreed" because some problems may require more time to resolve than the standard established in the contract. This additional wording provides flexibility and protects both the company and the vendor.
- *Ultimate rejection.* If, after rejecting the same deliverable multiple times, the company decides that the vendor will never meet the acceptance criteria, it may want to terminate the entire agreement. In that case, there should be a provision for refund of any fees paid for that deliverable. Under some circumstances, the company may want the right to return all deliverables that have been provided to date and to receive a full refund of any fees paid.

Ownership of Deliverables

Although the vendor typically owns the software and all documentation in a software license agreement, the company will normally want to retain ownership of service-based deliverables. This issue may be complicated if the deliverables are extensions or modifications to vendor software. In those cases, the vendor may reserve ownership rights to such work in the base software license.

Some vendors will agree that the company owns the rights to anything they deliver but will ask for a "perpetual royalty-free license" for those deliverables. In other words, they want the right to reuse the work and sell it to other customers. Company policy on granting such rights will vary, but in general, the company should not agree to such a clause unless it has received substantially reduced rates from the vendor for the work in question or believes that agreeing to this clause will result in concessions from the vendor on other, more important contract terms.

Changes in Scope

Although scope changes occur most frequently in long-term agreements, it is important to provide for them in the contract, even if it is expected to be a short engagement. In addition to describing the process for requesting, estimating, and approving a change in scope, the contract should answer the following questions:

■ *Who can propose a change in scope?* Some companies reserve that right for themselves, although it is more common to allow either the vendor or the company to propose one.
■ *What form will be used?* Although not mandatory, it is useful to have a standard form for changes in scope because that ensures that all important information is included and standardizes the process. Exhibit 8-2 shows a sample scope change form.
■ *What timeframes are associated with the change in scope?* There should be clearly defined periods in which the vendor will respond with the cost and schedule impact of a change request and in which the company will either approve or disapprove the proposal.
■ *Who will approve scope changes?* The company should specify who has the authority to either approve or disapprove the vendor's proposals. Because some changes may be extensive, approval authority may vary, depending on the costs associated with the change.

Exhibit 8-2   Request for Change in Scope

To Be Completed by Company				
Project name:			Change No.:	
Vendor name:		Vendor program manager name:		

To Be Completed by Requester				
Requester's name:		Phone No.:		Date:
Description of requested change in scope:				
Reason for change in scope:				
Benefits of change:				
Costs of not doing change:				
Priority:	High ☐ Medium ☐ Low ☐			

To Be Completed by Vendor	
Project elements impacted	Description of impact (cost, schedule, other)
Risk impact: High ☐ Medium ☐ Low ☐	
Schedule impact of this change:	
Cost of this change:	

ACCEPTANCE or REJECTION	
Company	
Acceptance ( )	Rejection ( )
Accepted / Rejected by:	Date:
Title:	Rejection reason:
Vendor acceptance	
Approved by:	Date:
Title:	

Reporting

If, as part of the work being done, the company expects the vendor to provide periodic status reports or metrics, the type and frequency of reporting should be specified in the contract. If the company has a specific format that it prefers for these reports, that format should be included as an exhibit and explicitly referenced in this clause.

Use of Company Resources

If the consultants will be working at a company site, any resources that they will require should be described. "Resources" may include office space, telephones (including explicit inclusion or exclusion of international calls), administrative assistance, PCs and LAN access, as well as specified percentages of the company's subject matter experts' (SMEs) time.

Where?

One of the questions that both the company and the vendor need to answer in service-related contracts is where the work will be performed. In some cases, particularly when there is a need for extensive SME contact, such as during the requirements definition phase, work is best done at the company's site. In other cases, especially when coding is being outsourced to lower cost regions, work will be done at one of the vendor's sites. There is no one correct answer, but the contract should include clauses specifying the company's expectations.

Fee Related

Service-based contracts are normally priced in one of three ways: fixed price, time and materials (T&M), or T&M not-to-exceed. As shown in Exhibit 8-3, there are advantages and disadvantages to each. Specific considerations that should be addressed are shown below.

Fixed Price

In addition to specifying the total amount that the company will pay for the deliverables, the contract should include a payment schedule, ideally tied to acceptance (not delivery) of the deliverables. If the deliverable is software, it is helpful to reserve final payment until the end of the warranty period. This provides the vendor with a financial incentive to correct bugs quickly.

Exhibit 8-3   Comparison of Fee Structures for Service-Based Agreements

Component	Fixed Price	T&M	T&M Not-to-Exceed
Total cost	Highest[a]	Lowest	Middle
Ability to make changes in scope	Difficult[b]	Easy	Difficult
Level of company oversight required	High[c]	Low	Low
Ease of budgeting	High	Low[d]	High

[a] Because the vendor assumes the risk of schedule and cost overruns, it will include a "fudge factor."
[b] Any changes require recalculating fees and the impact on the schedule, which may be cumbersome for both the company and the vendor.
[c] It is important that someone ensure that work is proceeding on schedule and that payments match the deliverables.
[d] Costs are somewhat unpredictable.

Although vendors may ask for a portion of the fee upon signing of the contract, many companies refuse that request, pointing out that they have received nothing of value at that point.

Time and Materials

Although it may appear simple to calculate the fees for a T&M contract, that is not always the case. The basic calculation is time expended multiplied by the rate. To clarify that calculation, the contract should answer the following questions:

- *Which rates will apply?* Most vendors have various levels of consultants, each with a different hourly or daily rate. As a result, the mix of consultant levels can have a major impact on the overall cost. The contract should indicate how many consultants of each level will be assigned to the account, and the company should understand how the vendor determined that mix.
- *Can base rates be increased?* If the term of the agreement is several years, the vendor may ask for periodic adjustment of rates. The contract should specify when such adjustments may occur, what the maximum increase will be, how it is calculated, and whether existing work is affected. Rate increases are typically tied to a major index of prices but may be limited to *the lesser* of that index's increase and a predetermined percentage. The company may also stipulate that engagements with less than a certain number of months left will be excluded from rate increases.

- *What happens if a consultant is promoted?* If an engagement is a lengthy one, it is possible that a consultant will receive a promotion during it. Should the company pay a higher rate for that person after the promotion? Many companies object to this policy, pointing out that the consultant is actually performing the same work, regardless of the title.
- *What constitutes a day?* When rates are specified as "daily" rather than hourly, it is important to have a clear definition of a day. In many cases, the company will argue that a professional day is more than eight hours.
- *What about overtime?* Even if a professional day is defined as ten hours, there may be times when consultants work longer than that. The contract should specify whether overtime is billed at the normal rate, or if there is a premium for hours in excess of a specified number per day or per week. Whether or not the company agrees to pay a premium, it should protect itself from cost overruns by requiring that all overtime be approved in advance.
- *Are travel hours billed?* Some vendors will not have sufficient staff with the required skills in the same city as the company's main location and will propose to fly in consultants for the engagement. Many will go home for weekends, returning each Monday. Should their travel time be billed to the company? It is obviously to the company's advantage to argue that travel time is not billable.

Time and Materials Not-to-Exceed

This fee structure is a hybrid, combining major elements from T&M and fixed price. All the points discussed above apply to it.

Expenses

In most cases, expenses are in addition to professional services fees. Because expenses can be substantial, it is important that the contract answer the following questions:

- *What expenses are included?* It is normal for a company to pay travel expenses, if consultants are coming from a different location. Some vendors, however, also charge an administrative fee that covers their billing, copying, and some overhead expenses. This may be priced as a percentage of the professional fees, whether or not actual expenses were incurred. There may be other costs, including licensing of software for the consultants' use. If the company is willing to incur any of these costs, the contract should clearly specify which costs will be reimbursed and whether there are caps to any expense.

- *Whose travel policy will be used?* It is to the company's advantage to review the vendor's travel policy and compare it with its own. If the company's policy is more restrictive, it should insist that the vendor's consultants follow it.
- *Is preapproval required?* Again, it is to the company's advantage to require that all travel and other expenses be approved in advance.
- *How often will expenses be billed?* Most companies will ask that expenses be billed no more frequently than monthly.
- *Are receipts required?* Although the company may not require that receipts be included with each invoice for expenses, the contract should include a clause that specifies that receipts will be provided upon request.

Miscellaneous

Although the majority of the clauses in this section are identical to those in a software license, several are of particular importance.

- *Insurance.* Because consultants may be working at the company's locations, it is important that the vendor have comprehensive insurance. This includes general liability and automobile, as well as "errors and omissions" coverage. Although the company is responsible for negligence on its part, it needs to ensure that the vendor is covered in the event of an accident or deliberate destruction of property by one of its consultants.
- *Indemnification.* Again, because consultants may be on-site, the contract should include provisions that the vendor will indemnify the company for any damage caused by its consultants.
- *Force majeure.* There should be a clear definition of the company's rights, should the vendor be unable to produce the expected deliverables because of a *force majeure* event. This may include terminating the contract and assigning the work to another company if the *force majeure* event extends beyond a specified timeframe.

When negotiating a professional services agreement, the company should review all the clauses described in Chapter 7 as well as the points outlined above to ensure that the proposed contract is complete and adequately protects the company's interests.

Chapter 9

Service Contracts and Statements of Work

The final category of contracts to be reviewed is the service contract. Along with professional services agreements, service contracts can be classified as service-based agreements. As discussed in Chapter 8, the primary difference between a professional services agreement and a service contract is the length of the engagement. Although a professional services agreement is typically written for one-time efforts, such as when the company engages an advisor or a consultant to assist with a specific portion of the project, a service contract is longer term. It consists of either on-going work of the same nature or multiple pieces of work of a similar nature. Although many companies consider service contracts synonymous with on-going support agreements, as shown on Exhibit 9-1, they can used for either development or support engagements.

The critical element in service contracts is not the content of the work — support versus development — but the timeframe. The longer term of a service contract creates complexities that are not present in a professional services agreement and may result in a different contractual structure.

Two-Tiered Contracts

All contracts discussed in previous chapters have been monolithic; that is, each consists of a single legal document. Although there may be

Exhibit 9-1 Examples of Use of Service Contracts

Development	Support
Assistance with phased implementation of multiple modules	Outsourcing of running of the software on company's computers
Assistance with implementation of full functionality, phased by location or division	Total outsourcing of running of the software, including use of vendor's computers (ASP)
	Outsourcing of maintenance and help desk for base software
	Outsourcing of maintenance and help desk for custom work

appendices and exhibits, they are drafted and negotiated at the same time as the body of the contract. In contrast, service contracts are frequently designed as two-tiered agreements.

Two-tiered contracts consist of two or more separate legal documents that together form the entire agreement between the company and the vendor. Although it is possible for both portions to be negotiated and signed at the same time, it is more common for there to be separate negotiations for each part. For the purposes of this book, the two tiers will be referred to as the master services agreement (MSA) and the statement of work (SOW).

Unlike the MSAs discussed in Chapter 6, these MSAs do not include all aspects of the relationship between the company and the vendor. In a two-tiered agreement, the MSA contains all the standard terms and conditions, including the rates that will be used to calculate fees. It does not include specific details of the work to be performed. Those, along with the associated costs and schedule, are described in the SOW. The MSA outlines the conditions under which the company and the vendor will do business; the SOW describes the actual work that the vendor will perform and the fees that the company will pay for that work.

It should be noted that there is a many-to-one relationship between the SOW and the MSA; that is, any one MSA may have multiple SOWs associated with it. Although unlikely, it is possible that an MSA may have no SOWs, in which case the MSA will have little value, because no work is being done under its terms and conditions (Ts and Cs).

Because of the greater length of service contracts and that phased work is frequently the subject of these contracts, a two-tiered contract is often easier to manage than a monolithic one.

Other advantages of a two-tiered agreement are the following.

Terms and Conditions Are Negotiated Only Once

Even when the term of the overall agreement is multiple years, with engagements expected to begin throughout that period, it is necessary to negotiate the bulk of the contract only once. Because Ts and Cs are often the most controversial part of contract negotiations, it is helpful to address them once and only once. It should also be noted that vendors are frequently more willing to compromise at the beginning of a relationship — the "honeymoon period" — than they are several years into it. This is another reason to develop a single set of Ts and Cs.

Master Services Agreement Negotiations Are Streamlined

Because details of the actual work are not included, there is less to negotiate. This allows the team to develop the framework for the overall relationship without being bogged down in details of specific engagements.

Attorney Time May Be Reduced

This is a corollary to the previous point. Because the SOW contains primarily business-related aspects of the work as opposed to contractual terms, it is frequently subject to minimal — if any — legal review. This can reduce costs as well as elapsed time for SOW creation. As noted below, an SOW template with the standard wording drafted and approved by an attorney is one way to streamline SOW development.

It Is Not Necessary To Know All Work That Will Be Involved at the Beginning of the Project

When the company initiates a project, it may know that it would like the vendor to provide assistance in development of reports, interfaces, conversions, and extensions (RICE) for the pilot implementation and that, if the pilot is successful, it may want the vendor to provide similar assistance for the next phase. Without a two-tiered approach, the company would either have to guess at the scope of all the work to be performed or invoke the contract's change of scope provision each time a new piece of work is identified. The first approach is risky; the second can result in a contract with so many revisions that it becomes unwieldy and difficult to understand.

In contrast, because the two-tiered approach anticipates multiple SOWs, it is necessary to know only the type of work that will be included, not all the details. There is no risk to the company because work is defined as the requirements are identified. Changes in scope are minimized because individual SOWs can be written for specified pieces of work.

The primary disadvantage to a two-tiered approach is that vendors may be reluctant to negotiate rates without knowing the extent of work they will be given. Because rates are part of the MSA, it is essential that they be determined before that contract is finalized.

Discounts are typically based on volume. Although the company will want to obtain the lowest possible rate for all work, it is not uncommon to include a volume discount schedule as part of the rate section of the MSA. Because discounts are typically based on annual expenditures, it is important to specify whether the year used for that calculation is a calendar year or is based on the effective date of the MSA. It is also important to determine whether discounts apply only to work in excess of the volume threshold or whether, once a predetermined volume is reached, the discounts are given retroactively to all work.

Master Services Agreement

Because MSAs are software-related contracts, they will contain many of the clauses described in the previous two chapters. In addition, an MSA should include the following:

References to Statements of Work

The MSA should explicitly reference the fact that SOWs are expected to exist. Because they may be subject to renewal and termination separate from the MSA itself, there may be additional clauses defining those terms.

Definition of Types of Work To Be Performed

It is important to have a clear understanding of the type of work that the vendor will perform in accordance with the Ts and Cs established in the MSA. Simply stating that "implementation services" will be provided can lead to confusion and conflict during the term of the agreement. The vendor might argue that program management is not an implementation service but a specialized type of work that demands a higher rate than those negotiated in the MSA, whereas the company expects the vendor to provide this service at the agreed-upon rates. To avoid problems, the company should list all the work that it includes under "implementation services," along with an explanation of each.

Format of Statement of Work

Although SOWs can be free-form documents, it is advantageous to have a standard format for them. Like the standard scope change form, having a predefined format increases consistency and helps ensure that all key elements are included. At a minimum, the MSA should include a table of contents for the SOW.

Order of Precedence

When a contract has multiple parts, as envisioned in an MSA-SOW structure, there is the possibility for conflict between those parts. For example, the MSA may state that the company must review all deliverables within ten business days, but an SOW may show a three-day review cycle. The MSA should specify which portion of the overall contract (MSA plus SOW) prevails in the event of such a conflict. To prevent changes to key sections of the MSA, such as rates, payment terms, and ownership of deliverables, it is desirable to have the MSA take precedence over the SOW. To allow flexibility for business-related issues such as deliverable review time, it is helpful to have the corresponding section of the MSA include the wording "unless otherwise specified in the SOW."

Termination for Convenience

As noted in Chapter 7, when the contract is for support services, termination for convenience should be unilateral. Because the services being provided may be critical to the company, only the company should be able to invoke this clause.

There are other considerations for termination for convenience. Because the MSA is the parent contract with SOWs as children, it is important to specify whether the termination will occur immediately or whether it will take effect when all SOWs reach their contractual termination or expiration date. If the company wants the right to terminate a single SOW for convenience but leave the MSA and all other SOWs in force, the MSA should include that stipulation.

Termination for Force Majeure

Support services can be mission critical for a company. As a result, the company needs recourse if the vendor is unable to provide those services because of a *force majeure*. The vendor cannot be held responsible for events beyond its control, but the company should have the right to terminate the contract and find another vendor to provide the same services.

Like termination for convenience, there may be circumstances under which the company wants to terminate a single SOW but to keep other SOWs and the MSA itself in force. Because this is a multipart contract, the MSA should provide for that possibility.

Reporting

Communication is a key element in any successful relationship. Although it is likely that the vendor and the company will have frequent informal communications during the life of a service contract, periodic formal reporting is also needed. Professional services agreements may include some reporting elements; however, reporting becomes more important in long-term agreements, especially those related to support. The company should clearly define the type of reports it expects, their content, and frequency and include that information — along with templates, if available — in an appendix to the MSA. This is particularly critical when dealing with service-level agreements (SLAs) because payments to the vendor may be based on achieving specific quantity and quality measures.

Auditing

Although software licenses with fees based on the number of users or seats provide for the vendor to audit the company, the tables are turned on service contracts. Many service-related agreements (both professional service agreements and service contracts) include the ability for the company to audit the vendor's records. Although auditing may be to verify that the vendor actually expended the number of hours which it billed in time and materials (T&M) contracts, auditing is also used to determine whether the service levels being reported are in fact accurate.

Service Level and Deliverable Credits

It is possible that the vendor will not meet its contractual responsibilities, either by failing to meet the agreed-upon date for a deliverable or by not providing the specified level of service. The company needs recourse in the event of such nonperformance. Because financial penalties are those that often have the greatest impact on a vendor's performance, the consequences for nonperformance normally involve the vendor paying the company some agreed-upon amount. This is often termed a credit.

In the event that the vendor does not meet the agreed-upon service levels or delivery schedule, the contract should provide for a correction period and, if the performance is still unsatisfactory, credits to the company. To avoid disputes, the calculation of the credits and the timeframe in which they will be assessed and paid should be clearly identified.

Steering Committee

Long-term support agreements typically have various levels of management to review the progress of individual SOWs and the health of the overall relationship. One of the most important review groups is a steering committee that consists primarily of key end users. The purpose of the steering committee is to review the vendor's performance, prioritize work, if needed, and resolve disputes. If a steering committee will exist, its composition, responsibilities, and frequency of meeting should be defined in the MSA.

The one thing that an MSA should not include is a guarantee that the company will spend a specified amount of money with the vendor. Although this is a clause that most vendors will request, it increases the company's risk and should be avoided.

Statements of Work

Because the company enters into a two-tiered contract with the expectation that multiple SOWs will be associated with the MSA, it is useful to create a template SOW that includes all standard wording as well as the format for the detailed business-related information that will constitute the bulk of the SOW. This template should be reviewed and approved by the company's legal staff and presented to the vendor. Because the SOW will not include Ts and Cs, there should be minimal negotiation involved in the creation of the template.

The advantages of an SOW template are:

- *Consistency.* Each SOW will have the same format as well as a common set of contents. This simplifies drafting of individual SOWs and ensures that all needed elements are included.
- *Reduced legal review.* As discussed above, use of a template with preapproved standard wording should have the effect of reducing or eliminating legal review of each SOW as it is drafted.
- *Increased vendor comfort during MSA negotiations.* Because the MSA does not include the specific work to be performed, vendors may be uncomfortable with references to an SOW format they have not seen. Providing the proposed template may alleviate some concerns and help expedite MSA negotiations.

Because the nature of work being provided under a development SOW differs from that of a support SOW, the two types of SOWs will not be identical. However, all SOWs should include the following information:

- *Incorporation with MSA.* Although a statement of work is a separate and legally binding contract, it is also part of an MSA. Typically, the first page of an SOW includes a phrase similar to, "This SOW is an addendum to the MSA for *fill in the blanks* services dated *fill in the date* between *fill in the name* (The Company) and *fill in the name* (The Vendor)." Although seemingly innocuous, that statement means that the Ts and Cs negotiated in the MSA also apply to the SOW.
- *Effective date.* Because SOWs are by definition addenda to the MSA, although it is possible for their effective dates to be the same as the MSA, normally SOW effective dates will be later than that of the MSA. To avoid confusion, it is important to specify the effective date rather than have it default to the date the SOW was signed because the signatures may be obtained either before or after work is begun.
- *Termination or expiration date.* Although an SOW for development services might terminate when the company has accepted the last deliverable or the warranty period has ended, a support SOW typically expires after a specified number of months or years, unless the company renews it. In either case, the method for determining the end date should be clearly specified.

Development Statements of Work

Because the heart of a development SOW is the deliverables that the vendor will provide, an SOW for development services will normally include a number of sections related to those deliverables. The information should be provided in sufficient detail to avoid confusion and possible disputes. A development SOW should include the following information:

- *Detailed description of deliverables.* As has been discussed in previous chapters, specificity is essential. "Design me a house" is unlikely to result in the same deliverable as, "I want a 2000-square-foot center all colonial with three bedrooms, two and a half baths, and a two-car attached garage." The more information the company can give the vendor, the more likely the deliverables are to meet the company's expectations. If, for example, the vendor is coding based on a requirements document, the requirements document should be referenced in the SOW so that there is no confusion over what is to be delivered.

■ *Format of deliverables.* If the company has coding standards, wants documentation provided in a specific format, or expects training to be delivered in a particular manner, the SOW should indicate that, including references to standards and formats.

■ *Schedule for delivery.* A detailed schedule, showing the date on which the final version of each deliverable will be given to the company, is needed. If the company wants to review interim versions of the deliverable, those may be added to the schedule; however, penalties for late delivery normally apply only to the final version.

■ *Schedule for review.* The date on which the company will complete its review of each deliverable should be included in the SOW. As noted above, the review period may vary from the default established in the MSA.

■ *Acceptance criteria.* Each deliverable should be accompanied by a clear indication of the criteria that will be used to determine whether or not the company will accept it. Chapter 8 provides more information about acceptance criteria.

■ *Fees.* The fees and the dates on which they are payable form an important part of the SOW. It is to the company's advantage to tie payments to acceptance rather than delivery of deliverables because there is no guarantee that the vendor will provide a quality product the first time. It is also helpful to establish a warranty period and to make final payment contingent on resolving all problems identified during the warranty period.

Support Statements of Work

Although development SOWs have deliverables, support SOWs normally refer to services that the vendor will provide. These services may include total outsourcing of the system's running to an application service provider (ASP) or provision of more limited services, such as a help desk or maintenance of custom code. In any case, the SOW should include the following information, much of which is similar to the clauses needed for vendor-provided maintenance of the base software (Chapter 7):

■ *Description of services to be provided.* Like the description of deliverables in a development SOW, it is important that these services be clearly defined. "Ninety percent of all problem tickets closed within three hours" may produce different results from "Resolution of all problems to the user's satisfaction within three hours of opening the problem ticket." The first clause encourages the vendor to close tickets quickly, whether or not the user is happy. The second addresses the critical question of user satisfaction and is probably closer to the end user's expectations of the service to be provided.

■ *Hours of support.* Not all services are provided twenty-four hours a day, seven days a week. If not, the days and hours that support is needed, including the time zone, should be specified. If company holidays are excluded, the SOW should either include a list of those holidays or a reference to them.

■ *Resolution time.* Although the time to answer a call is important (and is frequently included in the description of services), the end user's primary concern is how quickly problems are resolved. Because the agreed-upon resolution time will normally vary by the severity of the defect, severity codes should be defined, along with the resolution time for each.

■ *Quality measures.* This is the support SOW's equivalent of development's acceptance criteria. It is important that both the vendor and the company understand how the company will determine whether or not the vendor has met its commitment. Typically, this is done through an SLA.

Service-Level Agreements

SLAs are normally part of support SOWs and reflect the reality that the vendor will not meet the agreed-upon system uptime, defect resolution time, and other quality measures 100 percent of the time. The SLA identifies the lowest level of support that the company will accept.

When writing SLAs, there are several factors to consider.

■ *The company should draft the SLA.* This is analogous to having the company draft the contract. Although the vendor may have more experience writing SLAs, those that vendors draft will be written to their advantage. The ideal situation is for the project team, which includes key members of the end-user community, to draft proposed SLAs and then review them with a larger group of end users to ensure that the service levels are ones that will meet the users' needs before they present them to the vendor.

■ *All SLAs should be SMART.* The acronym shown in Chapter 2, Exhibit 2-2 applies to SLAs as well as problem definition. Exhibit 9-2 evaluates several SLAs against the SMART criteria.

Exhibit 9-2 SMART SLAs

Proposed SLA: 80 percent of the defects will be resolved within one day; the remaining 20 percent will be resolved within three days.

Criteria	Comments
Specific	No. How is "day" defined? Business day? 24/7?
Measurable	Yes; the vendor can count defects reported and calculate the percentage resolved.
Attainable	Probably.
Relevant	No. Because there is no distinction among severities of defects, the vendor can work on the easiest ones first, rather than resolving those of greatest importance to the end user.
Timebound	Yes, assuming that all reporting and calculation is done on a monthly basis.

A SMARTer SLA: 80 percent of the defects will be resolved within the timeframes shown below, working the hours shown below, according to their severity level. The remaining 20 percent will be resolved in no more than three times the timeframe shown.

Severity Level	Resolution Time	Working Hours
1	24 hours	24/7
2	48 hours	Normal business hours (8 AM to 5 PM eastern standard time, Monday through Friday, excluding company holidays)
3	96 hours	Normal business hours as defined above

Proposed SLA: The system will be available for use 98 percent of the time between 8 AM and 5 PM.

Criteria	Comments
Specific	No. What time zone is involved? Is uptime being measured seven days a week? What about holidays?
Measurable	Yes; the vendor can measure uptime.
Attainable	Probably
Relevant	No. The system might be "available for use" but have unreasonably slow response time. Furthermore, if the two percent downtime occurs during a critical time, such as month end for a financial system, the end user's satisfaction level will be low.
Timebound	Yes, assuming that all reporting and calculation are done on a monthly basis.

A SMARTer SLA: The system will be available for use with response time not to exceed two seconds 98 percent of the time between 8 AM and 5 PM, Pacific daylight time, Monday through Saturday, including company holidays. During the month-end financial close (as defined in Appendix A), the system will be available for use with response time not to exceed two seconds 99.7 percent of the time.

■ *Each SLA, other than system uptime, should total 100 percent.* Because it is unrealistic to expect the vendor to meet the SLA 100 percent of the time, the basic SLA will be for a percentage less than 100; however, it is essential that the remaining percentage be accounted for. Otherwise, the vendors need never satisfy those support calls or resolve those defects, yet they will be able to claim that they have met their SLA. Nothing should be allowed to fall into the black hole of unmeasured services.

■ *SLAs should not include averages.* Although vendors like to refer to "mean time to repair" and "average uptime," the company should not allow an SLA to be written in those terms. An average defect correction time of three days could mean that one problem was resolved in half an hour, undoubtedly pleasing the end user, although another required almost six days and created a dissatisfied customer.

■ *SLAs should not include ranges.* The SLA "Between 70 and 90 percent of all severity 1 problems resolved within ten business hours" has two problems. First, it encourages the vendor to resolve no more than 70 percent of the problems, because there is no incentive for a higher resolution. Second, if the vendor did resolve more than 90 percent of the problems, he would be in technical violation of the SLA — undoubtedly not the company's intention.

As with all contracts, it is important that everyone who is involved in drafting service contracts understand each of the clauses and the reasons they are needed. Once the contracts are drafted, negotiated, and signed, the team can proceed to what they may perceive as the "real work" of packaged software implementation: establishing the roadmap.

IMPLEMENTATION CONSIDERATIONS

While the contract is being negotiated, the team members who are not involved in the actual negotiations can begin planning the implementation. As is true of all aspects of packaged software implementation, prior planning prevents poor performance. This planning involves making several critical decisions as well as ensuring that the project is approved and accepted.

The first two chapters of this section review a number of the key implementation-related decisions that must be made. Chapter 10 discusses *how* the implementation will occur, that is, whether it will be phased or big bang, and if it is phased, how those phases are determined. Chapter 10 also raises the question of where the software will reside, discussing the use of application service providers rather than in-house hosting. In contrast, Chapter 11 outlines the *who* component, explaining the roles involved in implementation and reviewing the pros and cons of using outside firms for assistance.

No project can occur without funding approval. Chapter 12 presents a process for selling the solution to the key decision makers, suggesting a format for a business case and explaining the calculation of return on investment.

One aspect of packaged software implementation all too often given short shrift is the preparation of the user community. Chapter 13 reviews the fundamentals of change, conflict, and communication and provides recommendations for increasing user acceptance of the new software.

Chapter 10

Establishing the Roadmap

Once the company has made the decision that it will implement packaged software and has selected the commercial off-the-shelf (COTS) package, the next major question becomes, "How will the implementation be done?" Earlier steps have focused on the end state, in journalistic terms, the "what." The project charter, the requirements document, and the product selection steps have all had the objective of creating a picture of the changes that will occur and the benefits that will accrue once the software is in full production. Although it is essential to have that "big picture," it is also necessary to determine which route the project team will take to reach that end state.

Some companies use the analogy of a cross-country road trip and describe the master plan to reach their destination as a roadmap. Whether it is called a roadmap or simply a plan, it is important to have a clearly developed and communicated description of how the actual implementation will occur. (Methods of communication are discussed in Chapter 13.)

Developing the plan or roadmap can be simplified by answering a series of questions. The first deals with where the software will reside.

Will the Company Use an Application Service Provider or Install the Software on Its Machines?

Like fashion, information technology (IT) has cycles. In the 1970s time-sharing option (TSO) services were popular, with companies relying on large service providers to run some of their software applications. In the following decades, the pendulum swung, bringing most software back in-house. Now there is a renewed interest in the use of application service providers (ASPs) or, as some refer to it, "hosted software." Like the TSO services that were popular a generation ago, ASPs provide companies with an alternative to the traditional COTS implementation approach. Instead of installing the software on the company's own computers, the company relies on an ASP.

The ASP has three primary responsibilities.

1. It develops the software or licenses it from a third party.
2. It runs the software on its own servers or mainframes.
3. It is responsible for applying upgrades and enhancements.

The company pays for these services either on a fixed price or on a per-user basis. In either case, payments may be made monthly, annually, or at some other agreed-upon frequency. Because the costs continue for as long as the company is using the software, the company can be seen as "renting" the software, whereas software licenses, which normally involve a single payment, are "bought."

As with any option, there are advantages and disadvantages to using an ASP.

- ◾ Advantages
    - *Shorter implementation schedule.* Because the software is already installed, tested, and running on the ASP's machines, the overall project schedule may be reduced.
    - *Faster upgrades.* At least in theory, the ASP, whose staff is dedicated to the product, will have more time to apply, test, and implement upgrades than in-house staff with competing demands.
    - *Reduced demand on in-house staff.* Because the ASP is responsible for all operational aspects of the software, including backups as well as installation of bug patches, upgrades, and enhancements, the company's in-house IT staff can focus on other projects.
    - *No increase in in-house computing resource requirements.* If the company's servers or mainframes have limited excess capacity, use of an ASP may obviate the need to acquire new hardware.
    - *Increased scalability.* This is a corollary to the previous advantage. Because the ASP has responsibility for the computing platform, the company can begin slowly or ramp up quickly

without worrying about overloading servers or training additional staff to respond to end users' questions.

- *Guaranteed performance and availability.* Contracts with an ASP are service based and typically include SLAs similar to those discussed in Chapter 9. Because there are (or should be) financial penalties for not meeting the agreed-upon performance levels, the ASP has a greater incentive to meet those service levels than in-house staff do.

- *Possibly lower cost.* Some companies have found that using an ASP is less costly than implementing packaged software on their own machines. Because, as is discussed in Chapter 12, there are numerous elements involved in total cost of ownership (TCO), lower cost is not guaranteed and will vary by company and implementation.

■ Disadvantages

- *Less control.* It is the ASP rather than the company that decides when and how bug fixes are applied and whether or not new functionality is added. The ASP's schedule may or may not meet the company's needs.

- *Less ability to customize.* Although some ASPs provide for customization, others limit the company's ability to tailor the software for its unique requirements. Standard software such as payroll may require no customization and could be a good choice for an ASP, whereas applications that automate processes that are unique to the company may not fit well within the ASP model.

- *Increased security risks.* Whether or not the risk is real, companies may believe that they are more vulnerable to security breaches because they have less control over the environment in which the software is running. Contracts with an ASP should include sections defining the security to be provided as well as the company's recourse if security is breached. Although the ability to audit the ASP's operations should be included in the contract, the company should also evaluate the ASP's security prior to signing any contract.

- *Greater dependence on vendor.* If the ASP suddenly ceases operations, which has been known to occur, the company may encounter a temporary hiatus in processing while it finds another source of the software or brings the system in-house. Because there is no easy way to mitigate this risk, the company should use only ASPs with a proven track record and good financial backing for its mission-critical systems.

Exhibit 10-1 Application Service Providers versus Software Licensing

	ASP	Software Licensing
Location of software	ASP's servers	Company's servers
Location of data	ASP's servers	Company's servers
User interface	Web browser	Web browser or client/server
License/Use payment frequency	Ongoing for as long as the company uses the software	One-time licensing plus annual maintenance (optional)
Demand on in-house IT staff	Low	Medium to high
Time to install software	None	Medium to high
Dependence on vendor	High throughout the length of the contract	Low, once software is installed

Before deciding to use an ASP, the company should answer the following questions:

- Is there an ASP that provides software with the basic functionality needed for this project or that hosts one of the COTS solutions the company is considering?
- Is all the functionality that the company needs included in the ASP's offering?
- If some functionality is lacking, does the ASP provide the ability to customize the software?
- Is the company aware of the potential risks and willing to assume them?

If the answer to all these questions is positive, the ASP option may be a valuable one for the company.

Exhibit 10-1 provides a summary of the differences between use of an ASP and traditional software licensing.

Will Implementation Be "Big Bang" or Phased?

The second major implementation question is relevant only if either of the following assumptions is true:

- The software has multiple modules.
- The company plans to use the software at more than one site or in more than one department.

Exhibit 10-2 Implementation Strategy Options

	Big Bang	Phased by Site	Phased by Functionality	Hybrid (Both Site and Functionality)
Time to deliver first benefits	Longest	Medium	Medium	Shortest
Time to deliver full benefits	Shortest	High	High	High
Complexity of implementation	Greatest	Lowest	Medium	Medium to high
Overall risk	Greatest	Lowest	Medium	Medium to high
Need for throw-away interfaces	None	High	Low	High

Single-module packages installed at a single site are by definition "big bang."

In a "big bang" implementation, all functionality is installed at all locations at the same time. Phased implementations, as their name implies, deliver either portions of the functionality at different times or install software at some locations earlier than others.

Although the question of phasing applies primarily to traditional packaged software implementation projects, where software is being installed on the company's machines, there is also some applicability to the points discussed below when implementing an ASP solution.

As with most decisions, there are advantages and disadvantages to each approach. Exhibit 10-2 provides a summary of the options.

Big Bang

Advantages

There are two major advantages to a full functionality, single-phase implementation.

- *Fewer interfaces.* Because there is no transition period when some sites are using a legacy system and others are using the new COTS package, there is no need to develop interfaces from those legacy systems.
- *Faster full-benefit realization.* Unlike phased implementations when the full benefits are not realized until all phases are complete, in a big bang approach, once the software is implemented, the company will be able to determine exactly what benefits have

been derived. This faster benefit realization may also translate into lower overall project costs.

A third advantage, although not so significant as the previous two, is that the entire company is involved from the beginning. There is no need to choose an initial site or to delay others' implementation. As a result, none of the company's locations can be perceived as less important than another.

Disadvantages

Although there are several disadvantages, they can be summarized in two words: increased risk. A big bang approach can be likened to the proverbial putting all eggs in one basket. If it is successful, the rewards are great; however, failure can be equally spectacular.

Big bang's disadvantages include:

- *Greater risk of failure.* Even though the company is installing packaged software that has been tested and successfully implemented at other companies, there is always the possibility of problems. These may result from company customization, incompatibilities between the software and the operating environment, or simple misunderstanding of how the software is designed to work. The cause is almost irrelevant; the effect is not. Big bang by definition does not include a pilot. The lack of that pilot implementation means that any errors will be magnified because they will appear across the company, rather than being contained.
- *More complex implementation.* There is no doubt that trying to install multiple modules at multiple sites or even at one site at the same time is more difficult than installing a single software module. Multisite implementations include logistical challenges such as concurrent preparation and training of users at a number of sites. Unless there is a large project team or the sites are relatively close to each other, travel time may become an issue. Although it is possible to conduct training online, it is also likely that sites will require some hands-on assistance. Multiple module implementations present different challenges, one of which is the ability of end users to adapt to massive change. Preparing for change is discussed in Chapter 13. Similarly, if the company is reengineering its processes as part of the overall project, all new processes must be implemented concurrently. This may or may not be a realistic goal.

■ *Longer time to realize any benefits.* It is true that in big bang, full-benefit realization occurs more quickly than in a phased implementation; however, there is also a longer period without any visible benefits. This is a result of the time required to implement the full functionality at all sites. Depending on the overall length of the project, this delay may result in a credibility gap as end users doubt that the software will ever be installed, and it may cause a loss of commitment for the project. Furthermore, extended schedules carry more risk of turnover of key personnel, which can delay the project.

What Will Be Included in Each Phase?

If the company decides to mitigate its risk by choosing a phased implementation, it must determine how those phases will be defined. The choices are to phase the implementation by location, by functionality, or by a combination of the two.

Phased by Site

In this type of phased implementation, the team installs full functionality at one site, works out the bugs, then expands the implementation to other sites in several waves. (A pilot implementation, that is, a single site followed by full implementation at all other sites, is a variation on phasing by site. It has the advantages of phasing and somewhat mitigates the risks associated with a big bang approach.)

■ Advantages
  – *Decreased risk.* The primary advantage of phasing by site is decreased risk. This occurs because the first (or first few) implementations give the project team the opportunity to work out problems on a small scale. Only a few end users are impacted, and because the initial implementation is normally clearly defined as a pilot or learning experience, their expectations do not include perfection. The pilot allows training approaches, conversions and interfaces, and reengineered processes to be evaluated and modified, as needed, for subsequent implementations. Subsequent waves can also be delayed, if necessary, until all bugs are resolved. As a result of the initial implementation, the roadmap is turned into a detailed itinerary with information about how to achieve success.

– *Reduced time for initial benefit realization.* Although the company will not see all benefits from only one site, having an initial implementation will validate benefits relatively early in the life cycle. This visibility has the added benefit of keeping interest in the project high.

– *Public relations opportunity.* Having an initial site up and running provides the project team the opportunity to celebrate success and communicate that success to the rest of the company. Because there is always some measure of skepticism about a new software system, the project gains credibility when the team can point to an internal success. There is, after all, a major difference between seeing software running at a vendor's site or even at another company and seeing it running within the company.

■ Disadvantages

– *Need for temporary interfaces.* If reporting and other functions depend on having all sites using the same system, it may be necessary to develop interfaces from legacy systems for those sites that are not yet using the new system. These "throw away" programs increase the cost of the project and add time to the initial implementation schedule.

– *Possibility of incomplete functionality.* Although the entire system may be installed at the initial sites, if some functionality depends on having all sites installed (if, for example, the software is designed to allow one site to transfer inventory from another), it may not be possible to use that functionality in the initial implementation. This problem decreases in importance as more sites are added.

– *Possibility of resistance to change.* As was true of a big bang implementation, installing full functionality at a site may result in end users being overwhelmed by change and being unable or unwilling to deal with it. Although this is less likely at a pilot site where expectations have been properly established, it is possible at subsequent sites.

– *Second-class citizen syndrome.* Sites that are not part of the initial implementation may feel that they are considered less important than others. Not only may this have a negative impact on morale, but it also may result in those sites trying to sabotage their own installations when they finally occur. On the other hand, if the project's benefits have not been sold to all sites, the early sites may be reluctant to participate and may wonder why they were chosen to be pioneers.

Phased by Functionality

In this scenario, the team installs a subset of the full system at all sites, then expands the functionality in groupings of modules.

- ■ Advantages
  - *Few, if any, temporary interfaces.* Because all sites will have the same functionality at the same time, the need for temporary interfaces to legacy systems is decreased.
  - *Full-benefit realization for each module.* As each module is installed, it will be possible to determine the related benefits.
  - *Streamlined interactions among sites.* If the system functionality includes interactions among sites, such as inventory transfers, that functionality will be available immediately.
  - *Involvement of all sites.* Because all sites are involved at every stage, there is no feeling of being excluded. This may increase morale. The risk is that all sites may not be at the same level of readiness at the same time, which could complicate and delay the overall implementation.
- ■ Disadvantages
  - *More complex implementation.* As with the big bang approach, a multisite operation requires training and installation at multiple sites at the same time. If a problem occurs, its severity will be magnified by the fact that all locations are involved.
  - *Longer time for full implementation.* Because of the need to revisit sites as new functionality is implemented, the overall schedule may be longer than phasing by location.

Phased by Both Functionality and Site

In this approach, a subset of functionality is installed and proven at one site, then deployed to other sites in "waves." (Site groupings can be based on geography, the corporate structure, or other factors, including site readiness.) While the first round of functionality is being deployed at other sites, more functionality is installed at the initial site, and the process is repeated until all functionality is installed at all sites.

- ■ *Advantages.* Although it is a hybrid approach, the benefits of this type of phasing are more closely related to those of phasing by site than by functionality.
  - *Decreased risk.* As with total phasing by site, the major advantage is decreased risk. Implementing only a subset of the functionality further simplifies the installations because the team

has the ability to focus on that functionality and the associated process reengineering. This may reduce end users' resistance to change because they will have time to adjust to one set of revised processes before having to learn the next.

- *Reduced time for initial benefit realization.* This approach allows the company to validate benefits for each module as it is installed, provided that that module does not require interactions between sites. Because it is easier to install a single module at one site than full functionality at one or more sites, hybrid phasing produces the shortest initial implementation and thus the earliest opportunity to demonstrate benefits.

- *Public relations opportunity.* As with full-site phasing, there is a distinct advantage to being able to point to a successful implementation, even if it is of limited functionality. The initial site starts the momentum and can help ease the concerns of other sites about their implementations because the company now has a proven model for success.

■ *Disadvantages.* The disadvantages of this approach are a combination of those for phasing by site and phasing by functionality.
  - Need for temporary interfaces
  - Possibility of incomplete functionality
  - More complex implementation
  - Longer time for full implementation

How Are Phases Chosen?

If the project team decides to phase its implementation, the next question becomes, "How are the phases determined?" It is important to select the correct site and the right modules for the initial implementation because the team wants to do everything possible to guarantee success.

Choosing the Initial Site

When selecting the site for the initial or pilot implementation, the team should consider the characteristics of effective team members (Chapter 2, Exhibit 2-4) because a site that exhibits many of these characteristics will have a greater probability of success. Although references are to "the site," it is the individuals who will be responsible for the implementation at that site and the end users of the system who comprise "the site" and who should display these attributes.

The most critical characteristics are:

■ *Commitment.* It is important that the site believe in the benefits that the COTS package and any related process reengineering are designed to provide and that they are willing to be the initial site. As with software selection, it is possible for a site to sabotage the implementation if it is not committed to the project's overall success.

■ *Flexibility.* Reengineering requires change, as does the use of a new software product. Furthermore, it is likely that some problems will be uncovered as the package is installed, new processes are implemented, and training is delivered. The pilot site needs to be able to cope with those problems and help find ways around them. They should be enablers rather than barrier builders.

■ *Personal influence and respect.* Although a site cannot have "personal" influence, its leaders should be well respected throughout the company because they will be asked to assess the project and to help sell the benefits to other sites.

In addition, the pilot site should be representative of the company. A site that is smaller than the average location or one that has less complex processes may provide an easy initial installation, but it will not be a true demonstration of the project's capabilities and the benefits that will be derived.

Choosing the Initial Functionality

If phasing is to be done by functionality rather than site or as a hybrid phasing, the project team should consider the following points when selecting the initial modules to implement:

■ *Importance to company.* This is analogous to selecting a site that is representative of the company. If the team chooses modules that are not of critical importance to the company as its initial implementation, the project will lack credibility.

■ *Number of interfaces.* If there are two modules of equal importance, the team should select the one that requires fewer interfaces to be developed because that will streamline the initial implementation and produce results more quickly.

■ *Demonstrability of benefits.* This is a corollary to "importance." Because one key objective of the initial implementation is to demonstrate benefits, the team should select a module for which benefits can be easily quantified and demonstrated. Tangible benefits, such as cost reduction, are easier to prove than cost avoidance or improved customer satisfaction.

Will There Be Parallel Runs?

Whether the team is doing a big bang or a phased implementation, they need to decide how to validate the initial results. In some cases, this will be done by running the old and the new systems in parallel and verifying that the outputs are the same. Although this is a traditional approach, it may not be feasible if one or more of the following is true:

- *Processes are changed dramatically by reengineering.* In this case, it would be difficult for the end users to perform the same function in two different ways.
- *Data entry is extensive.* Even without reengineered processes, it may be difficult for an end user to enter the same data into two systems. Although it is possible to create a program to capture data entry from the old system and convert it into a format that can be entered into the new system, the programming introduces the possibility of errors that are not related to the system's functionality.

If the company can perform parallel processing, the roadmap should identify the length of time the two systems will run concurrently and who will be responsible for verifying the results.

Communicating the Roadmap

Once the team has decided on the implementation strategy, the next step is to develop a formal plan, showing the schedule for each major step and — if the implementation will be phased — clearly identifying what will be included in each phase. This plan should be approved by the project champion as well as other key stakeholders, notably the heads of all affected departments, then communicated to everyone who will be impacted by the project.

Having addressed the question of "how" the COTS package will be implemented, the team is ready to decide who will be involved.

Chapter 11

Who Is In Charge?

As the preceding chapters have discussed, the initial steps in a successful packaged software implementation project involve making a number of key decisions. This chapter continues the planning and decision-making process by addressing another issue that impacts how the implementation is carried out. Previous chapters have dealt with the "what," "when," and "how" aspects of software implementation. This one addresses "who." In addition to deciding which commercial off-the-shelf (COTS) package is the best for the project, the team needs to decide who will be involved in the actual implementation.

For a single-site implementation of a package with either monolithic functionality or multiple modules that are so closely integrated that they should not be installed separately, the answer to that question is frequently simple. Because the implementation is relatively straightforward, internal staff can often accomplish it with minimal assistance from the vendor. However, more complex COTS projects, such as enterprise resource planning (ERP), normally result in a different answer to the same question. In those cases, it is not uncommon for the company to use outside firms (OFs) to either supplement its own staff or provide all implementation support.

To make an informed decision about whether to seek assistance, the project team should understand the types of work that may be involved as well as potential sources of assistance for that work.

Architect, General Contractor, or Skilled Trade?

System development, including packaged software implementation, requires the contribution of people with a variety of skills. There are managers, coders, testers, and trainers, not to mention subject matter experts. Although there is no doubt that the skills are important, it is also helpful to consider the roles that these people play. Some companies use a home-building analogy, dividing the roles into three categories.

Architect

As the name suggests, whoever fills this role will design the finished product, determining which functionality will be included and, in the case of packaged software implementation, how much customization will occur as well as how processes will be reengineered to take best advantage of the software's capabilities. The architect creates the blueprint, including the high-level schedule, that is used to sell the project to senior management as well as the end users.

General Contractor

This is the group that determines how the architect's design is turned into reality. The general contractor is responsible for validating the high-level schedule, then creating and monitoring a detailed schedule. The general contractor also hires and manages the trades people who will perform the actual implementation and is responsible for ensuring that the final product meets the agreed-upon schedule as well as all quality standards.

The general contractor may also modify the blueprint based on end-user requests or problems encountered during the actual implementation. As is true of house building, minor modifications to the blueprint are common and do not create a problem, although they may extend the schedule. Major structural changes, such as the addition or deletion of an entire module, should not be undertaken without reengaging the architect.

Skilled Trade

These are the people who install the software, customize it as directed by the general contractor, test it, develop and write new procedures, and train users. In short, they are the workers.

It is possible to have OFs perform any or all these roles in their entirety or to provide assistance with portions of each. Before discussing the advantages and disadvantages of each approach, it is important to under-

Exhibit 11-1   Implementation Assistance Options

	Systems Integrator	*Boutique Firms*	*General Purpose Staffing Company*
Cost	High	Medium to high	Low
Breadth of services provided	High	Medium to high	Low to medium
Depth of knowledge of specific package	Medium to high	High	Low to medium
Flexibility	Low to medium	Medium to high	High
Suitability as architect	High	High	Low
Suitability as general contractor	High	High	Low to medium
Suitability as skilled trade	Low to medium	Medium to high	High

stand potential sources of assistance. Exhibit 11-1 provides a summary of three of the most common types of implementation assistance providers besides the vendor.

Sources of Assistance

Some companies use the software vendor for all work related to the package. Although the vendor may be a logical choice for assistance, the company may want to consider alternatives if any of the following are true:

- The vendor's support is too costly for the company.
- Vendor staff is not available within the timeframe needed to meet the company's desired schedule.
- The company wants the perspective of a more impartial group.

The good news is that there are normally choices besides the software vendor.

Other OFs that provide implementation support can be grouped into three categories.

Systems Integrator

These are large companies that provide the full range of implementation services. What differentiates them from the vendor is that they provide these services not just for the specific software package that the company has chosen but typically for a number of other packages. The greatest strength of systems integrators (SIs) is their ability to provide services for more than one COTS package. If the company anticipates a number of packaged software implementation projects, it may want to use an SI because the company would be able to use the same firm for all of the projects. This should reduce the learning curve and, at least in theory, shorten the schedule.

Although SIs have distinct advantages, there are also potential drawbacks to them. As shown in Exhibit 11-1, SIs tend to be expensive, and may, in fact, be as costly as the vendor, particularly for skilled trade work. Their depth in a specific skill (that is, the number of staff members with the needed expertise) may vary by the package. Because they are large companies, they frequently have their own processes and may be unwilling to adopt the company's standards. Depending on how they are used, this lack of flexibility may be of minimal importance.

Boutique Firms

These companies, which are frequently smaller than SIs, specialize in providing implementation services for a specific software package. As a result, their greatest strengths are their focused expertise and that their entire staff has experience in a single package, normally in all aspects of the implementation, including those defined above as skilled trade. Although their smaller size may increase their flexibility, their costs may equal those of SIs.

General Purpose Staffing Company

These firms, as their name suggests, provide staff for a number of purposes, not simply software implementation. They are the firms that companies typically call when they need to augment their staff on a temporary basis. General purpose staffing companies' technical hourly costs tend to be the lowest of the three alternatives, in part because the expertise they bring is in a skill (coding, testing, documentation, training) rather than knowledge of a specific COTS package. As a result, they are used most effectively in the skilled trade role. It should be noted, however, that these firms may have individuals with the skills and the specific software background needed to serve as architects and general contractors. In these cases, the company's reliance would be on those individuals rather than the firm as a whole.

If the project team decides to use outside assistance for its packaged software implementation, the next step is to determine the role the OF will play. As noted above, there are several options.

The Turnkey Alternative

This is the most dramatic outsourcing of responsibility. In a turnkey implementation, the company hires an OF, typically the software vendor or an SI with expertise in the specific package, to perform all functions from architect through skilled trade. The OF has complete responsibility for the project, with the company's role being on the periphery, as a consumer of the services rather than an active participant.

Although this may sound extreme, there are cases when a turnkey approach is useful. These include:

- Implementation of shrink-wrapped software that needs no customization.
- Software implementation at companies with small or overcommitted information technology (IT) staffs.

As is true of most alternatives, there are pros and cons.

- Advantages
  - *Simplicity.* Using one firm to provide all services provides a single point of accountability and can simplify the implementation process because there is no question about who is responsible for either individual tasks or adherence to the overall schedule.
  - *Prior experience.* If the company has done its due diligence properly, the selected firm will have experience implementing the software for multiple companies, including — in an ideal situation — others in the same industry as the company. This experience can help the company avoid pitfalls.
  - *Shorter schedule.* Although not guaranteed, the OF's experience should reduce the time required to implement the software.
- Disadvantages
  - *Cost.* Compared with in-house staff and general purpose staffing companies, vendors and SIs are normally more expensive. Although their experience with the specific package should reduce the elapsed time (and actual work hours involved), their

higher hourly rate often outweighs the lower number of hours they expend, making them more expensive than in-house staff or general purpose staffing companies.

− *Lack of understanding of the company.* Although the SI has experience with the specific package being implemented and potentially with the company's own industry, it does not understand the nuances of the company's current processes and any idiosyncrasies associated with them. The risks that this lack of understanding brings are that the final product may not fully meet the company's requirements or that the schedule may need to be extended to provide the SI with a detailed knowledge of the company's processes. Use of the vendor or an SI in an architect role on complex projects places the company at risk of receiving a plain vanilla solution when it needed fudge ripple.

− *Lack of continuity.* Unless the SI or vendor is going to assume responsibility for the ongoing running of the software, including maintenance and end-user support, having the company play only a peripheral role during implementation means that company staff will not understand the rationale behind key decisions. When responsibility is ultimately transferred to in-house staff, there may be a lengthy transition period a staff needs to learn the system, and there is the possibility that not all critical information will be transferred. This can translate into slower response to end-user questions and confusion over the value of specific software updates.

Sources of Assistance

Because the company has little direct involvement in a turnkey implementation, it is essential that the OF it selects have both technical skills and a high level of expertise with the specific software package chosen for the project. In most cases that combination of skills and functional knowledge is more readily obtained from the vendor, an SI, or a boutique firm than from a general purpose staffing company.

Company Ownership with Assistance from Outside Firms

Many companies are unwilling to accept the risks associated with a turnkey approach or are reluctant to relinquish control of the project, particularly during the development of the blueprint. Although they want to serve as the architect, developing the overall strategy, they may also realize that they require outside assistance, either because their own staff does not have enough time to work on the project or because they need resources with prior experience implementing the COTS package.

This scenario is the most common one for large packaged software implementations. The company performs the architect role. It may also serve as the general contractor and provide a portion of the skilled trade effort. All other work is provided by one or more OFs, some of which may serve as advisors during the development of the architecture.

- ■ Advantages
    - – *Vested interest.* It can be argued that this is the major advantage. The company has a greater interest in ensuring the success of the project than any OF can because it is the group most directly affected by the project. The OF risks bad publicity as well as a loss of revenue if the project fails. Although these risks are not insignificant, they are of lesser importance than the company's risks, which can — in the case of companywide systems such as ERP — include not being able to transact its daily business. The OF can walk away from a failure; the company must live with it. This vested interest may help drive the project and increase the likelihood of success.
    - – *Greater control.* Because the company is assuming overall responsibility for the project, it should be involved in all major decisions and thus be able to ensure that the project remains on track and that it delivers the expected benefits.
    - – *In-depth understanding of company.* Having company staff actively involved in the implementation mitigates the risk that the OF does not fully understand the company's processes and should result in an implementation that meets the company's requirements.
    - – *Continuity.* It is frequently to the company's benefit to have several members of its staff participate in and understand all decisions that are made. This "tribal knowledge" is particularly valuable in lengthy implementation projects during the actual installation. Benefits continue afterwards, if support is provided in-house.
    - – *Lower cost.* By performing some of the work with internal staff, the overall costs may be reduced because in-house staff may be less expensive than an OF. The actual savings will depend on the spread between fully burdened internal costs and the fees being charged by the OF. Lower costs are not guaranteed.

If the OF provides some of its services offshore in lower cost regions, it may actually be less expensive to use them, particularly in the skilled trade role.

■ Disadvantages
  - *Potential for conflict.* Whenever there is shared responsibility, there is the potential for disagreement. This is particularly true if more than one OF is engaged to perform services. Even when each group performs a different role, there will be handoffs, and one group will depend on work from another. This can create conflict and a lack of cooperation both among the OFs and between the OFs and company staff. In these cases, the company, which has overall accountability for the project's success, must serve as a mediator. To mitigate this risk, the program manager should hold regular meetings with all parties, encouraging cooperation and communication.
  - *Need for specific skills.* Even though it may want to perform this role, it is possible that the company may not have staff with the skills required to serve as architect or general contractor. In this case, risk is increased by assuming that responsibility. That risk can be reduced by using an OF with the needed skills in an advisory role.

Sources of Assistance

Because the company is serving as the architect, it has more flexibility in choosing assistance partners than in a turnkey approach. It may hire an SI or boutique firm to serve as the general contractor and stipulate that a general purpose staffing company be used for skilled trade work. Depending on the skill level and availability of its staff, the company may also serve as its own general contractor and use a combination of boutique firms and general purpose staffing companies for the various skilled trade tasks.

The Program Management Office

If the company has decided not to use a turnkey approach but rather to take an active role in the project, one of the next decisions it needs to make is how to manage that project. At this point, the initial project team is sometimes reconstituted into a program management office (PMO). Like the product selection team, this is a small group of people who have overall accountability for the project. The project or program manager will be a member of the PMO, as will key representatives of the user community. For the sake of continuity, it is desirable that some members of the PMO be chosen from the team that guided the software selection process, although it is normal to add new players at this point in the project. A project charter (Chapter 2, Exhibit 2-1) is helpful in defining the expectations of the PMO, and members should exhibit the characteristics of effective team members (Chapter 2, Exhibit 2-4).

Although the product selection team may have had part-time participants, membership in the PMO is typically full time and may extend beyond the final implementation into support of the software.

Responsibilities

The PMO has a variety of responsibilities, including:

- *Ensure the project's success.* This is the single most important role that the PMO plays, and because of its importance, it is key that all members be fully committed to the project's goals.
- *Select, monitor, and manage OFs.* Even if the company is not officially serving as the general contractor, the PMO is the organization that ensures that the OFs are meeting their schedules and providing the expected quality of services. Because of this responsibility, some PMOs include a contracts administrator as one of their members.
- *Establish and enforce standards.* Successful packaged software implementation means more than having the software installed within budget and on schedule. It also means having the implementation done the right way. The definition of "the right way" may vary by company and may not be consistent with the OF's normal processes. As discussed further in Chapter 14, it is important to create and publish formal standards, then ensure that they are adhered to.

If the implementation will be multisite, another of the PMO's standard-related roles is to ensure consistency across the sites. Chapter 20 provides more information about multisite implementations.

Other Key Decisions

If the company has decided that it will employ one or more OFs to assist with the project, it needs to answer another series of questions.

How Much Control Will the Outside Firms Have?

Whether the OF will assume the role of general contractor or simply provide periodic assistance, it is important that the company establish expectations and boundaries. Expectations can be established in a statement of work, but boundaries are more difficult to document because they typically address what the OF cannot do rather than what the company requires it to do. They are, nonetheless, important. As is true of all communication, the more that can be written and distributed to all parties, the better.

How Much Involvement Will In-House IT Staff Have?

As has been noted several times, it is important that at least some members of the IT department be involved in the project so that they develop tribal knowledge and can provide continuity once the software is fully installed. If, in addition to those core team members, the company wants to use its staff as skilled trades, it needs to weigh its staff's existing commitments and skills with the company's desire to provide career advancement opportunities for them.

Some companies choose to outsource support of legacy systems to allow their staff to participate in the COTS implementation; others hire OFs to provide all implementation support, leaving in-house staff to continue maintaining the legacy systems. Either approach is a viable one, although there are different risks associated with each.

- Outsource legacy systems.
  - Service levels may decrease during the transition period from in-house to outsourced staff.
  - Depending on the length of time the legacy system will be needed, it may not be cost effective to transition knowledge.
- Outsource the implementation.
  - In-house staff may consider their jobs to be dead ends and may leave, resulting in insufficient support for critical legacy systems.

Who Will Coordinate the Outside Firms' Work If There Is More Than One?

As noted above, even if one OF is serving as the general contractor, it will be necessary for the company to serve as an escalation point if there is more than one OF working on the project. A member of the PMO with experience in mediating disputes is the logical choice for this role.

Exhibit 11-2 Staff Augmentation versus Outsourcing

Characteristic	Staff Augmentation	Outsourcing
Company contracts for	Individual contractor's work	Predefined service or product
Selection of staff to perform work	Company's (interviews prospective contractors)	Outsourcer
Day-to-day direction of staff provided by	Company	Outsourcer
Pricing	Time and materials; hourly rate or *per diem*	Fixed price, typically payable monthly or on completion of specific deliverables
Location of staff	Company site	Either company or outsourcer's site
Coemployment concerns	Possible, if lengthy assignment	None
Measure of success	Individual tasks	Deliverables
Key to success	Individual contractor	Outsourcer

Will the Company Outsource Work to the Outside Firms or Use Them for Staff Augmentation?

Before answering this question, the company needs to have a clear understanding of the distinctions between the two. Exhibit 11-2 outlines key differences, the most critical of which is day-to-day management of the staff.

In staff augmentation, whether they are called contractors or consultants, the people who are hired function as an extension of the company. Except for the fact that their salaries and benefits are paid by a different company and that their services are temporary, they are virtually identical to permanent staff. This is the reason that coemployment concerns can arise.

Outsourcing is different. In outsourcing, the company contracts for a service or deliverable, not for an individual. Responsibility for a specific body of work is given to the OF. It is the OF's responsibility to decide who will perform specific tasks and to ensure that deadlines and quality standards are met.

If the company chooses to use the OF for staff augmentation, it needs to be certain that in-house staff are available to manage their day-to-day work and that potential coemployment issues are reviewed with both human resources and the law departments.

The Champion

No matter how the company plans to staff the project implementation, it is essential to have a champion. As discussed in Chapter 1, the presence of a champion is one of the critical success factors for successful packaged software implementation.

In some companies, this person is referred to as the sponsor rather than a champion. Although the distinction may appear to be nothing more than semantics, there is a difference. The term *champion* implies a more active role than *sponsor*. The Merriam-Webster Collegiate dictionary defines *champion* as "a militant advocate or defender," whereas *sponsor* is "a person or organization that pays for or plans and carries out a project or activity." In the context of packaged software implementation, what is needed is a champion, a person who will fight whatever battles are needed to ensure success.

Champions are the people who use their credibility, clout, and charisma to ensure that the project is successful. Their responsibilities are to:

- *Sell the solution.* The champion's first role is to convince others of the value of the project and to obtain approval for funding.
- *Provide ongoing public relations.* Throughout the life of the project, the champion is responsible for communicating progress and cheering successes, keeping key decision makers aware of the project's status and reiterating the value to be derived when the implementation is complete.
- *Break down barriers.* In any lengthy project, problems are inevitable, and some cannot be resolved within the project team. Whether they are related to schedule slippage, cost overruns, disputes among OFs, or other issues, the champion should have the ability to resolve them.

The champion is normally the highest ranking person within the end-user department because that is the group most directly affected by the project and the one that stands to gain the most. For some projects, there are cochampions: one from the user department, the other from the IT department. Unlike the project leader role, which should not be shared, this is one case where shared responsibility may be helpful because both departments have a vested interest in the project's success.

Although not involved in the day-to-day work on the project and not a member of the project team or the PMO, the champion is still a critical factor in the project's success. This is the person who keeps the project visible at the decision-making levels of the organization, who obtains funding, and who is able to resolve problems.

The Implementation Team

If the company is going to play a major role in the implementation, it may be necessary to form a new team in addition to the PMO. There may also be subteams with responsibility for individual portions of the project.

When selecting members for the implementation team, the team leader should consider the characteristics of effective team members that were outlined in Chapter 2, Exhibit 2-4. In addition, the team should include people with backgrounds that enable them to analyze and reengineer processes, configure or customize software, and adapt training materials to make them more relevant to the company, if those are the tasks they will be performing.

Some team members will come from the IT department; however, many should be part of the end-user community. It is essential that users be involved in the project at every step. Not only do they provide a "real world" perspective, but they are the ones whose lives will be most changed by the new software. They are the ones who need to define their requirements and then ensure that those requirements are being met by the proposed solution. The IT department is key in defining "how" requirements are satisfied, but only the end users can specify "what" is to be done.

Depending on the project, implementation team membership may require full-time participation or be a part-time responsibility. As was true for the selection team, it is helpful to document expectations and obtain commitments from managers prior to convening the first team meeting. A project charter (Chapter 2, Exhibit 2-1) is an effective way of documenting and communicating team roles as well as the boundaries of the project.

If the software will be implemented at multiple sites, it is important to have representation from each site. Wars have been fought over taxation without representation, and projects have failed because of implementation without representation. Each site needs to have at least one person involved in key decisions so that the site not only understands why the decisions were made, but also has a stake in those decisions.

The implementation team also needs to include individuals who will be responsible for actual installing the software, applying any updates, and performing system administration tasks such as defining user access.

Packaged software implementation can be a resounding success or a miserable failure. Having the right people working on it increases the probability of success.

Chapter 12

Selling the Solution

In most companies, once the team has selected the software and developed a basic project plan, there is still one key hurdle that must be crossed before the project can begin: the project must be funded. The process for gaining funding approval varies by company and by project size. For small projects, all that is required may be completion of a return on investment (ROI) form that is submitted to the finance department. Multiyear, expensive projects typically require more formal approval, sometimes at the highest levels of management. This chapter addresses the steps involved in obtaining that approval.

What Is Involved?

As noted above, each company has its own procedure for documenting potential projects and determining whether or not to fund them. For the purposes of this chapter, the assumption is that the company requires a formal business case document that will be read in detail by the finance department as well as a summary presentation that will be given to senior management.

Although the champion is normally the person who presents the business case and seeks funding, the preparation of the materials for that presentation is typically done by the project team. In most companies, because the team will have only one chance to obtain funding, it is important to create a bullet-proof business case and a compelling presentation. The five Ps (Prior Planning Prevents Poor Performance) definitely apply to this process.

When developing the business case and the related presentation, it is important to understand the perspective of the audiences. Although the finance department will want to ensure that every calculation is correct and that all benefits assumptions are valid, senior management will focus primarily on two questions:

■ Why is this project important?
■ How much will it cost?

These are designed to help senior management balance competing priorities and choose the projects that will provide the greatest benefit, relative to their cost.

An eight-step process will help the team answer those questions as well as provide the level of detail the finance department needs to evaluate a project. Those steps are:

■ Step 1: Calculate the costs of the proposed solution.
■ Step 2: Calculate the costs of the current process.
■ Step 3: Identify the benefits of the proposed solution.
■ Step 4: Calculate return on investment.
■ Step 5: Outline the implementation schedule.
■ Step 6: Develop the business case and presentation.
■ Step 7: Presell the solution.
■ Step 8: Present the solution.

Step 1: Calculate the Costs of the Proposed Solution

It is intuitive that any business case will include the costs of the proposed solution. The confusion sometimes arises over what should be included in those costs. Although it may be tempting to show only the costs of the actual installation, a more accurate calculation includes not only the initial outlay, but also the ongoing support costs. This is typically referred to as total cost of ownership (TCO).

Calculating the total cost is important for two reasons. First, it is the true representation of the project's costs, which can — and probably will — be used to evaluate this project's merits compared to others. Second, because it is unlikely that first-year benefits will exceed the initial costs, the subsequent years' costs are needed to calculate the break-even period. (Step 4 describes this calculation.)

When determining costs, it is important to include labor as well as hardware and software. Outside labor costs are relatively simple to obtain because the vendor and outside firms should have provided good estimates by this stage in the project. It is, of course, wise to include a contingency factor to provide for possible cost overruns.

Internal costs may be more difficult to capture because at this point the company has only estimates of how much time will be needed to support the system (assuming that that support will be performed by in-house staff). Recognizing that these estimates may not be 100 percent accurate, it is still important to include them as part of a complete picture of costs.

All internal costs should be shown, including an inflationary factor for salaries in subsequent years. Internal staffing costs should also be "fully burdened," that is, they should include benefits, training expenses, service and occupancy charges, and other internal costs that are assessed on a per capita basis.

Exhibit 12-1 provides a checklist of costs that may be part of a packaged software implementation project. In his book *Maximizing ROI on Software Development,* Vijay Sikka[1] also recommends including what he terms "intangible costs." These include such unplanned costs as downtime as well as end-user costs. End-user costs are real and should be shown in the business case; however, depending on the company's practices, they may or may not be included in the cost calculations (Steps 1 and 2). If the company normally shows only the costs directly associated with installing and running the system as opposed to using it, end-user costs will not be considered part of the cost equation. It should be noted, however, that reductions in end-user effort will be part of the benefits (Step 3).

Step 2: Calculate the Costs of the Current Process

To present a complete picture of the costs, it is essential to identify the costs of the current solution. Although the costs identified in Step 1 may appear high, it is important to understand that the current process is not free and to be able to compare those costs, which represent the cost of doing nothing, with the costs of the proposed solution. Both costs will be used to calculate ROI (Step 4).

When calculating costs of the current process, the team should consider the items shown in the "Ongoing" column of Exhibit 12-1. If the current solution is an in-house system, there will be no software maintenance fees, but there are likely to be internal costs for maintaining and upgrading the software. Because these costs will continue *ad infinitum* unless the

Exhibit 12-1   Project Costs

Cost Element	One Time	Ongoing (Annual)
Software license	X	
Software maintenance fees		X
Software support (charges for applying changes, etc.)		X
Database licenses	X	
Database maintenance fees		X
Database support (charges for applying changes, etc.)		X
Software modifications (internal and external)	X	
RICE programming (internal and external)	X	
Installation labor (internal and external)	X	
Installation travel (internal and external)	X	
Training labor (internal and external)	X	
Training travel (internal and external)	X	
Training materials (duplication, etc.)	X	
Help desk		X
Servers (initial cost)	X	
Servers (operations)		X
Workstations (initial cost)	X	
Workstations (operations)		X
Depreciation (servers and workstations)		X
Telecommunications (LAN and other charges)		X
Contract negotiations (internal and external)	X	
Process reengineering (internal and external)	X	
Severance costs (if staff is eliminated)	X	
PMO costs	X	X
Other third-party costs (identify)	X	X

proposed solution is implemented, the cost model should include inflationary increases for salaries and other charges that are not fixed. The time periods for these cost calculations should be the same as those used in Step 1.

Besides presenting a balanced picture, identifying current costs is important because some of those costs may be eliminated when the proposed solution is implemented. This is particularly true when labor-intensive tasks are being automated and when old systems running on expensive hardware (typically a mainframe) are being replaced with less costly software. Identifying these costs will simplify the calculations in Step 3.

Step 3: Identify the Benefits of the Proposed Solution

Costs are only a part of the total picture. Benefits are the reason the project was initiated. Although some initial projection of benefits may have been outlined on the project charter (Chapter 2, Exhibit 2-1), to create a complete business case all potential benefits need to be identified and quantified. At the conclusion of this step, the project charter should be updated with the revised numbers.

Benefits are typically grouped into four categories: cost reduction, cost avoidance, quality improvement, and increased functionality.

Cost Reduction

For many projects, this category of benefits is the most important because reduced costs can be used to justify the expenditures involved in acquiring a new software package. Certain cost reductions are easy to quantify. Among those are retirement of hardware and elimination of maintenance fees on old software. Other cost reductions may occur if cycle time or back orders are reduced or inventory turns are increased.

It is also possible that the proposed solution will reduce in-house efforts by streamlining processes or reducing the potential for error, thus eliminating the rework time associated with those errors. This is where end-user time becomes important. As with costs, it is important to use fully burdened salaries and to include an annual inflation rate for salaries. When including manpower savings, the team should distinguish between time that is freed up for other work (which does not translate into a reduction of the bottom line) and the ability to eliminate one or more positions.

Cost Avoidance

Although less concrete than cost reduction, cost avoidance is also a key benefit area. The costs that are avoided are typically acquisition of new hardware and additions to staff, whether temporary or permanent. Stream-lined processes that require less effort may not only reduce costs, but also help avoid them. If, for example, the company anticipates a dramatic growth in sales but does not want to increase its staff of order takers, a new system that allows the current staff to take more orders in the same time or that encourages customers to enter their orders online may avoid staff increases. When calculating the costs that were avoided, the team should include not only the fully burdened salaries, but also hiring costs (employment agency fees, managers' time to interview candidates, preemployment physicals, etc.) and the costs of acquiring workstations or other equipment for the new hires.

Quality Improvement

Although it is more difficult to assign a dollar value to this category and the following one, the team should try to quantify all benefits. Almost no one doubts that improved quality is important. The challenge is to quantify its value. The vendor or an outside advisor may be able to assist in this process. If the quality impacts external customers, there may be research that demonstrates either increased sales due to improved quality or less erosion of the customer base. This same research may help quantify the extent of those changes.

Increased Functionality

Like quality improvement, increased functionality can be a difficult category to quantify. Sometimes increased functionality, like the early customer relationship management (CRM) applications which provided demographics of customer purchases, is instrumental in identifying new products and new markets. This can be translated into increased sales. In that case, those projected revenue increases should be shown as a benefit.

Similarly, new functionality may reduce the time to get a product from the conceptual stage to market. The revenue that would be generated during the time between the streamlined introduction date and the one that would have been the result of the old system can be quantified as a benefit of increased functionality.

If, on the other hand, the new functionality is needed to meet governmental regulations, the benefits can be categorized as cost avoidance because failure to meet those regulations would result in penalties.

Even when cost reduction alone is sufficient to justify the project, it is helpful to include all categories of benefits to present a complete picture of the project and its benefits.

Step 4: Calculate Return on Investment

Sikka[1] lists a number of reasons why project teams try to avoid calculating ROI, then counters with, "Resources spent on analyzing ROI will be better informed and aligned with the business goals and objectives and will actually help get the project completed on time and under budget." In addition to fostering the sense of ownership that Sikka describes, ROI is an important calculation because it helps answer both of senior management's questions.

The calculation of ROI is relatively simple, once the team has completed the preceding two steps. The basic equation is:

$$ROI = [(benefits - costs)/costs] * 100$$

The costs are those identified in Step 1. These costs represent the investment that the project team is asking the company to make. Benefits are quantified in Step 3. It should be noted that if the calculations are done correctly, the following equation should be true:

$$Proposed\ costs = Costs\ of\ the\ current\ system -$$
$$(Cost\ reductions + Cost\ avoidance)$$

ROI is normally calculated for each year as well as the entire project. Exhibit 12-2 shows the calculation of ROI of a hypothetical project. That project will have cost reductions due to the elimination of an expensive mainframe. Because the new system is less labor intensive than the old one, the same number of employees will be able to process more orders, resulting in increased revenues (shown as "Other Benefits").

When reviewing ROI, the finance department will typically ask for two additional calculations: payback period and net present value (NPV). Payback period is the number of months or years until the cumulative benefits equal the cumulative costs. Exhibit 12-3 shows a graph of the cumulative costs and benefits from Exhibit 12-2 which have been used to demonstrate the payback period.

NPV recognizes that there is a value to the money that is being invested in this project. If it were not being spent on the project, it could be invested in something that would generate income. The percentage of income that the money would earn is referred to as the internal rate of return (IRR). The NPV calculation discounts projected benefits by this rate because their value is decreased by the delay in when the benefits are achieved. This is commonly referred to as the time value of money. A dollar received today is worth more than one received five years from now.

Step 5: Outline the Implementation Schedule

In addition to asking how much the proposed solution will cost, both the finance department and senior management will want to know the total duration of the project and, if there are multiple sites involved, in which

Exhibit 12-2 ROI Calculation

Year	Proposed Costs	Costs of Current Solution	Cost Reduction	Other Benefits	Total Benefits	Annual ROI	Cumulative Proposed Costs	Cumulative Costs of Current Solution	Cumulative Benefits	Cumulative ROI
1	300	200	-100	50	-50	-117	300	200	-50	-117
2	100	215	115	60	175	75	400	415	125	-69
3	105	230	125	65	190	81	505	645	315	-38
4	110	245	135	70	205	86	615	890	520	-15
5	115	260	145	75	220	91	730	1150	740	1

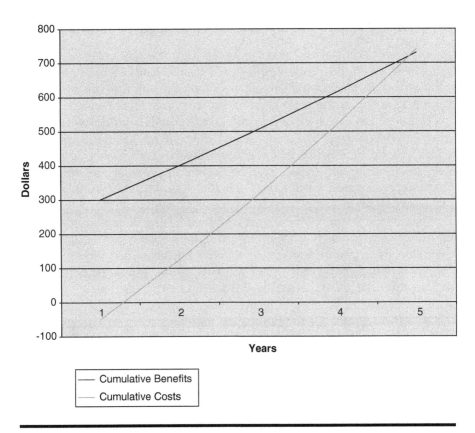

Exhibit 12-3   Break-Even Analysis

order the sites will be implemented. When developing the implementation schedule, the team should show all major tasks, indicating responsibility for each. Although it is not necessary to list accountability by individual, it is important to distinguish among tasks being performed by the company, by the vendor, and by outside firms. Typically the implementation schedule is presented in a simple GANTT chart, a bar chart that graphically displays the project schedule and the progress that has been achieved on each task.

The major challenge associated with creating the schedule is determining how aggressive to make it. Chorafas[2] argues, "The principle is that the more lead time one gives for deliverables, the higher will be the costs, the more elusive the benefits and the lower the implementation accuracy." Although there is truth to his assertion — and it is one of the reasons why projects should be divided into tasks of short durations — it is also important that the schedule be realistic and achievable. An overly optimistic schedule that promises benefits in early years simply to gain funding approval is a dangerous one. As has been noted above, unrealistic schedules can demoralize the team and result in project failures.

Step 6: Develop the Business Case and Presentation

The five previous steps provide much of the material that is needed for a business case and funding approval presentation. There is, however, additional information that should be included in the business case. Exhibit 12-4 shows the table of contents from one business case.

The business case itself is normally a text document. Because business cases can become lengthy, many of the details are relegated to appendices, which can be read as needed. Although the base document is primarily text, some of the appendices may be graphical, providing readers with a visual representation of the facts. Exhibit 12-5 shows a sample of the Deficiencies, Impacts, and Consequences Appendix.

Also, because the business case may be a longer document than some of the decision makers choose to read, it is customary to include an executive overview in addition to the full business case. The executive overview, which is placed first in the packet of information, should not exceed three pages and typically has the following sections:

- *Introduction.* A summary of the problem and proposed solution. Although costs are not included in the introduction, this section provides a condensed version of the whole overview.
- *Background.* A description of the problem that is being addressed and a very brief summary of the events that led to the recommendation. If, for example, the team evaluated ten different packages and benchmarked with three companies, those facts would be included in the background section.
- *Recommendation* The proposed solution, including the name of the software package as well as the names of any outside firms that will be employed to assist with the implementation.
- *Cost versus benefit.* A summary of the ROI calculation, including the payback period.

The formal presentation that is delivered to senior management is typically accompanied by slides that summarize the key points that are detailed in the business case. The break-even analysis shown as Exhibit 12-3 is an example of one possible slide.

The sections of a presentation are similar to those of the executive overview; however, there is no summary at the beginning. Instead, the presentation builds the business case, explaining why a change is needed, what steps the team took to reach their recommendation, what those recommendations are, and the cost and benefits to be derived.

Exhibit 12-4   Business Case Table of Contents

1.0   Project Background
    1.1   Problem or Mission Statement
    1.2   Scope of Project
    1.3   Project Objectives
    1.4   Actions to Date
2.0   Drivers for Change
    2.1   Deficiencies of Current Solution
    2.2   Need for New Functionality
    2.3   Other
3.0   Overview of Proposed Solution
    3.1   Description of Proposed Solution
    3.2   Mapping of Recommendations to Objectives
4.0   Alternative Solutions
    4.1   Identification of Alternative Solutions and Reasons Not Selected
5.0   Benchmarking
    5.1   List of Companies Contacted
    5.2   Results of Benchmarking
    5.3   Independent Advisors' Recommendations
6.0   High-Level Project Plan
7.0   Critical Success Factors
8.0   Assumptions
9.0   Risks and Recommended Mitigating Actions
10.0   Overview of Costs
11.0   Benefits
    11.1 Cost Reduction
    11.2 Cost Avoidance
    11.3 Improved Quality
    11.4 Increased Functionality
    11.5 Other Benefits
12.0   Cost-Benefit Analysis
Appendices
    List of Team Members
    Visual Representation of Deficiencies, Impacts, and Consequences
    Mapping of Deficiencies and Recommended Resolutions
    Sample Process Flow (Showing Steps Eliminated by the Proposed Solution)
    Base System Schematic (Linkage between Modules)
    System Interfaces
    ROI Details
    Detailed Project Plan

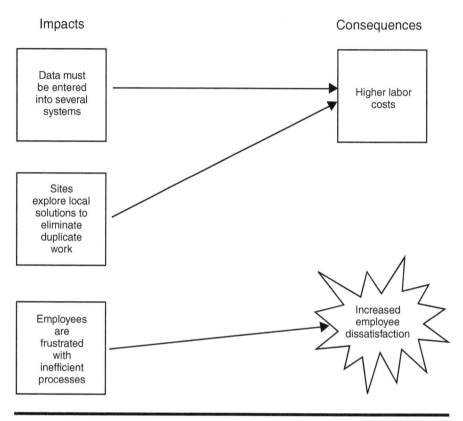

Deficiency 1
Duplicate effort is required to perform routine tasks

Impacts   Consequences

Data must
be entered
into several
systems   Higher labor
                                                    costs

Sites
explore local
solutions to
eliminate
duplicate
work

Employees
are   Increased
frustrated   employee
with   dissatisfaction
inefficient
processes

Exhibit 12-5   Visual Representation of Deficiencies, Impacts, and Consequences

Step 7: Presell the Solution

Although not mandatory, when there are a number of competing priorities for funding or when the project is politically sensitive, some companies increase their likelihood of gaining approval by preselling the solution to key members of the decision-making group. This preselling consists of one-on-one meetings, normally between the project champion and the decision maker, to outline the project and obtain commitment. If preselling is effective, Step 8 becomes almost a formality.

Step 8: Present the Solution

The final step is to deliver the presentation and obtain funding approval. This is the culmination of all the previous steps and represents a major milestone for the project. Depending on corporate culture, the champion may present the business case alone or may be accompanied by key members of the software selection team. In addition to the presentation itself, the champion will typically provide copies of the full business case to all members of the decision-making group.

If approval is given, the team is ready to begin the next task, preparing for the changes that will result from the implementation of their COTS solution.

References

1. Sikka, Vijay, *Maximizing ROI on Software Development*. Boca Raton, FL: Auerbach Publications, 2005, page 64.
2. Chorafas, Dimitris N., *Integrating ERP, CRM, Supply Chain Management and Smart Materials*. Boca Raton, FL: Auerbach Publications, 2001, page 111.

Chapter 13

Organizational Readiness

This chapter could be subtitled "dealing with change." Although change management may not, on the surface, appear to be part of packaged software implementation, it is actually a critical component. One of the differences between simply installing packaged software and implementing it is that a true implementation recognizes that change will occur and addresses the issues associated with those changes.

The fact is, any new software implementation involves change, and those changes impact people. In some cases, the changes are dramatic, including major process reengineering and the potential of staff layoffs. In others, even if the underlying processes are not altered, screens and reports will be different. Packaged software typically involves more change than custom development, simply because the company is implementing a standard package that is designed to meet many companies' needs rather than one that was developed specifically for the company. Although the functionality — the "what" — of packaged software may be the same as custom development, the "how" is likely to differ.

Because change is such a key part of software implementation, it is important to understand how change affects people, what roles different individuals play during change, how those roles impact their acceptance of change, and how to avoid having poorly managed change derail the whole project.

The Basics of Change

Although some people welcome change in their work environment, many others resist it, at least to some degree. The reasons are not hard to find. Change is difficult. There is a learning curve associated with any new system, and that means that people who were experts feel as if they are novices. Even if the functionality that is part of the new system will ultimately make their jobs easier, there are still the initial hurdles of unfamiliarity to overcome. Many people experience discomfort and frustration, knowing that speed and quality are suffering during the early stages of a new system.

A classic book that reveals different reactions to change through a parable is Spencer Johnson's *Who Moved My Cheese?*[1] In this parable of two mice's responses to change, Johnson presents what he calls "the handwriting on the wall." These are seven statements that range from "change happens" to "enjoy change." Although not everyone will enjoy change, it is in the team's best interests to make the changes that are associated with implementing a new system as painless as possible. The first step is to understand how change affects people.

One exercise that is sometimes used in change management classes is to give participants a piece of paper and a pencil and ask them to write their names as if they were signing a check. Although this frequently elicits puzzled looks, it rarely creates a problem. When the facilitator tells the participants to move the pencil to their other hand and repeat the activity, the reaction is different. Nervous laughter and groans can sometimes be heard.

The third step is for the participants to discuss the difference between the two experiences. Common responses when describing the second attempt are:

- It took longer.
- I felt awkward.
- It was hard.
- I had to think about it; this used to be instinctive.
- My signature is illegible.
- Why would anyone do this?

The point of the exercise is to understand that change — even as simple a change as writing with the nondominant hand — is difficult, and that when change is first imposed, quality may suffer and schedules may not be met. Furthermore, people may resist change because it takes them out of their comfort zone.

When asked if they think they could master writing with their non-dominant hand if given enough time to practice, almost all participants will nod. The challenge in software implementation is to minimize the amount of time needed for end users to learn the new processes and to accept the changes.

Roles Associated with Change

Just as people have different roles in the organization and play different roles on a project team, so too are there different roles associated with change. In *Managing at the Speed of Change*,[2] Daryl Conner identifies four categories of roles: sponsors, agents, targets, and advocates.

- *Sponsors* are the champions of change, the ones who instigate it. They are the people who identify the problem and seek a solution. It is important to note that Conner's sponsor may not be the same person as the champion discussed in Chapter 11. A sponsor in Conner's terms may be a lower ranking person within the company who recognizes the need for change and persuades others of the value of that change, rather than the person who becomes its primary defender.
- *Agents* are the activists who make change happen. They are the people who are charged with translating the sponsor's vision into reality. In the case of packaged software implementation, the project team members are the primary agents.
- *Targets* are those who are changed. In most cases, these are the ultimate end users, the people whose jobs will be altered, at least to some degree, by the new system. They may also be members of the information technology (IT) department whose jobs are being eliminated because the new system replaces a labor-intensive legacy system.
- *Advocates* support the change. They may be members of the IT or the end-user departments who are not directly impacted by the change, as well as members of other departments who see the value of the change. Although not directly involved in the project, they are vocal about its benefits and may help sell the solution to the targets.

It should be noted that some people may play more than one role. It is possible for an end user or someone within the IT department whose job will be changed as a result of the project (in other words, a target) to also serve as an agent.

Exhibit 13-1   The SARAH Model

Stage	Characteristic Behaviors
Shock	Surprise and disbelief are the hallmarks of this stage. Irrational behavior is also possible. During shock, it is impossible to predict what a person will do.
Anger	Productivity suffers as the individual lashes out at either the company as a whole or at specific people. Anger may also be internalized.
Resistance	During this stage, the employee will do the absolute minimum that is required to avoid being fired.
Acceptance	Although productivity may still not be normal, the employee has begun to cooperate.
Hope	In this stage, the employee recognizes that there may be benefits to the change.

The Impact of Change

The impact of change, of course, varies based on the magnitude of the change and the person's role. Typically, targets are the people who feel the greatest effects of change. In her best-selling book *On Death and Dying,* Elisabeth Kubler-Ross[3] defines the stages that people go through as they face their own death or that of a loved one. Further research[4] revealed that not only do people who are faced with mortality experience these stages, but any major life change can trigger these stages. Being laid off or having responsibilities dramatically changed, both of which can be the result of a new system, are among those major life changes.

Kubler-Ross defines the stages as denial, anger, bargaining, depression, and acceptance. When related to loss of a job or a major change in responsibility, the names of the stages are slightly different. As shown on Exhibit 13-1, they are sometimes referred to as the SARAH model: shock, anger, resistance, acceptance, and hope.

When reviewing the SARAH model and trying to understand people's reactions, it is important to recognize the following:

- *The speed with which people progress through the stages varies.* Some people will appear to skip stages completely, others to remain mired in one of them.
- *Relapses occur.* The progression through the stages is not linear. It is possible that a person may have reached acceptance but that an event triggers anger, and the person returns to that stage.

- *Not everyone reaches hope.* Although that is the ultimate stage, there are no guarantees that each person will reach it.
- *Survivor guilt is real.* It is not only the targets who experience these stages. Particularly in the case of layoffs, those who remain may feel many of the same emotions.

It is beneficial for the project team, as agents of change, to understand how people may react when faced with dramatic change and to be prepared for the various stages of coping with that change.

Components of Successful Change

Change is not always successful. Virtually every company can cite an example of a major change that failed, whether it was the introduction of a product that fizzled or an attempt to implement a new version of a software product that created a rebellion in the end-user community. Because of the failures — some of which have been spectacular — people have tried to identify the root causes of the problems.

In *Managing Transitions*, William Bridges[5] points out that for any change to be successful, it must have the four Ps: purpose, picture, plan, and part.

- *Purpose.* If the reason that the change is being implemented is not clear — and clearly communicated — the likelihood of success is diminished. Why would targets support a project whose value they do not understand, particularly when it will cause them more work or might even result in their losing their jobs? There should be no doubt in anyone's mind why a project has been undertaken and what benefits are expected to result.
- *Picture.* It is not sufficient to understand why a change is occurring. It is equally critical that everyone involved have a clear vision of the end state. What will the company or their department or their individual jobs look like once the change is complete? Trying to implement change without this vision is a bit like trying to assemble a jigsaw puzzle without having seen a picture of the finished product. Although it is possible to assemble the puzzle or implement change, the process is more frustrating and will take longer.
- *Plan.* Simply knowing what the end state will be is of little value if the team does not have a plan to reach it. "Plan" is sometimes written "Plan/Process," because processes are needed to implement the plan. As with purpose and picture, it is vital that the plan be communicated to everyone who is impacted.

■ *Part.* Last, it is important that everyone who is involved in the change understand the roles they are expected to play and the tasks they are expected to accomplish. Without that understanding, people may be working at cross-purposes or simply not working at all.

Other components of successful change include commitment and sustainability.

Commitment

Ken Blanchard stresses the importance of commitment in *The On-Time, On-Target Manager.*[6] *Commitment* stands alone. It has no subcomponents. If a change is to be successful, all stakeholders — and that includes agents as well as targets — must be fully committed to turning the vision into reality. Mere acceptance is not enough.

One aspect of gaining commitment is ensuring that everyone involved understand their "Part." That is only the beginning. The project's champion and the entire team need to ensure that the stakeholders "buy into" the project and work to achieve its success. The key to this commitment, as discussed below, is effective communication.

Sustainability

Sustainability is the final aspect of successful change. Everyone knows of New Year's resolutions that produce short-term change but that are forgotten by February 1. When the resolutions were made, the person had direction and commitment. What as lacking was sustainability. It includes the attributes that ensure change will be lasting. Like direction, sustainability has three subcomponents:

■ *Methods.* Simply having a vision and commitment will not make change happen, whereas effective procedures and tools combined with that vision and commitment will. Methods are similar to the four Ps' "Plan/Process." They are key not only to making change happen, but, when combined with the next two attributes, to ensuring that the change is permanent.
■ *Measurement.* Although sometimes overlooked, measurement is essential. How else will the project team and the company know whether the change has been implemented and whether it has achieved the expected results? Typically, the team measures and

reports its progress against the schedule and budget during the actual implementation. This is, of course, important, but it is only the beginning. The team should also be measuring benefits as they are achieved, not only during the early stages of the system life cycle, but also — and arguably more importantly — after the system is fully installed and running. Unless the results of change are monitored, backsliding and reversion to the old ways are possible. Measurement adds a needed incentive to sustain change. It also helps quantify and communicate the results of the change, underscoring the validity of the initial reason for the change.

■ *Control.* Even measurement is not sufficient to prevent backsliding. The team needs to develop and implement a plan to bring the process back onto course if the measurements demonstrate that there is a problem. Chapter 22 provides more information about the development of a formal control plan.

The Critical Element: Communication

Change is difficult, and some people will resist it. Those are facts. Nothing will change them; however, effective communication can help ease the change and reduce resistance. When seeking successful change, it is not enough to develop the four Ps or to establish a direction. Unless these elements are communicated effectively, the likelihood of obtaining commitment is low, and there will be no change to sustain. In short, the change will not be successful.

Realtors stress the importance of three things: location, location, and location. The packaged software equivalent is communication, communication, communication. Realtors really mean "good location," and project teams need effective communication. Simply preparing a PowerPoint slide show or hosting a town meeting is not enough. To be effective, communication must be clear, consistent, targeted, and ongoing.

Clear

Whether it is a PowerPoint presentation, a newsletter, or an oral briefing, it is important that there be no ambiguity. The KISS (keep it simple, Stupid) principle applies to all communication but is particularly relevant when explaining major changes such as those often accompanying packaged software implementation.

Consistent

It is important that everyone who has a role in communicating information about the project deliver the same message. This point is so critical that some companies provide scripts for anyone who will be providing oral briefings and channel all written communications through a single person to ensure consistency. Mixed messages not only create confusion; they can also hinder the development of commitment.

Targeted

All projects have a variety of audiences. Just as the business case contained an executive summary designed for senior management as well as more detailed descriptions of costs and benefits for the finance department, so too is it important to consider the needs of everyone who will be impacted by the project. Although everyone has a need to know the overall schedule and progress in meeting it, the detailed information provided to the IT department will differ from that provided to the end users. Even within the end-user community, there may be different communications to managers and to workers.

The format as well as the content may vary based on the target audience. Although a poster hung on the breakroom door may serve the production-line workers' needs, managers may require additional detail in the form of a memo or newsletter.

Ongoing

Simply delivering the message once is not enough. People have short attention spans and competing priorities. They need to be reminded of what is happening, why and when. Not only is it important to reiterate the reasons for the project and the overall schedule, but it is also critical to provide regular updates on progress. Although some people may believe that no news is good news, many equate an absence of news with an absence of progress.

The Rumor Mill

Spinoza said, "Nature abhors a vacuum."[7] So too do employees, particularly those involved in change. It is important to understand that there will always be communication about a major project. The question is whether the information disseminated will be accurate or a product of the rumor mill. Unless the project team takes ownership of communication, the information being circulated throughout the company may be misleading or even totally wrong. The rumor mill and grapevine are active in most companies, and it is in the project team's best interests to preempt them by providing clear, consistent, targeted, and ongoing communication.

The rumor mill is expensive. Its information is frequently inaccurate, based only on speculation or grains of truth. This means that instead of simply communicating the facts, the project team will be involved in damage control, denying the misinformation, and then presenting the facts. Additionally, transmission of information through the rumor mill requires more time and effort than properly designed communications, because there are numerous people both relaying the information and discussing the possible implications.

When delivering their messages, the project team will probably use both types of communication, formal and informal. It is important to understand the differences and the uses of each. Although informal communications are normally verbal, formal communication can be either written (memos, e-mails, updates to Web sites) or verbal (speeches, teleconferences, meetings). The primary distinction between the two classifications is that formal communications are planned, whereas informal ones are not. Both have their uses and advantages.

Formal Communication

The majority of official communication about a project is typically formal and may be delivered in a number of different ways. Exhibit 13-2 shows some of the communication mechanisms that are often used and their target audiences.

When designing communications, the team needs to consider whether to make them "push" or "pull." Communications that are "pushed" are delivered to the target audience without any need for action on their part, whereas "pulled" communications require the recipient to do something to obtain the information. In general, it is preferable to push communications during a project, because that ensures that the audience receives them.

Meetings, briefings, memos, newsletters, and posters are examples of pushed communications, whereas Web pages typically require pulling. If key information is contained on the Web page, it is advantageous to send an e-mail alert to all stakeholders, announcing the update.

In the case of a major change, particularly one that involves staff changes, it is frequently desirable to develop a written communication plan. The purposes of a formal plan are as follows:

- Ensure that the right people are involved.
- Develop a common message.
- Identify the correct timing for delivery of the message.

In other words, a communication plan outlines *what* will be communicated, *by whom* and *when*. If layoffs or other major personnel changes are anticipated, it is critical that they be announced at the right time and that the law and human resource departments be active participants in both developing and delivering the message.

The contents of a communication plan include the key messages, a schedule of events, and a list of frequently asked questions (FAQs) and answers. All are prepared in advance and reviewed with the key communicators prior to the kickoff of the project. This helps increase the consistency of the messages being delivered.

Key Messages

Particularly when sweeping changes are planned, it is essential to ensure that everyone affected understands the major elements, the five Ws (who,

Exhibit 13-2   Communication Mechanisms

Communication Mechanism	Target Audience	Uses
Memos	Managers	Explain details of specific decisions, plans, etc.
Posters	End users	Outline key points and progress
Newsletters	All stakeholders	Review progress and plans; share success stories
Web page	All stakeholders with Internet access	Provide summary of project; may include the same information as posters and newsletters
Town hall and departmental meetings	All stakeholders (either together or in separate groups)	Provide status (typically through a formal presentation); encourage two-way communication
Briefings	Senior management	Provide status (typically through a formal presentation); respond to questions and concerns

what, where, when, and why). The message should focus on the following questions:

- What changes are being planned?
- Why is the change needed?
- When will it happen?
- Who will be impacted?
- Where will it happen?

In many cases, the "where" aspect is of less importance, although for companies that are combining previously decentralized groups, it is a critical component of the message.When developing the key messages, it is important to keep them simple. Details will be presented in subsequent communications, and, as noted above, different audiences may receive different pieces of information. The key messages, however, should be communicated to everyone at the project's initiation and should be repeated regularly until they have become incorporated into a shared vision.

Schedule

It is also important to know who will communicate what, to whom, and when. Building commitment begins by getting buy-in from advocates and agents at an early stage. These groups may be included in "preannounce-ment" meetings so that they are prepared for the reactions when the general announcement is made. Exhibit 13-3 illustrates a sample commun-ication plan schedule.

Frequently Asked Questions

Any announcement of change will elicit a number of questions. To ensure that messages are not "lost in the translation," it is helpful to have a brainstorming session to outline all possible questions that may be raised and to develop answers for them. Putting both the questions and the answers in writing helps prepare whoever will actually deliver the message and helps ensure consistency.

Some companies prepare an FAQ document and distribute it to the affected groups. Others simply give the document to those who will be delivering the messages.

Although a communication plan is not necessary, it embodies the five Ps (Prior Planning Prevents Poor Performance) and helps increase the project's chances of success.

Exhibit 13-3 Communication Plan Schedule

Date	Audience	Medium	Key Messages	Accountability
11/1 – 2 PM	Department heads	Meeting (travelers to dial in)	Overview of project Impact on employees Timing Overview of communications process Next steps: Schedule meetings with HR reps to review process for documenting RIF decisions	Sharon sponsor
11/2 – 11/6	HR reps	Memo Meeting with HR reps (Dept heads to use memo as basis for discussion with their HR reps)	Overview of project Impact on employees RIF selection criteria Alternative assignments Timing Overview of communications plan	Department heads
11/8	Affected departments (all employees)	Meeting	Overview of project Vision and reason for project Impact on employees Some layoffs Enhanced severance Internal posting for other jobs Communications plan Weekly updates of project status Send questions to central e-mail box Answers posted weekly	Department heads

Informal Communications

Informal communications are often nicknamed the "watercooler" communications, because they tend to be *ad hoc*. Although those conversations are important to helping employees feel involved, they can also result in feeding the rumor mill because employees may misinterpret what they have heard and repeat incorrect information. A more effective informal communication mechanism is the rumor control session (RCS). During a period of major change, the champion, department manager, or other person in a leadership role schedules regular RCSs. (Typically these are held weekly.) Attendance is optional, there are no planned messages to be delivered, and the leader makes no speeches. Instead, he or she may begin the session by asking, "What's the latest rumor?" and either confirming or denying it. The leader also responds to questions. An honest "I don't know" or "I can't tell you that yet" is a valid answer; silence is not, because the objective of an RCS is to allay fears and give employees a chance to gripe.

When dealing with change, it is important to understand that resistance is often because the employee feels a loss of control. Whether it is real or not, the employee's perception is critical. The project team are agents of change and may not be able to restore any real control, but they can — by keeping all affected people informed of progress and including them in decision-making meetings — help mitigate the sense of loss. This will help build commitment, which in turn fosters more successful change.

Coping with Conflict

In a lengthy project or one that involves major change, it is likely that conflict will arise, both within the team and between the team and others, including end users and outside firms (OFs), if they are used. If there are multiple OFs, it is also possible that there will be disagreements among them. Conflict may be major; it may be minor. It cannot be prevented, but it can be — and must be — managed.

The first step in dealing with conflict is to understand the nature of the specific point of contention. As shown in Exhibit 13-4, conflict ranges from disagreements over facts to battles based on values. As the cause of

Exhibit 13-4   The Conflict Continuum

	Facts	*Goals*	*Methods*	*Values*	
Rational					Emotional

the conflict moves from the rational to the emotional side of the continuum, it becomes more difficult to resolve.

Some disagreements, such as the planned date for implementation at a specific site, are easily settled. Others, such as the validity of the plan to outsource all support or laying off company staff, may never be resolved. The difference between them is their position on the conflict continuum. Disputes that revolve around facts like the scheduling question are more easily resolved than those that are based on personal values, like the displacement of internal staff. The reason is that factual questions relate to a person's rational side. A person's opinion can be changed by demonstrating a fact. ("The implementation must occur over that particular weekend because it is the only time that the production lines will be shut down.") In contrast, values are intrinsic to the individual and will not be easily changed.

When faced with conflict, the person who is attempting to mediate should identify the type of conflict. If it is factual, it should be relatively easy to resolve simply by listing the facts. If the conflict is not factual, the objective should be to move the dispute toward the rational end of the continuum by finding common ground. For example, if the disagreement is over the right way to accomplish a task (method), the dispute may be resolved by getting both parties to agree on the goal they are trying to accomplish.

In some cases, it may be necessary to go all the way back to facts to obtain agreement. In the case of the hypothetical outsourcing of support, the fact may be that eliminating x jobs through outsourcing will save the company y million dollars, preventing the closing of a plant with $3x$ employees. Although the person's value (saving jobs) has not changed, the facts presented illustrate that the proposed outsourcing will actually save more jobs than it will eliminate and should resolve the conflict.

Conflict will occur, but it can be minimized by having effective communications and attempting to mediate problems as soon as they are evident. Once again, prior planning prevents poor performance.

References

1. Johnson, Spencer, M.D., *Who Moved My cheese?* New York: GP Putnam's Sons, 1998, p. 76.
2. Conner, Daryl R., *Managing at the Speed of Change.* New York: Villard, 1992, pp. 106 and 107.
3. Kubler-Ross, Elisabeth, *On Death and Dying.* New York: Collier Books, 1969.
4. Borgen, William A., "A Model for Group Employment Counseling," *ERIC Digest*, 1995. (www.ericfacility.net/ericdigests/ed404588)

5. Bridges, William, *Managing Transitions*. Cambridge: Perseus, 2003, p. 60.
6. Blanchard, Kenneth H. and Steve Gottry, *The On-Time On-Target Manager*. New York: William Morrow, 2004.
7. Spinoza, Benedict, *Ethics*, cited in *Bartlett's Familiar Quotations*. Boston: Little, Brown, 1980, p. 308.

IMPLEMENTATION V

At this point in the project, team members are understandably eager to begin what they believe to be the "real work" of implementation, that is, actually loading software on servers and beginning the tailoring of it. This section outlines that "real work" but begins with another chapter of planning. Chapter 14 stresses the importance of developing ground rules that will ensure consistency and higher quality throughout the actual installation.

Chapters 15 through 18 outline the decisions to be made and the actions to be taken during the installation process, with Chapter 15 devoted to base software installation and Chapter 16 to configuration of the software to match the company's processes. Chapter 17 discusses interfaces and conversions, and Chapter 18 reviews the most problematic aspect of packaged software implementation: customizations.

No matter how complete the software's functionality is or how flawless the actual installation was, the system is of little value if the end users cannot use it effectively. The key to that effective use is training, the subject of Chapter 19. Chapter 19 also discusses the importance of training the project team.

And, because many companies will be implementing the software at many sites and perhaps in multiple countries, Chapter 20 addresses the challenges of multisite and multinational projects.

Chapter 14

The Ground Rules

The Need for a Rule Book

It is an unfortunate fact of packaged software implementations that some fail. It is possible to have selected the correct software, negotiated a favorable contract, and put together the Dream Team, yet still have the project fail. Failures typically fall into three categories:

- *Incorrect implementation.* The functionality as installed does not meet the users' needs.
- *Schedule overrun.* By the time the project is complete, requirements have changed or the users have found other solutions.
- *Cost overrun.* Even though the functionality satisfies the requirements and was delivered on time, excess costs reduce the return on investment (ROI) to the point where the project is not considered a success.

One of the keys to avoiding these problems is to establish procedures that the project team will use throughout the implementation and to ensure that the procedures are followed. These procedures are the plan processes and methods described in Chapter 13 as essential components of successful change. The goal is to ensure consistency throughout the project, leaving nothing to chance or individual interpretation. These procedures can be considered the ground rules under which the team operates, and — like all important aspects of the project — they should be written, communicated to the team, and easily accessible throughout the life of the project.

There are four primary steps in creating the ground rules.

1. Establish and publish standards.
2. Develop and monitor the schedule.
3. Define and implement change management.
4. Create and follow communication protocols.

Step 1: Establish and Publish Standards

Although it might appear that the need for standards applies only to custom development, it is important to have standards for packaged software implementation projects as well. In fact, it can be argued that standards are even more critical for commercial off-the-shelf (COTS) solutions because it is likely that there will be multiple groups involved in the project: namely, the company, the vendor, and one or more outside firms. Without standards, chaos can result. Standards are a primary key to consistency.

Many companies have existing standards for development and may want to use them. Others may prefer to use the vendor's. Still others may choose to create new standards, specifically for this particular COTS implementation. Exhibit 14-1 shows the advantages and disadvantages of each approach. What is important is not the source of the standards but their existence.

Although the project team may establish other standards, the three most important categories for which standards should be developed are coding, testing, and documentation.

Coding

It is true that the greatest portion of the software that is being implemented should be provided by the vendor; however, the majority of projects require some coding, typically for the reports, interfaces, conversions, and extensions (RICE) elements. Even though some of these programs are designed for one-time use, it is important that they be coded consistently because this may permit reuse of either entire modules or components thereof.

Coding standards should address, at a minimum:

■ *The language and version of the language to be used.* If multiple languages are allowed, there should be a clear definition of when each is used.

Exhibit 14-1   Sources of Standards

Source	Advantages	Disadvantages
Existing company standards	No additional work is required to create them. Company staff is familiar with them. Consistency is ensured with in-house developed systems.	May not address all issues involved in a COTS implementation. Outside staff will require training.
Vendor standards	No additional work is required to create them. All issues involved in this COTS implementation are addressed. If vendor staff will provide most of work, training in use of standards is minimized.	Company staff will require training. Inconsistent with in-house developed systems.
Customization for project	Requires additional work to create them. Addresses all issues involved in this COTS implementation.	Both company and outside staff will require training. Inconsistent with in-house developed systems.

- *Naming conventions*, including data element names as well as program and file names.
- *Identification and use of reusable components*. Because one of the objectives is to deliver the software at the lowest possible cost and in the shortest possible schedule, reuse of code is important. The project team should define which types of modules will form part of a reusable code library as well as when and how they will be reused.

Testing

As is discussed in subsequent chapters, testing is an essential component of successful packaged software implementation. Both vendor-supplied and custom code must be tested to ensure that the project delivers the expected functionality. When creating standards for testing, the team should address the following questions:

- *Who will develop the test cases?* Will the company rely solely on those supplied by the vendor, or will they create their own?
- *Who will conduct the test, entering the test cases and recording the results?* Will it be team members or a separate quality assurance (QA) group?
- Who will review the results?
- *How will defects be reported, repaired, and retested?* This question and the previous one are discussed in more detail in the next section.

Documentation

Although few information technology (IT) professionals' favorite part of a project, complete and accurate documentation is essential. When developing standards, the team should include the following:

- *Identification of types of documentation to be provided.* Will there be design documents, functional specifications, user documentation, training materials, or other documents?
- *Content of each type of documentation.* All items that are expected to be included in each form of documentation should be listed, along with a table of contents, showing the correct order.
- *Format.* If a specific format is required — and, for consistency, it should be — the standards should indicate that. Formats may include the word processing or other program to be used to create the documentation and the specific version of that program as well as type fonts, margin sizes, etc., if those are important to the company.
- *Examples.* Because it is possible to have multiple interpretations of the level of detail required if all that is provided is a table of contents, the team should develop a sample of each type of documentation, showing the desired contents and format. In addition to maintaining consistency, these samples should reduce confusion, which will in turn reduce the time required to create the documentation.

Need for Review and Approval

It is not enough to create standards. The team must also ensure that those standards are being followed. Typically, this is done through the review and approval cycle. As each standard is developed, it is important to address the following questions:

- *Who will review the code, documentation, and test cases?* Will there be a peer review? Will an independent QA group be established?
- *How many levels of review will be implemented?* If only specific pieces of code or documentation require multiple levels of review before final sign-off, they should be clearly identified.
- *Who has final sign-off authority?* If this varies based on the component being reviewed, the decision tree for matching those components with approvers should be defined.
- *How often and when will reviews occur?* Will drafts be subject to review, or will only final versions be included? Will reviews be scheduled on a regular basis, with any components that are ready for review added to the agenda, or will they be scheduled on an as-needed basis?
- *What happens if a component does not pass the review?* Who will be notified? How long will the author have to correct the defects? How many defect correction and review cycles are allowed before the issue is escalated? If escalation is required, to whom is each type of component escalated?

Step 2: Develop and Monitor the Schedule

Although the project team developed a schedule as part of the business case, that schedule is normally a high-level one, outlining the major tasks and milestones, with responsibilities established at the organizational level (vendor versus company versus outside firm). Once the project has been approved, the team needs to develop a more detailed schedule, showing individual tasks and accountability by employee, then ensure that that schedule is met. Like standards, it is not enough to create a schedule. It must be monitored and, if needed, adjusted.

There are two points to consider when developing and monitoring the schedule.

Micromanagement

Although micromanagement is normally a pejorative term, it is important to divide tasks into small ones, ideally of no greater than one week in duration. Some companies refer to these as "inchstones" rather than "milestones." The reasons for having relatively short task durations are threefold:

1. *They help gauge progress.* Although large tasks seem to be perpetually 90 percent done, it is easier to determine whether or not an

inchstone has been met. Particularly on long projects, it is important to be able to demonstrate progress because the end date may be in the distant future.

2. *They serve as motivators.* Although it may not be intuitive, dividing the project into small tasks has a psychological benefit because agents gain satisfaction from completing work. Being able to mark tasks complete and demonstrate progress helps motivate the team and maintain the momentum of the project.

3. *They allow for immediate corrections.* A small deviation from plan may not seem significant, but if allowed to continue without correction, like the train track that is being laid only one degree off plan, it may result in reaching the wrong destination. By measuring progress no less frequently than weekly, it is possible to implement corrective action plans before the problem or slippage reaches epic proportions.

Review Regularly

Having tasks of short duration is of little value if the deliverables are not reviewed as soon as they are available. As discussed above, it is important to establish the standards for reviews and ensure that they are implemented. Ideally, an independent group should review deliverables and certify that each task has been completed.

Establish corrective action plans when problems arise. Despite the best plans, some deliverables may be rejected and schedule slippage may occur. It is important that, as soon as a problem is identified, the team develop and implement a corrective action plan. In some cases, the plan may be assigning additional staff to ensure that a dependent task does not slip. In others, the problem may be of such a magnitude that it may not be possible to adhere to the original schedule. In that case, replanning will be necessary. In either case, it is important to update the schedule, showing the changes that are being made, and, as discussed below, communicating the changes.

Step 3: Define and Implement Change Management

Change, whether it is caused by an expansion or contraction of the project's scope or slippage in the schedule, will occur. If the project is to be successful, it is important that all changes be documented, monitored, and controlled. In short, they need to be managed through a formal process.

There are various types of change that may be encountered, each of which should be addressed through a documented process.

Software and Documentation

It is essential to establish version control for any components that the vendor delivers, as well as programs and documents that will be created during the project. The questions to be answered when developing the version control procedure include:

- *Where will the various versions of code and documents be stored?* Most companies have separate libraries for test and production and, in the case of packaged software, keep a copy of everything that was delivered in a third library. That third library of "vanilla" items is never modified but serves as the ultimate backup if other versions are destroyed or corrupted.
- *Who can check out items?* If access to specific libraries is to be restricted, there should be a written policy explaining who has access. Typically, descriptions of access rights are shown based on job functions rather than individual names.
- *Who approves items?* Although it is likely that a number of individuals will be able to check out items, as noted above, it is important that there be a formal process for reviewing results and certifying them when they are complete.
- *Who can move items into production?* Normally, a group separate from those who are actually making changes has responsibility for updating production libraries.
- *How often and on what schedule will production be updated?* Other than emergency bug fixes, which are normally applied as soon as they are ready, most companies adopt a "release-based" maintenance schedule under which updates are made at specific times of the month or year.
- *How are changes documented?* The importance of documenting who made the change, what it was supposed to accomplish, and when the change was implemented cannot be overemphasized. Not only does this documentation provide an audit trail, but it also provides important information if a rollback is needed.
- *Under what circumstances can standard code be modified?* In many cases, source code is not provided, and this question has no relevance. However, if the vendor provides source code, the company should develop a formal, written policy outlining when that code may be modified. Because the effects of modifying code are far-reaching and will make applying subsequent updates and

releases more difficult, the answer to this question should be "never." The only exceptions should be when the company's process cannot be modified (in which case, another COTS solution that matches the process might be preferable) or when the modification is needed to provide the company with competitive edge.

If modification of standard code is permitted on an exception basis, each exception should require written preapproval by the program manager or someone else within the company who has a clear understanding of the implication of making changes to vanilla code.

Scope

Particularly in projects of long duration, changes in scope may occur. They may be small, the result of finding that the software does not operate in exactly the way the company had envisioned and that another interface is needed, or they may be as extensive as implementing a new module. In all cases, the team should have a formal procedure for requesting, approving, and implementing changes in scope. As discussed in Chapter 8, the change process may have been outlined in the contract. If it is not, the team should develop a written process, indicating who can request changes, who approves them, and the timeframe for receiving responses to change requests. Exhibit 8-3 in Chapter 8 shows a sample request for a change in scope.

Schedule

As noted above, the schedule may change either because of problems in delivering expected results or because of changes in scope. The team should have a formal process with clearly delineated responsibility for revising the schedule and, as discussed below, notifying affected groups of the changes.

Champion

Although uncommon, there is always the possibility that the project's champion may leave the company or accept another position within the company before the project is complete. Because of the importance of the champion's role, the team should have a predetermined process for dealing with such a critical change. Typically the process will include briefing the successor champion, including a full presentation of the business case, and obtaining his or her commitment to the project. If, for whatever reason, the new champion is not enthusiastic about the project (perhaps because of being drafted rather than volunteering for the role), the project team should escalate their concerns and attempt to obtain a different champion.

Step 4: Create and Follow Communication Protocols

There are two major themes to establishing the ground rules, namely, document everything and communicate it. To ensure that everything is properly communicated, the team should also develop a protocol for communication within the team when they are establishing the other procedures outlined in this chapter. This is in addition to the communication plan discussed in Chapter 13. That one is designed to ensure that key messages are delivered to stakeholders and other affected parties at the appropriate times.

Intrateam communication can be divided into two categories: routine and exception. In each case, the team must decide on the method and frequency of reporting.

Routine Communication

Just as it is important to divide the schedule into inchstones so that progress can be measured on a regular basis, so too is it important to establish a schedule for frequent communication among team members. That communication has two primary purposes: reporting progress and identifying problems before they become too complex to resolve, and keeping the team members involved and motivated.

On a large project, there are normally smaller work teams, although there is an overall team that may be composed of dozens of people. The most frequent communication (daily or weekly) is at the work unit level, and if the team is colocated, the method of communicating is in-person meetings. Other types of communication and their recommended frequency are outlined in Exhibit 14-2.

Exception Reporting

Steps 1 through 3 above all mention the fact that problems may arise. It is important to have a methodology for reporting those problems and a plan for escalating them when they cannot be resolved within a work unit or at the next higher level.

Exhibit 14-2   Routine Team Communications

Frequency	Medium	Participants	Purpose
Daily	Meeting or telecon	Work unit	Team members report progress, problems, and plans.
Weekly	Meeting or telecon	Unit team leaders	Team leaders report their teams' progress, problems, and plans.
Weekly	Meeting or telecon	Work unit	Unit team leader reports other teams' progress, problems, and plans.
Monthly	Newsletter or memo	All teams	Document reports overall progress of project, focusing on positive aspects and benefits to be derived.
Quarterly	Meeting or telecon	All teams	Champion addresses entire team, amplifying the monthly newsletters.

Exception reporting, by definition, is not scheduled but occurs whenever a problem is identified. However, not all problems are serious enough to be reported outside the project team. The communication protocol should classify problems by severity (including clear definitions of what constitutes each severity level) and indicate who should be notified, whether that notification is via e-mail or phone, and if by phone, whether that notification should occur outside of working hours or wait until the next business day. Escalation of unresolved problems should have a similar protocol established.

Implementing packaged software involves change on many levels. Having a clearly defined process for dealing with that change increases the likelihood of success.

Chapter 15

Software Installation

As has been stated previously, software implementation is more than simply installing software. Implementation is a multifaceted, multistep process; however, installing and testing software is a critical step in that process. It is essential that the "vanilla" software be installed and tested before any changes — no matter how small — are made and before any configuration is begun.

Although no one doubts the need to install the packaged software, in the case of projects with tight timeframes, it may be tempting to skip the testing step. That would be a mistake. As discussed below, the initial test is critical to validate the software and to establish a baseline for the project team.

Actual installation, if done properly, is a six-step process.

- Step 1: Prepare the infrastructure.
- Step 2: Install vanilla code.
- Step 3: Test the vanilla code with vendor-supplied data.
- Step 4: Test the vanilla code with company-specific data.
- Step 5: Test the software in the real world.
- Step 6: Review the documentation.

Steps 1 through 5 are performed sequentially; Step 6 should be part of the first three steps.

Step 1: Prepare the Infrastructure

Before software can be installed and tested, the supporting infrastructure must be ready. As part of their response to the request for proposal (RFP), the vendor should have provided detailed information about the infrastructure requirements for the commercial off-the-shelf (COTS) package. Unless the software will be hosted by an application service provider (ASP), it is the company's responsibility to ensure that the correct infrastructure is in place. Even if the company has outsourced day-to-day running of the data center to an outside firm, the project team should be involved in reviewing the current infrastructure and ensuring that any needed upgrades are scheduled.

Infrastructure has a number of components, including servers, databases, the firewall, and user interfaces.

Servers

In some organizations, procuring servers or acquiring space on an existing server requires a substantial amount of paperwork and lead time. In others, the process is simple. In either case, there are several decisions to be made.

■ *Will the software be loaded on a dedicated server, or will it reside in a shared environment?* In most cases, the advantage of using a shared environment is lower costs. The potential disadvantages are conflicts among different systems, including problems when multiple systems have different versions of the same dynamic load library (DLL). A shared environment may also result in degraded response time because multiple systems are competing for the same resources. The project team should weigh costs versus potential risks and, if a shared environment is chosen, outline a migration plan to a dedicated server as a way to mitigate the risk.

■ *Will the test instance be a mirror of production?* It is not uncommon to have the test instance reside on a smaller and less powerful server than the one that will be used for production. The advantage to that approach is lower cost. The potential disadvantage is that the team may disregard problems — particularly performance-related problems — that occur in the test instance, believing that they will be resolved in the more robust production environment. The reality may be that the problems are not server related but are actually underlying errors in the software configuration that must be addressed.

■ *Is the correct version and release of the operating system installed?* If the software is to be loaded on an existing server, it is particularly important to ensure that the operating system is compatible with the new system and that, if upgrades are needed, they do not negatively impact any other systems currently loaded on that server. Upgrades should be applied and tested before the new software is installed to isolate the cause of any problems.

Database

There are several database-related questions.

- *Where will the database be loaded?* If it is on a separate server from the software, which is common, is that server installed and running? Will test and production databases be on the same server? As with many hardware-related questions, cost needs to be evaluated against risks of poor performance.
- *Is there sufficient space available?* The team should ensure that the database server is properly sized not only for the initial installation but, more importantly, for the projected size when the software is fully implemented. Most vendors provide tools to guide the team through the sizing process. Regardless of the amount of experience the in-house team may have with database sizing, it is always wise to use vendor-provided tools because there may be idiosyncrasies in the vendor's use of a standard database.
- *Is the correct version and release of the database management system (DBMS) installed?* As was true of the operating system, if the database will be in a shared environment, it is important to ensure compatibility with other systems using that same server.
- *Are there database administrators (DBAs) available to support the database?* If the DBMS needed for the software is not a company standard, it may be necessary to hire or train staff to serve as DBAs. This need should have been identified early in the selection process because it must be resolved before the software is installed.

Firewall

If the software is going to be available to employees, customers, and suppliers via the Internet, it is likely that the database itself will be behind the company's firewall, even though the software is available as part of the "extranet." In this case, the team must ensure that the firewall is properly configured to provide the maximum security for the data. Typically this includes designating a specific port in the firewall that will be used for database calls as well as establishing firewall access rules. It is also important to be able to predict the volume of calls that will be placed through the firewall to ensure that the firewall can support them.

User Interface

Although questions related to servers, the database, and the firewall may not apply if the software will be hosted by an ASP, the user interface is almost always the company's responsibility. In addition to ensuring that everyone who will use the software has an appropriately configured workstation (sufficient disk space, memory, processing power, etc.), it is important to ensure that the correct version and release of the operating system and Web browser are installed. As was true of the other components of the infrastructure, if new releases or versions are required, it is important to ensure that existing software will continue to run properly.

Step 2: Install Vanilla Code

The second step is the obvious one: install the software. This is one of the steps where reviewing the documentation (shown below as Step 6) is important. Even though the company has installed countless other software packages, they should follow the vendor's instructions explicitly and report any problems that may occur. The reasons for reading and following the vendor's instructions are twofold:

- *There may be unique steps.* It is possible that this vendor's software requires special steps that other COTS packages do not and that failing to perform them in the proper sequence may result in an incorrect installation.
- *The instructions may be inaccurate.* One of the objectives at this stage of the project is to evaluate the quality of the product as it is delivered, not just as it was presented during the selection process. If the vendor provides erroneous installation instructions, the company may want to hold back payment until the problems are resolved or reconsider its choice of a vendor. Poor quality at this stage may be a fluke; it may also be indicative of underlying problems that will plague the entire implementation.

Dealing with Problems

Although every project team hopes that its implementation will be bug free, the reality is that problems do occur. They may be actual errors;

they may simply be misunderstandings. Regardless of the cause, they need to be addressed.

The team should be prepared for problems and have a method for recording them and reporting them to the vendor. Although it is tempting to simply call the vendor or send an e-mail with a brief explanation, the team should have a formal problem log similar to the one shown as Exhibit 15-1. Not only will this ensure that problems are not forgotten, but it will also give the team a way of quantifying both the number and type of problems and the vendor's responsiveness.

It is possible that to install the software in the company's environment some changes to the vendor's standard instructions are needed. If this is the case, the circumstance and resolution should be recorded on the problem log. In addition, the standard installation instructions should be annotated with the changes because if similar instructions are used for installation of future releases, they will require the same changes.

Step 3: Test the Vanilla Code with Vendor-Supplied Data

As part of the overall installation package, the vendor should have provided test data along with expected test results. It is essential that the team run these test cases, verify the results, and document any discrepancies on the vendor problem log.

There are two reasons for testing with vendor-supplied data:

1. *To prove that the software works as promised.* Until this point in the project, the team has typically been working with copies of the software loaded at the vendor's site. Although that software may appear to meet all the vendor's claims, there is no guarantee that the software being demonstrated is the same software that will actually be delivered to the company. Running the vendor's test cases and reviewing the results will ensure that the code and documentation are in sync and that there are no problems with the vanilla code.

2. *To establish a baseline.* Having a baseline allows the team to monitor the effects of any modifications they make. This is also a reason why vanilla code should be kept in a separate directory so that the team can run the unmodified software and compare results to the problem code should problems occur. As changes are made to the software, whether through configuration or customization, the team should evaluate the test standard cases, document which ones will have different test results as a result of the modifications, then rerun the test cases with the modified code, ensuring that the

Exhibit 15-1   Vendor Problem Log

Problem Number (1)	Problem Area (2)	Type of Problem (3)	Description	Date Reported to Vendor	Reported By (4)	Date Resolution Received	Resolution	Root Cause (5)	Date Closed	Closed By

(1) Should be a sequential number.
(2) Problem area
  1 – Software module
  2 – Test case
  3 – Technical documentation
  4 – User documentation
  5 – Online training
  6 – Instructor-led training
(3) Type of problem
  1 – Missing
  2 – Incomplete
  3 – Defective
  4 – Ambiguous
(4) Initials or last name of person reporting problem. Note that "closed by" should follow the same format.
(5) Root cause
  1 – Erroneous code
  2 – Incorrect documentation
  3 – Lack of training
  4 – Misunderstanding

expected changes were indeed observed. Both functionality and performance should be documented as part of the baseline because both may be affected by company modifications.

Step 4: Test the Vanilla Code with Company-Specific Data

Step 3 proved that the software performs as the vendor claimed it would. Although important, that is not the only test that needs to be conducted. The team also needs to create company-specific data. This step is critical because it demonstrates whether or not the software performs as the company needs it to. The distinction is a key one. Vendor-supplied test cases are generic, designed to showcase the system's functionality. The ones that the company creates should be tailored specifically for the company and should reflect real-world data.

Prior to actually running the test cases, the team should develop a test plan outlining the processes that they will follow for all testing, not simply the testing of base system code. At the same time, they should create a test case log. Exhibit 15-2 shows the contents of a sample test plan. A test case log is included as Exhibit 15-3.

There are several questions to be answered when drafting the test plan.

- *Who will test?* Although it is important to have end users as well as members of the information technology (IT) department participate in the testing process, the most effective testing is done by independent, trained testers, typically part of a quality assurance organization. End users and IT members, particularly the members of IT who were responsible for developing the reports, interfaces, conversions, and extensions (RICE) elements, have a natural bias to test to prove that the system works. Professional testers, on the other hand, test to prove that the system *does not* work. They are the ones who devise convoluted and illogical test cases that test the system's boundaries. As a result, their tests are more comprehensive and challenging to the system. Whenever possible, professional testers should be included as part of the testing team, both to develop test cases and to conduct the actual test.
- *What types of testing will be performed?* Exhibit 15-4 refers to five different types of testing, any of which may be conducted. Each one of these has a different objective, as shown in Exhibit 15-4. Unless the system is being installed with no configuration or customization, it is likely that all five levels of testing will be needed. If one or more types of testing are not to be conducted, the test plan should indicate the reason for their omission.

Exhibit 15-2   Contents of Test Plan

Section Number	Section Name	Information to be Included
1	Introduction	List of types of testing to be performed
2.0	Base code test plan	
2.1	Test strategy	Scope of testing to be performed; objective of testing
2.2	Roles and responsibilities	List of all individuals who will participate in the test; this includes reviewers as well as actual testers
2.3	Test environment	Environment in which test will be performed; any special requirements (testing software, special security, etc.)
2.4	Test schedule	High-level schedule of when tests are to be performed
2.5	Test cases and expected results	A list of all test cases to be entered along with the expected results
2.6	Other acceptance criteria	A list of acceptance criteria that may not be linked to an individual test case; e.g., response time
2.7	Critical success factors	A list of all assumptions that may affect the completion of the test; may include assumptions about the maximum time required to review and approve test results, maximum vendor response time, and accuracy of data conversions, etc.
3.0	System test plan	Will include all the subsections shown for the Unit Test Plan
4.0	Integration test plan	Will include all the subsections shown for the Unit Test Plan
5.0	Stress test plan	Will include all the subsections shown for the Unit Test Plan
6.0	Acceptance test plan	Will include all the subsections shown for the Unit Test Plan
7.0	Approvals	A listing of all approvals that are required for the document

Once the test plan and test cases have been developed and approved, the team can conduct the test of base system code using the test cases the company created. Discrepancies between expected and actual test results should be reported to the vendor. Unless these problems are resolved, the team should not proceed with configuration or any package customizations.

As was true of the testing that occurred in Step 3, the results of this test should form part of the system baseline.

Exhibit 15-3 Test Case Log

System						Initially Tested By					
Module						Date					
Case Number (1)	Type of Test (2)	Data Entered	Expected Results	Actual Results	Problem Number (3)	Date Retested	Retested By	Retest Results	Comments	Date Closed	Closed By

(1) A sequential number
(2) Type of test
  1 – Base code
  2 – System
  3 – Integration
  4 – Stress
  5 – Acceptance
(3) Next sequential number from the vendor problem log

Exhibit 15-4   Types of Testing

Testing Category	What Is the Objective?	What Is Being Tested?	When Is It Performed?	Who Should Participate?
Base code	Verify that the system performs according to the vendor's specifications and the company's needs	Entire system	As soon as the system is delivered and installed	Project team, Quality Assurance
System	Verify that the configured or modified system operates according to its specifications	Entire system, excluding interfaces	When all modifications have been made	Project team, Quality Assurance
Integration	Ensure that the interfaces between systems function as planned and that the system meets the required performance levels under normal conditions	Interfaces to and from external systems; operation in the "real-world" environment	At the completion of system testing	Project team, Quality Assurance
Stress	Test the system's limits and performance under extraordinary circumstances	System robustness under high volumes of data or low resource availability; ability to recover from system failures	During base code testing and again at the completion of integration testing	Project team, Quality Assurance
Acceptance	Verify that the system meets all end-user requirements	Functionality and ease of use	At the completion of integration testing	End users, Quality Assurance

Step 5: Test the Software in the Real World

It is not enough to prove that the system has the functionality the vendor claimed it would and that the functionality meets the company's requirements. It is also essential to conduct "real-world" testing. The objectives are:

■ To demonstrate that the system will perform at acceptable levels under real-world conditions.

■ To determine what will cause performance to degrade to an unacceptable level.

These are part of the integration and stress tests shown in Exhibit 15-4, although at this point interfaces will not be available for integration testing. Both tests will be rerun once all modifications are completed. Whereas the first two tests were conducted using a small number of test cases, normally entered via automated test software or keyed manually by a few operators and are typically run in the test environment, real-world testing is conducted on the infrastructure that will be used in production, beginning with expected volumes and increasing to the point where system performance is no longer acceptable.

There are two components to real-world testing.

1. *Normal environment.* These tests attempt to simulate the production environment once the system is fully installed. As such, they include the volume and type of transactions that are anticipated when the system is implemented, and they are run on multiple servers in different physical locations, if that will be the ultimate production environment. If the system will be used in multiple time zones, transactions are designed to reflect that reality. The purpose of this testing is to ensure that there are no surprises when the system has been rolled out.

2. *Extraordinary circumstances.* Not only is it important to understand what system performance will be under normal circumstances, but it is equally important to know how much growth the system can handle and how it will react to disasters. These are commonly referred to as stress and disaster recovery testing.

    – *Stress.* In this test, the team deliberately enters multiple times the expected volume of transactions, trying to break the system. It should be noted that testing in earlier stages attempted to break the system through the entry of invalid transactions. In stress testing, the majority of the cases entered will be valid because what is being tested is performance rather than functionality. The objective is to determine at what level the system will become so sluggish that users will refuse to use it or whether, with a heavy enough load, the system crashes.

    – *Disaster recovery.* Whether or not the system will crash under normal circumstances, the team must be prepared for the possibility of a system crash or a disaster such as an earthquake or hurricane that destroys the data center. The company should have formal disaster-recovery procedures in place and tested on a regular basis. When new software is being added to the company's portfolio, it is important to ensure that the procedures are updated to include the new application and that a test is performed.

In disaster-recovery testing, the team creates and executes disaster scenarios, including "crashing" a server, to determine whether or not the recovery procedures that the vendor or the company's IT staff have developed actually work as planned.

Full disaster-recovery testing is normally run at the conclusion of integration testing; however, at these initial stages, it should be scheduled and procedures documented.

Step 6: Review the Documentation

Although the other steps were conducted sequentially, portions of the documentation review can, and should, occur as part of Steps 1, 2, and 3. The remaining documentation, including training materials and user manuals, should be read carefully and assessed for its completeness, accuracy, and ease of comprehension. As noted above, any discrepancies should be reported to the vendor by using the vendor problem log.

At the conclusion of these steps, the team should assess the open items on the problem log and determine whether or not to proceed with the next steps before they are resolved. Minor discrepancies in documentation may not warrant a schedule delay, but if the system fails the real-world performance test or if there are unresolved problems from earlier testing, the team should consider waiting until they are complete because configuration and customization, the next steps, may complicate problem resolution.

Chapter 16

Configuration

Configuration is, or should be, an important part of every packaged software implementation project. Gone are the days when the vendor provided one-size-fits-all software that addressed basic needs but gave companies with unique requirements little recourse other than changing source code. In place of those fairly rigid systems is software that can be easily tailored to meet each company's requirements without having to modify any vendor code.

For the purpose of this book, configuration is defined as the use of vendor-provided capabilities to tailor the base system. This tailoring typically includes such elements as definition of calculations; creation of an organizational structure or, in the case of financial software, the chart of accounts; and the establishment of user access rules, in addition to the specification of basic code tables. Conversions and interfaces are addressed in Chapter 17, reports in Chapter 18.

The Configuration Conundrum

Depending on the package, configuration can be as simple as completing a half dozen tables with readily available information or as complex as a task that consumes months of effort. In general, the more comprehensive the system, the more complex configuration will be.

The following information may be easy to obtain:

- Company codes, including individual region and country codes
- Organization structure, including sales and distribution chains
- Bank data
- Monetary currencies to be used
- Customer data, including historical information
- Vendor data, including historical information
- Bill of materials

All that information is typically available in existing files, either electronic or paper. Configuration of those elements may involve no more than mapping the data elements of an existing file to specific fields in one of the new system's tables.

Complexities arise when processes are involved. The powerful configuration tools provided with many enterprisewide systems allow — and expect — the company to map its processes to the system, showing the sequence in which each process will be executed. An efficient mapping requires a thorough understanding of not only the company's current processes, but also the new system's design. This is the stage at which process reengineering becomes a reality as companies recognize that there may be better ways to accomplish tasks than their existing process.

The good news is that some vendors, recognizing the time and effort involved in configuration, have developed preconfigured systems for each of the major industries they support. Although the tailoring in those preconfigured solutions may not be a perfect match for each company, it will normally shorten the configuration process.

On the surface, configuration is simple because it consists of only three steps:

1. Define the requirements, including the specific changes to be made.
2. Make those changes.
3. Test them.

Although streamlined, these correspond to the system design, construction, and testing and quality assurance phases of the traditional waterfall system development life cycle (SDLC) in Chapter 1, Exhibit 1-1.

Definition

Definition is arguably the most difficult and time consuming of the three steps. The high-level identification of configuration requirements should have been completed prior to selection of a commercial off-the-shelf (COTS) solution. What is needed at this stage is the translation of those requirements into enough detail for coding. As noted above, in some cases the creation of that detail is relatively simple. The mapping of existing country codes, for example, to the vendor's format should provoke little discussion. However, the definition of other components of the configuration may be less straightforward.

The flexibility that is inherent in modern packaged software can be a double-edged sword. Although it allows a great deal of tailoring without modifying source code, it also presents the project team with myriad choices, the implications some of which they may not fully understand.

This is one step where companies frequently hire the vendor's consultants as advisors even though they are not using them for other functions. The reason, as Dimitris Chorafas states in his book, *Integrating ERP, CRM, Supply Chain Management and Smart Materials,*[1] is that "while ERP [enterprise resource planning] systems are not necessarily difficult to install in an average way, they do require significant effort to get the best of out them." The project team's objective is not simply to implement the software but to implement it in the best way possible.

The problem Chorafas describes is not confined to ERP but exists for any complex software package. One way to simplify the task and achieve the team's overall goals is to use a version of the software that is preconfigured for the company's industry. However, one may not be available, and even if it is, the project team may not have enough package-specific expertise to make the correct choices. Outside advisors can fill the gap. Using the vendor or a systems integrator with specific industry experience with the chosen COTS solution can reduce the time required to define configuration and help the company understand the effects of the choices they are making.

As with all aspects of the project, the detailed requirements and the resulting design that are developed prior to configuring the software should be documented and subject to the same quality assurance and review cycles as any other critical document. Although some companies may choose to create both functional and technical design specifications, as they do for custom development, that level of detail is not always necessary for configuration because elements such as the specific processing to be performed and the system architecture have already been established in the software package.

It is, however, important to document all decisions. As an alternative to functional and technical design specifications, the company may create a configuration specification. Exhibit 16-1 provides a sample table of contents.

Exhibit 16-1   Contents of Configuration Specification

Section Number	Section Name	Information to be Included
1	Introduction	Project name; scope of configuration
2	Assumptions	A list of any assumptions, including availability of specific staff or other resources
3	Critical success factors	A list of the key elements that must be occur or be present for the configuration to succeed
4	Risks	A list of potential risks as well as the plan to mitigate them
5	Resources required	A list of all staff (both external and internal) who will participate, along with the percentage of time for each Any infrastructure requirements System or other software requirements
6	Schedule	A high-level schedule, including milestones
7	Process modifications	If the end-user's process will change, a description of the current and proposed processes
8	Detailed design	A description of the actual configuration to be done. The format of this will vary based on the vendor and the component being configured.
9	Test strategy	A description of the testing that will occur; may refer to an overall project test plan
10	Approvals	A list of all approvals that are required for the document
11	Revision history	Chart showing the dates on which the document was revised, the person responsible for each revision, and the changes that were included

Although it is important that end users be involved throughout the project, it is critical that they participate in the creation of the configuration document because configuration directly impacts their daily work. They are the ones who understand the intricacies of the current process, and if reengineering is needed, they are the ones who can validate the feasibility of proposed changes.

This is one portion of the project where end-user subject matter experts (SMEs) are vital to the project's overall success. Their subject matter expertise combined with an in-depth knowledge of the system's internals, whether provided by the vendor, a systems integrator, or trained in-house staff, is what is needed to ensure accurate configuration of the system.

Coding

Unlike traditional programming, which requires logic to be developed, configuration is normally a simpler process, in essence requiring the project team to specify parameters rather than create entire programs. Although the process for incorporating the configuration into the overall system varies by vendor, the key to success does not. There is one simple rule: follow the vendor's process. Vendor documentation should include step-by-step instructions on how to perform the configuration tasks. As was true of the installation of the base software, it is important to follow the defined process and to document and report any problems that are encountered. The vendor problem log (Chapter 15, Exhibit 15-1) should be used to report discrepancies and errors.

Testing

The baseline that was established during the installation of the base software will be a key component of this step. When the configuration is complete, the team should retest the system, using the company-specific data that was developed for Step 4 of Chapter 15, comparing the results to those developed during the baseline. The objective is to ensure that the configuration is accurate and that it achieves the company's goals.

Results should vary from the baseline because the system is now tailored to meet the company's specific requirements. Consequently, it is important that the team document each change that is observed, ensuring that the variations in output are the ones they expected. Any deviations from those expectations should be documented on the test case log and reported to the vendor.

In addition to the testing described above, the team may want to create a more robust set of test data based on the detailed configuration. When those cases are created, they should be added to the test case log along with expected results. This will form a new baseline.

In addition to testing functionality, the team should also observe system performance and compare it with the performance during the baseline. Although output will change because of the increased functionality that results from configuration, system performance should be unchanged. Any degradation in response time should be reported to the vendor by using the vendor problem log.

At this point in the project, the team should have a fully functioning system that meets the company's basic requirements. The next step is to connect that system to the company's other software applications.

Reference

1. Chorafas, Dimitris N., *Integrating ERP, CRM, Supply Chain Management and Smart Materials*. Boca Raton, FL: Auerbach Publications, 2001, p. 12.

Chapter 17

Interfaces and Conversions

Once the initial configuration is complete, the team can begin developing interfaces and conversions. These are sometimes referred to as part of the reports, interfaces, conversions, and extensions (RICE) elements. Interfaces and conversions are particularly important because they provide links to and from existing systems. As noted in Chapter 16, the commercial off-the-shelf (COTS) solution, no matter how powerful and comprehensive it may be, rarely exists in a vacuum. To become fully functional it must be connected to the company's other systems, drawing data from them or sharing its data with them. This is the purpose of interfaces and conversions.

Although in many cases the vendor toolset simplifies the development of interfaces and conversions, both require careful planning to ensure that the final product meets the user's expectations. The tasks involved in the two activities are similar, and in some cases the same tools can be used. A primary distinction is that whereas data conversion is run once — normally before the system is placed in full production — interfaces are executed multiple times and do not begin to be run until the system is in production mode.

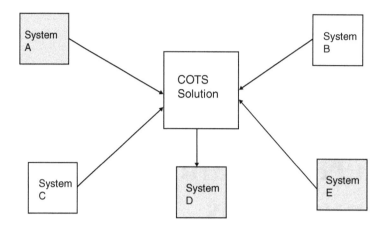

Shaded boxes represent
temporary interfaces

Exhibit 17-1   System Interfaces

Interfaces

Although comprehensive software packages such as enterprise resource planning (ERP) will replace many legacy systems, interfaces are frequently required from (and in some cases to) existing systems. Because these interfaces are critical to the functioning of the COTS solution, it is helpful to create a pictorial representation of them. A high-level version of this is typically included in the business case (Chapter 12, Exhibit 12-4). A sample system interface chart is shown as Exhibit 17-1. The value of such a graphic is that it is easy to see both the direction that data is being transferred as well as the expected life span of the interface.

As discussed in Chapter 10, interfaces may be either permanent or temporary. Temporary interfaces are most often needed when the implementation is being phased by site. The effort involved and the questions to be answered do not vary based on the expected life span of the interface.

There are four basic steps involved in the creation of interfaces: planning, definition, coding, and testing.

Planning

As is true of all aspects of packaged software implementation, the five Ps (prior planning prevents poor performance) apply to developing interfaces.

17-2 Legacy System Interface Inventory

Legacy System	Type of Interface (1)	Direction (2)	Frequency of Execution (3)	Retirement Date

(1) Type of interface: B = Batch; O = Online.
(2) Direction: to or from legacy system.
(3) Frequency of execution: A = Annual; S = Semiannual; Q = Quarterly; M = Monthly; W = Weekly; D = Daily; H = Hourly; T = Transactional (whenever a transaction is generated); O = Other (frequency must be specified).

As part of the planning process, the team should consider the following series of questions and document their responses. If the vendor's toolset does not include a comparable form, the team can use an interface inventory similar to the one shown as Exhibit 17-2 for documentation.

Which Legacy Systems Require an Interface?

To answer this question, the team needs to consider the overall project objectives and how those objectives will be met in both the short and long term. If one of the objectives of the project is to provide consolidated head-count reports, showing how many employees the company has in each location, country, and region with breakdowns of salaried versus hourly and if the initial implementation addresses only the United States-based plants of a multinational company, the team will need to develop interfaces from the payroll or human resource systems in Europe and Asia.

The initial planning stages of the project should have identified major interfaces. At this point, it is important to review those proposed interfaces and to determine whether any additional ones are required.

What Type of Interface Is Needed?

Interfaces come in two types: batch and online.

1. *Batch.* Batch interfaces are used when one or more of the following is true:
   - The sending system is updated in batch mode.
   - The data being transferred does not require immediate updating.
   - The volume of data being transferred is so high that it would slow response time if the transactions occurred during peak system use time.

A primary advantage of batch interfaces is that they can be scheduled to run during the slowest shift, causing minimal impact on system response time.

2. *Online.* Online interfaces are most common when both of the following are true:
   - The sending system is an online system.
   - The data being transferred is time critical to the receiving system.

An example of a situation that lends itself to an online interface is the transfer of orders from an existing order entry system into the new ERP system so that inventory can be updated in close to real-time mode. The potential disadvantage of an online interface is that high volumes may impact performance.

Which Direction Is Data Transferred?

Although most interfaces are from legacy systems to the new COTS solution, it is possible that some data will be transferred from the new system to a legacy application. An example of that is the case where the company wants to have a single point of entry for its chart of accounts and has decided that the COTS solution will be that point of entry. If the company has existing financial systems that need to be kept in sync until they are replaced, an interface would be developed from the new system to the legacy applications.

How Frequently Will the Interface Be Run?

Typically, the frequency depends on how often the source system is updated and how critical the information is to the destination system. It should be run no more frequently than the source system is updated. Exhibit 17-2 shows a list of potential frequencies.

How Long Will the Interface Be Needed?

As noted above, some interfaces are permanent, in which case their retirement date, as shown on Exhibit 17-2, will be N/A. Others are designed to be run only until the legacy system is retired. The purpose of listing a retirement date is to aid in decommissioning legacy systems. (Chapter 22 discusses this decommissioning.)

Definition

As was true of configuration, the team should develop formal written specifications for all interfaces. The need for specifications and the standards to be followed should have been identified as part of the project's ground rules (Chapter 14). If the vendor's toolkit does not provide a template and if the company does not have an existing standard for specification documents, a format similar to the configuration specification (Chapter 16, Exhibit 16-1) can be used. Although it is critical to list the details of the interface, notably the translation of data into the specified transaction form for the receiving system, it is also important to note assumptions and critical success factors along with the planned schedule and needed resources. Complete documentation is important to the team because these programs will be in existence for some period after installation and may need to be modified.

In addition to defining what will be done, the team must consider who will perform the work of creating each interface. Development of interfaces is one aspect of the project where the team typically expands its resources to include members of the information technology (IT) department who are currently supporting the existing systems. Even if outside firms are being used for basic coding, the support staff's in-depth knowledge of the legacy systems makes them the logical candidates for writing interfaces. At a minimum, they should be involved in developing the specifications because they understand the legacy applications' file structure and any idiosyncrasies in the current systems.

Coding

Interfaces typically consist of two steps:

1. Extracting the data from the sending system and formatting it into the receiving system's format
2. Reading the interface file and applying the transactions to the database

Most vendors provide toolkits that perform the second step. As a result, the team is required to do little more than ensure that the file is in the correct format and schedule the running of the interface. The first step, however, normally requires custom programming to deal with myriad file formats. It is here that the existing support staff excels. It is also here that the coding and documentation standards established as part of the ground rules should be employed.

Testing

Two types of testing are needed for interfaces: unit and integration. Unit testing, which is similar to the base code test shown in Chapter 15, Exhibit 15-4, verifies that the interface itself works properly. Integration testing ensures that the interface functions as expected when all other components of the system — including all interfaces — are installed.

The team should develop a test plan for each interface, including test cases and expected results. Exhibit 15-2 in Chapter 15 presents contents of a sample test plan. When interfaces are online, it is also important to ensure that normal system response time is not adversely impacted by the additional transactions from the interface. Results should be recorded on a test case log (Chapter 15, Exhibit 15-3), with any vendor-related problems reported to the vendor by using a standard problem log (Chapter 15, Exhibit 15-1).

Data Conversion

Although it is possible to populate the data in a new system "from scratch," in most cases, the company will want to use data from legacy systems, converting them into the format that the new system requires. The four steps that were used and many of the precepts that were established for interfaces also apply to data conversion routines. Even though they will be run only once, these are key programs.

Planning

As was the case with interfaces, there are a number of questions that the team should answer as they plan the conversion. These will help them determine the type of conversion that is most appropriate. If the vendor toolkit does not include a conversion inventory form, the team should record their decisions on one similar to that in Exhibit 17-3.

What Data Will Be Converted?

This is a key decision because it determines both the volume and complexity of the actual conversion programs as well as the functionality that will be available in the new system. There is normally no question about active records. They will almost always be converted. All current employees and suppliers, for example, would be deemed to be active for the new system.

Exhibit 17-3 Data Conversion Inventory

Source System	Scope of Data to Be Converted	Volume of Data	Degree of Cleansing Required (1)	Complexity of Code Translations Required (2)	Type of Conversion (3)	Responsibility

(1) Degree of cleansing required:
  1 – Clean, no additional effort required
  2 – Automated cleansing possible
  3 – Majority can be automated; manual exception processing is required
  4 – Requires manual cleansing

(2) Complexity of code translations required:
  1 – Completely automated, no special programming required
  2 – Completely automated; special programming will be required
  3 – Majority can be automated; manual exception processing is required
  4 – Requires manual translation

(3) Type of conversion: automated or manual

The primary question the team faces is whether or not inactive records should be transferred. In answering this question, the team will weigh the possibility that these records will be needed for reporting against the cost of converting and storing them in the new database.

Similar questions apply to historical transactions. Should the company convert one or more years of history or simply transfer balances? There is no right or wrong answer; as with the question of inactive records, the team must weigh the costs and benefits, then record their response in the "Scope of Data" column of the data conversion inventory.

Where Does That Data Currently Exist?

It is possible that data will exist not only in a number of automated systems, but also in manual files. All sources should be identified in the "Source System" column. It is possible that multiple conversions will be needed for the same type of data if it resides in different systems with different file formats.

What Is the Volume of Data To Be Converted?

The primary reason for determining the volume of data is to aid in the decision of whether to convert that data manually or to use an automated conversion program.

How Clean Is the Data?

Unfortunately, even when data comes from existing systems, it may not be as "clean" as it should be. Codes may be inconsistent or fields that are now validated against tables may have been entered as free-form test. These problems can be the result of incorrect conversions from other systems or simply the evolution of coding rules. Whatever the cause, the team will want to avoid GIGO (garbage in, garbage out) by planning for data cleansing. In some cases, the data cleansing can be automated. In others, manual intervention will be required.

If Needed, Can Code Translation Be Automated?

It is possible that the codes the team established for the new system are different from those in legacy systems. If this is true, the team must determine whether or not the translation is a simple one that can be done by either the conversion program or the vendor's conversion toolkit or whether manual intervention will be required.

Will the Conversion Be Automated or Manual?

The answers to the previous questions will help determine the type of conversion that will be needed. Automated conversions should be used whenever the following are true:

- Data exists in electronic file format.
- Volume is high.
- Data is clean, or rules can be developed for the cleansing.
- Code translations can be automated.

Low-volume data, data that exists only in paper format, or data that requires extensive manual intervention for either cleansing or translation is better suited for a manual conversion.

Who Is Responsible for the Conversion?

As was true of interfaces, this is a task that typically includes members of the existing system support staff because of their knowledge of the legacy systems. When data cleansing or manual translations are required, end users should be part of the team because they own the data and have the greatest incentive for ensuring that the conversions are accurate. It is also critical to establish responsibility for reviewing the output of the conversion.

Definition

The same considerations that exist for interfaces apply to data conversions. Both manual and automated conversion activities should be fully documented and subject to the normal project review cycle. In addition, it is important to include end users in all data-mapping activities because they know the actual data better than anyone else.

Coding

There are two types of coding that may be needed for data conversions. The first is the traditional program coding, as outlined in the section about interfaces. The second is the manual entry of data into the new system following the rules that the team has established for conversion and cleansing. When addressing manual conversions, the team may want to consider using an automated tool that permits the creation of scripts rather than keying data directly into the system. Use of scripts allows rerunning of the data without rekeying. This is of use if problems occur during the conversion process and it needs to be rerun.

Testing

As noted above, the team should plan for both unit and integration testing of data conversion routines. Because of the importance of valid data, review of the test results should be particularly rigorous and should be done by end users as well as the quality assurance staff.

With interfaces and conversions planned, the team can proceed to the remaining RICE elements: reports and extensions.

Chapter 18

Customizations

This chapter addresses the "R" and "E" components of RICE, namely reports and extensions, as well as pure customization of the commercial off-the-shelf (COTS) package. These represent the two extremes of programming that the team may perform. Reports, because they simply extract data from the system, are noninvasive. Other than possibly affecting system performance, they will have no negative impact on the base system. Extensions or customizations are on the opposite end of the spectrum. By definition, they are designed to modify the functionality of the base system, and, as such, they have the potential for creating problems.

Reports

Reports come in two flavors: scheduled and *ad hoc*. Because the second category of reports is developed and run by end users, who will use either the company's standard report writer tool or the one provided by the vendor, the project team does not have complete control over it. Their primary responsibilities are to provide adequate training (cf. Chapter 19) and to ensure that the reporting tools are equipped with overload controls that halt runaway, looping, or excessively long reports.

Scheduled or standard reports are the project team's responsibility. The good news is that there are fewer complexities associated with reports than with extensions or customizations because reports do not change the basic logic of the system but instead provide views of existing data. It is, however, advisable to use a defined process for identifying and creating reports and to follow the coding and documentation rules that were established in Chapter 14. As was true for interfaces and conversions, the report creation process has four steps: planning, definition, coding, and testing.

Planning

There are several steps that the team should take before proceeding with the development of reports.

Review All Existing Reports

Most COTS packages come with myriad standard reports. In addition to the ones that may be required for governmental reporting (payroll withholding, tax returns, etc.), there are normally a number of reports that other companies have found valuable. Although the format of these reports may not be identical to the ones the company currently produces, in many cases the content is the same.

The end-user members of the project team should review every report that is part of the standard package to determine whether or not it is needed and, if it is, whether or not it can be used in its basic format. A report inventory similar to that of Exhibit 18-1 can be used to record the results of the review.

The team's objective should be to use as many standard reports as possible rather than create new ones because that reduces implementation cost and time. If only minor modifications are needed to a standard report, the team should consider using the standard report as a template rather than developing a totally new one. "Cannibalization" is a good thing.

Develop an Inventory of All New Reports

It is possible that even though the base system has hundreds of reports, the company will need others. These new reports should be identified and treated like any other RICE component. A formal inventory similar

Exhibit 18-1   Standard Report Inventory

Report Number	Report Name	Needed? (Y or N)	Modifications Required	Scheduled Run Frequency

to those created for interfaces and conversions (Chapter 17, Exhibits 17-2 and 17-3) is useful. It should list the title of the report, the frequency of execution, and the mode of execution (triggered manually or scheduled).

Determine the Tool That Will Be Used To Create Reports

Once the team knows the magnitude of the report generation task and the complexity of individual reports, they can determine how to create those reports. The optimum solution is to use either the report writer that the vendor provides as part of the package or the company's standard commercial report writer. Because of the cost and time involved, hard-coding of reports should be done only on an exception basis when the standard tools are unable to perform the needed calculations or formatting.

Definition

Any modifications to the system, including the development of new reports, should be formally documented in a specification document similar to the one shown for configuration (Chapter 16, Exhibit 16-1). When this document is created, it is important to include a detailed mapping of database fields to the report fields, and to specify sort and selection criteria as well as any calculations that will be done. End users should be key participants in this process because they have a knowledge of the reasons why the report is needed and how it will be used, as well as a vested interest in the results.

Coding

Use of a report writer simplifies coding. Whether reports are generated with a standard tool or hard-coded, this is one of the project activities that is frequently outsourced because the work does not require frequent interactions with the project team and can be done offshore at lower rates. As always, it is important to ensure that the coding standards established in Chapter 14 are followed because reports may be subject to ongoing maintenance.

Testing

Although it may not be intuitive, both unit and integration testing are required for reports. Unit testing validates the report itself. Integration testing ensures that the overall system continues to meet desired performance levels. Although reports do not affect system functionality, they may impact performance. Improperly coded reports may generate the correct results but require excessive system resources, causing a degradation in response time.

In addition to the normal quality assurance testers, it is important that end users be involved in unit testing to ensure that the results are the ones they expected. Because integration testing for reports is concerned with performance rather than functionality, end-user participation is not normally required.

As was true of all other testing, the team should develop a test plan (Chapter 15, Exhibit 15-2) and record results on the test case log (Chapter 15, Exhibit 15-3).

Extensions and Customizations

Development of extensions and customizations of the base system is the most problematic aspect of packaged software implementation and should be approached with caution. Of the two, customization is far riskier because it involves changes to the vendor's source code. This is the reason Chapter 14 suggested having ground rules that make it difficult to implement any change to source code.

Whether the change is done as part of a vendor-provided user exit or whether the source code is modified, it is important that the team — and the company as a whole — understand the implications. Although reports, interfaces, and conversions all involve one-time efforts, extensions and customizations require work each time the base software is updated.

Each change that is made complicates not only the initial implementation but, more importantly, every upgrade or new software release. The reason is that as part of the upgrade process, it is necessary to review each modification that was made to determine whether it will be affected by the vendor's changes. It is possible that the functionality in the customization will be incorporated in the base system, obviating the need for it. It is also possible that changes in the base system may conflict with the customization, requiring additional modifications to the custom code. As a result, the cost of a customization is often many times greater than the cost to develop and implement it.

If the team decides to proceed with changes, the four-step process that was used for interfaces, conversions, and reports should also be followed for extensions and customizations.

Planning

Because of the long-term implications of customizations and the ongoing effort that is required to support them, it is important that the team evaluate each proposed customization carefully and, whenever possible, avoid implementing it.

A risk assessment similar to the one shown as Exhibit 18-2 can help the team identify the benefits and risks associated with each proposed change to the system. The information that should be gathered and assessed is as follows:

- *Proposed customization.* Provide a brief description of the change that is needed.
- *Current process.* If the change is to accommodate functionality that exists in a current system or manual process but that is not provided in the new system, the team should indicate how the process is currently performed.
- *Ability to continue current process.* The team should assess the feasibility and cost of continuing the current process rather than modifying the new system. In some cases, this will require continuing to run a legacy system, with a cost which may be prohibitive. In others, there may be little or no cost involved in maintaining the current process.
- *Cost of customization.* Because it is difficult to calculate the ongoing cost of supporting a customization, this column should show only the cost of the initial implementation of the modification. Although this cost cannot be compared with the cost of continuing the current process because it is a one-time rather than a repetitive cost, calculating this cost will give the team the ability to measure the magnitude of the change.
- *Schedule impact of customization.* If the overall project schedule will be extended because of this modification, the team should indicate the length of that extension.
- *Risk to company if customization is not implemented.* The team should make a realistic assessment of the impact of doing nothing, then rate that risk as high, medium, or low.
- *Functionality planned for future releases?* Before any customizations are undertaken, the team should ask the vendor whether that functionality is scheduled to be incorporated in future releases of the software and, if it is, when that release will be available.
- *Decision.* This column records the results of the risk assessment, namely, whether or not the customization will be made. In general,

Exhibit 18-2   Customization Risk Assessment

Proposed Customization	Current Process	Ability to Continue Current Process	Initial Cost of Customization	Schedule Impact of Customization	Risk to Company if Not Implemented	Functionality Planned for Future Release?	Decision

a customization should not be undertaken if any of the following are true:
- The current process can be continued without a major cost or effort.
- The risk to the company of not implementing it is low.
- The functionality is scheduled to be included in the next release of the software.

Once the team has made the decision that a customization should be made, the next consideration is who should make that change. Although in-house staff or the outside firm that has been hired to perform other programming-related tasks is a possibility, there is another option that will reduce the risk to the company and may result in a lower total cost for the change.

If the modification is significant and if the functionality that is included is not proprietary to the company, the team should consider approaching the vendor to determine whether they will agree to make the modification and to incorporate it into a future release. Even though the company would in all likelihood have to pay the vendor's consulting staff to make the change, the fact that it will become part of the standard product in the future means that the process of applying releases is simplified. Because of the life span of a typical software package, that reduced cost may outweigh the potentially higher cost of using vendor resources rather than in-house staff for the development of the modification.

Definition

Formal written specifications are particularly important for customizations because these programs may be in existence for the life of the software product and will probably be supported by a number of different staff members. If the vendor's toolkit does not provide a template for defining extensions, a format similar to the configuration specification (Chapter 16, Exhibit 16-1) can be used.

Definition of modifications is one task where it is helpful to use application experts for guidance. This expertise may come from either the vendor or a boutique firm with extensive experience in the package. In either case, the expert's in-depth knowledge of the system can help ensure that the extensions do not have unwanted effects on the base system.

Coding

Regardless of who performs the coding, it is important to follow the vendor's guidelines for modifications and to use the vendor's toolset whenever possible because both of these suggestions reduce the risk of erroneous changes. Company coding and documentation standards as established in Chapter 14 are also important when implementing customizations.

Testing

Testing of modifications is arguably the most important kind of testing that the team will perform. As was true of all aspects of system implementation, the team should develop a formal test plan (Chapter 15, Exhibit 15-2) with a test case log (Chapter 15, Exhibit 15-3) to record the results of the testing.

In addition to unit and integration testing, it is critical to perform a full regression test, ensuring that the changes that were made have no negative effects on the rest of the system. The regression test should use the test data that was developed for the baseline (Steps 3 and 4 in Chapter 15) to prove that the base system is still fully functional and that any deviations from the results observed during the baseline were expected.

Once reports and extensions are completed, the system is ready to be placed in production. The sole remaining task is to ensure that everyone who will use the system is fully trained.

Chapter 19

Training

Training may be the Rodney Dangerfield of packaged system implementation. It gets little respect, and yet it is a critical element in making that implementation successful. A perfectly installed and configured system is of no value if the end users cannot use it or if they find using it a frustrating experience. Without adequate training, either scenario is possible. Furthermore, without proper training, the project team will have difficulty producing that perfect installation and configuration.

Successful packaged software implementation involves training two different groups: the project team and end users. Although there are similarities, there are also different considerations for each category of training.

Project-Team Training

Unlike end-user training, which occurs at the end of the project, training of the project team needs to take place during the first stages. Unfortunately, it is at this point that excitement is at its highest and the team feels pressured to deliver tangible results quickly. As a result, there is often a tendency to minimize the training and delve directly into the "productive" portions of the project.

This is a mistake.

Just as untrained end users may find the system frustrating to use, so too may untrained team members find the vendor's proprietary tools difficult to understand and use. Previous chapters have stressed the value of using the vendor's methodology and tools, yet without training, the implementation team may believe it easier to use their current toolset. Even if the functionality is correct, failing to use the vendor's toolset may result in additional costs to integrate coding with the base system and to support the nonstandard programs. Inadequate training may also cause the team to use the vendor's tools incorrectly or inefficiently, creating performance or functionality problems.

The toolset and methodology are important, and the project team needs to be trained in their use. But even more critical is the need for training on the system itself. Although the team should have a high level of understanding of *what* the system does as a result of the selection process, successful implementation requires both a detailed knowledge of the functionality and a good understanding of *how* that functionality is delivered. Without this detailed understanding of the system, the team may make unnecessary customizations, adding to the overall cost, both in the short and the long term.

Although some companies believe that project-team training should be minimized to reduce costs and expedite the schedule, this is truly a case of "pay me now, or pay me later." The time and money invested in training the team will be paid back in an easier, simpler implementation.

Team training is a necessity, not a luxury, which is one reason why it is included on the project charter (Chapter 2, Exhibit 2-1). The necessity of training is also the reason why most vendors, particularly those of complex software such as enterprise resource planning (ERP) systems, have developed a complete curriculum for project team members.

Companies increase their risks of failure if they do not adequately train their team members.

When planning for team training, the following questions need to be answered.

Who Will Attend Training?

The simple answer is everyone on the project team who has not already been trained. Although that is true, it is also necessary to categorize team members because not everyone needs the same type of training. At a minimum, the team should be divided into the following categories:

- *Decision makers*, including leaders from both the information technology (IT) and the end-user departments.
- *Analysts*, a grouping that includes both end users and IT members.
- *Programmers*, a category that is typically comprised of only members of the IT department.
- *Operations*, including database administrators (DBAs) as well as the data-center staff who will be responsible for keeping the system running.

Which Subjects Will Be Included?

The different categories of team members need different training. Decision makers will typically be given an overview of the entire system because this will allow them to determine which modules should be implemented first and to evaluate at a high level how much customization will be needed. Analysts, who will be working on configuration as well as defining any modifications, need in-depth training on the specific modules for which they are responsible, whereas programmers need to be trained on the vendor's toolset. Operations' training will often be the least extensive because it will focus primarily on any differences between the commercial off-the-shelf (COTS) package and other packaged solutions.

Who Will Provide the Training?

Unless the company has in-house expertise, which is unlikely if this is the first implementation of the specific software product, training should be provided by the vendors or one of their authorized partners.

What Type of Training Will Be Used?

Training is typically delivered in one of two ways: traditional instructor-led (classroom) and computer-based training (CBT). A third method is instructor-led online training. Although this is gaining popularity in academic circles, it is less common in the corporate environment. Exhibit 19-1 presents a comparison of all three methods.

As shown in Exhibit 19-1, the hallmark of CBT is its scheduling flexibility, whereas the primary advantage of classroom training is the interaction with the instructor and among participants. Either type of training can be effective. To a large extent, the decision at this point in the project will be made based on the availability of vendor-provided training.

Exhibit 19-1   Comparison of Training Methods

Training Method	Advantages	Disadvantages
Computer-based	Self-paced; good for both quick and slow learners	
	Flexible scheduling allows student to train at most productive time of day; no need to wait until a class is available	Scheduling time to train may be difficult because of job commitments
	May be less expensive than classroom, particularly if only a few people need to be trained	May require special software
		No interaction with other students
Instructor-led classroom	Encourages interaction with other students and with instructor	
	Content can be modified during delivery to meet students' needs	
	Scheduled class ensures that training takes place	Time away from workplace may create conflicts with job assignments
		Pacing may not be ideal for all participants
Instructor-led online	Semiflexible scheduling allows students to read material at their most productive times.	Flexibility is not as great as CBT (Classes are held within specific timeframes, and assignments are due on a specified schedule.)
	Online chats encourage interaction with other students and with instructor	Body language and other interpersonal cues are not available; this may decrease the instructor's ability to gauge participants' rates of learning
	May be less expensive than classroom, particularly if only a few people need to be trained	
	Normally requires no special software	

Where Will the Class Be Held?

If the training is to be instructor led, the team must decide whether to have that training conducted at the vendor's facility or at a company site, assuming that the company has a training room. There are advantages and disadvantages to each.

- *Vendor's facility.* The advantages include (1) the possibility of having participants from other companies, which can be useful to the company because it may provide insights on how other companies plan to implement the software; and (2) distancing participants from their jobs (by having training off site, participants are able to focus on learning rather than their normal job responsibilities). The primary disadvantage to training at a vendor site is that, unless the vendor has a training facility in the same city as the company, each participant will incur travel expenses.
- *Company site.* The primary advantage is the elimination of travel expense and time. Disadvantages include the potential need to install software exclusively for the training as well as the tendency of participants to be distracted by job-related problems.

End User Training

End user training presents a number of challenges that differ from those associated with project-team training. Not only is the scope normally larger, but so, too, is the timeframe. In addition, the team has more options regarding the material to be covered, delivery methods, and trainers.

This training, like all aspects of the project, should be carefully planned and the results of that planning documented. Exhibit 19-2 provides a sample training plan overview that can be used to schedule the actual training. Because initial and ongoing training have different objectives, they are discussed separately. Both should, however, be planned for and documented on the training plan overview.

Initial Training

As was true of project-team training, the planning process is facilitated by answering a series of questions. Many of these are the same questions that were asked for project-team training. The answers may be different.

Exhibit 19-2   Training Plan Overview

Course Name	Length	Target Participants (1)	Training Method (2)	Trainer (3)	Participant Materials (4)	Other Training Materials (5)

(1) Target participants: Category of users to be trained (managers, superusers, transactional users, query users, support staff [Help Desk]).
(2) Training method: CBT or classroom.
(3) Trainer: Name of organization providing trainers.
(4) Participant materials: List of all materials that will be provided to participants.
(5) Other training materials: List of other materials that trainer will require to conduct the class.

Who Will Attend Training?

Like the project team, end users can be divided into different categories, depending on their roles and the ways in which they will use the system. The expectation is that different groups will have differing needs for training. A suggested categorization of end users is:

- *Managers.* This group includes supervisors and department heads who require a high-level understanding of the functionality of the system. They may or may not be active users of the system.
- *Superusers.* These individuals are expected to become the in-house experts on their portion of the system, serving as first-line resources to the other members of their departments.
- *Transactional users.* This group includes those individuals who use the system on a regular basis. They are differentiated from the next group by the fact that they update the database.
- *Query users.* This group uses the system on a regular basis, but only to extract data from it.
- *Support staff.* Although not truly end users, it is important to include the IT support staff (also known as the help desk) in end-user training.

It should be noted that some individuals will fill more than one role and will, therefore, attend different classes. A manager, for example, may also be a transactional user or a query user. Superusers, by definition, will receive the same training as transactional and query users, in addition to courses designed specifically for superusers.

What Subjects Will Be Included?

As was true of project-team training, the different categories of users should receive different training. In each case, it is important that the participants receive two types of training:

- A brief overview of the entire system, showing where their specific functionality fits into the overall scheme
- Training that is specific to their jobs

Will the Company Use Vendor-Provided Training?

Although the vendor will normally have a suggested curriculum for each category of user, the project team needs to decide whether or not to use the vendor's training and, if they do, whether or not to modify it. One key consideration is that vendor training is designed to teach participants *how to use the system.* Company-modified training can teach those participants *how to use the system to do their jobs at the company.* The distinction is an important one. At a minimum, the team should ensure that the training materials reflect the company's configuration and any customizations that the company has made rather than rely on generic screens. The ideal situation incorporates transactions that are representative of those the users will actually see with a database of company-specific data.

What Type of Training Will Be Used?

The same options are available for end user training as for project-team training, with the same advantages and disadvantages.

Who Will Provide the Training?

If the project team has selected instructor-led classroom training, they have several choices of groups to deliver the training. In most cases, the vendor has an educational division that provides training. For the more commonly used software packages, there are outside firms (OFs) that also provide training. The third option is to use in-house staff as trainers. The advantages and disadvantages of each are shown on Exhibit 19-3.

To mitigate some of the disadvantages of using either the vendor or an OF, some companies have training delivered by a team that consists of in-house staff as well as trainers from the vendor or OF. This can result in lower costs as well as provide the company perspective on the subject material. In some cases, this approach is used initially until the in-house trainers are comfortable with the course materials, at which time they assume full responsibility for training. This is sometimes referred to as "train the trainer."

When choosing trainers, it is important to ensure that whoever will deliver the training has the skill set to do that effectively. In the case of the vendor or an OF's staff, the team should check references and ideally audit a course to be certain that the facilitators understand the material and can communicate the concepts to participants. When selecting in-house staff to be trainers, it is important to realize that not everyone is comfortable teaching in a classroom environment. Simply understanding the material and being able to use the system does not qualify a person to be a facilitator. Some people who are very effective as one-on-one mentors fail in a classroom setting because it takes them out of their comfort zone and requires presentation skills they do not have.

Training is critical. In many cases, it will be the end users' first experience with the system that will become part of their daily routine. It is important that that first experience be a positive one because it will

Exhibit 19-3 Comparison of Trainers

Trainer	Advantages	Disadvantages
Vendor	Has in-depth knowledge of the system Is aware of planned new functionality Has experience with other companies' use of the system	Is typically the most expensive alternative May not be fully aware of how the system will be used at the company
Outside firm	May be less expensive than the vendor Has experience with other companies' use of the system	May not be fully aware of how the system will be used at the company Knowledge of the system may not be as extensive as the vendor's
In-house	Normally the least expensive alternative Trainers should be fully aware of how the system will be used at the company	Knowledge of the system may not be as extensive as the vendor's Requires ramp-up time for trainers to learn materials and system Trainers may not be as skilled at delivering courses

affect users' opinions of the system as well as their ability to use it effectively. Having the correct trainer helps ensure that the experience is positive.

Where Will the Class Be Held?

Although the same options are available as for project-team training, in many cases the most cost-effective decision is to conduct training at the company's site because of the number of people who need to be trained. This also facilitates the use of company-specific data because the training will use one of the company's databases.

What Materials Are Required, and Who Will Provide Them?

Classroom training typically utilizes props of various kinds, including PowerPoint slides, videos, and written descriptions of exercises as well as user manuals and quick reference guides that will be given to the participants. As was true of the course content itself, the team needs to decide whether or not to use the materials that the vendor or OF provides without modification. Once that decision is made, the team must also determine whether they will be responsible for duplicating handouts or whether the vendor or OF will provide that service.

How Will Training Be Evaluated?

It is not enough to simply conduct training and assume that participants have learned everything they need to know to do their jobs. The team should ensure that the training is effective. This is a two-step process.

The first step is to ask participants to evaluate the training itself. Typically this is done through a participant survey similar to that shown in Exhibit 19-4. The results of the survey will help the team determine whether or not the training has achieved the goals of being informative and providing a positive experience.

The second step is to conduct a follow-up evaluation, either through another survey or through focus groups, to determine whether or not the material had any long-term value. This follow-up evaluation, which should be conducted 60 to 90 days after training, addresses how well the participant is able to use the system and, with the perspective of "real-world" experience, what changes should be made to the training.

Ongoing Training

One of the primary differences between project-team and end user training is that, in addition to the initial round of training for end users, it is necessary to plan for the future. Not only will staff changes require some people to receive the full initial training, but it is also desirable to provide refresher training for those who were trained as part of the project implementation.

Exhibit 19-4   Training Survey

Course Name: _____

Location: _____   Date: _____

Instructor: _____

Participant's Name (optional): _____

We're glad you were here. We hope that the training met your expectations and that you'll help us make it even better. After all, we can't fix a problem if we don't know about it.

Please rate the following aspects of the training using a scale of 1 to 5, where 1 means you disagree totally and 5 you agree completely. You'll note that we've asked you to rate each of the lessons as well as the course as a whole.

Exhibit 19-4 (continued)   Training Survey

(continued)

System Navigation

The content of the lesson was applicable to my job.	1	2	3	4	5
The pacing of the lesson was correct.	1	2	3	4	5
The examples were relevant to my job.	1	2	3	4	5
I will be able to use the function after the class is over.	1	2	3	4	5

Comments:

Report Writing 101

The content of the lesson was applicable to my job.	1	2	3	4	5
The pacing of the lesson was correct.	1	2	3	4	5
The examples were relevant to my job.	1	2	3	4	5
I will be able to use the function after the class is over.	1	2	3	4	5

Comments:

General Ratings

The training materials were relevant and easy to use.	1	2	3	4	5
The instructor provided clear and complete explanations of the subject.	1	2	3	4	5
The instructor was able to answer all questions to my satisfaction.	1	2	3	4	5
The instructor encouraged learning.	1	2	3	4	5
I would recommend this course to others.	1	2	3	4	5

The Best Thing About This Course Was:

The Areas I Think Need Improvement Are:

The considerations for training new staff are the same as those for the initial training, with one exception. Because it is likely that there will be only a few people who need training at any one time, it may not be cost effective to conduct classroom training. The team may want to consider alternative approaches, including developing a CBT course and supplementing that with mentoring by one of the superusers.

Refresher training is different from initial training but equally critical to the project's success. Anyone who has done training knows the depressing statistics of how little participants retain from a class, no matter how well delivered it is. To increase users' knowledge of the system, it is important to provide continuing education. This can be done in a number of ways.

- *Refresher courses.* The team may want to offer the initial training one section at a time. Covering only one module in any one session allows employees to select the functionality they feel least comfortable with and does not require a major commitment of time. It is, after all, easier to leave the workplace for a half day than for the three to five days that may have been involved in initial training.
- *Newsletters.* In addition to touting the successes of the project, a regular newsletter can provide a "Did you know?" column, focusing on different ways to use the system. In some cases, this may be nothing more than a reiteration of the material that was covered in class. In others, it may be a more advanced function that was not included in the original training. As with other forms of communication, the newsletter can be delivered in either paper or electronic format, depending on the company's culture and user preferences.
- *Lunch and learn.* If the team wants to demonstrate specific functionality or teach users new techniques but does not want to develop or conduct a full course, a classroom environment may be preferable to a newsletter. Some companies have established monthly "Lunch and Learn" sessions in which users are invited to bring their lunch to a classroom and learn a new aspect of the system. The advantages of this approach are that they do not require employees to schedule time away from their jobs, and they provide hands-on experience.

Effective training is essential to the success of the project. By following the suggestions in this chapter, it is possible to ensure that the training is done properly and that both the project team and the end users are able to perform their jobs effectively.

Chapter 20

The Challenges of Multisite Implementation

There is no doubt about it. Installing packaged software in a multisite environment is more complex than implementing it at a single site, and the complexity increases when multiple countries are involved. Some of the issues associated with multisite implementations were discussed in Chapter 10 as part of the big bang versus phased decision-making process; however, there are others that the project team needs to consider.

How Much Variation Will Be Allowed?

This is the single most important question that the team will answer, and it affects many of the other questions. The simplest and easiest approach is to insist that all sites use the same configuration and that there will be absolutely no variation from site to site. Not only is this the easiest way to implement the software, but it also simplifies application of future releases because there is only one version of the software and one set of reports, interfaces, conversions, and extensions, or RICE elements.

Unfortunately, although this is the simplest solution, it may not be the correct one for the company. The reality is that some companies are highly diversified, and a single configuration may not be possible because of the differences among their business processes. The good news is that most modern software packages have multiorganizational capability to address this problem. In these cases, the individual sites can have different configurations without impacting the ability to apply future releases.

It should be noted, however, that many companies use the implementation of packaged software as an opportunity to review all processes and to establish common best practices across the corporation wherever possible. Having standard processes provides cost savings beyond those associated with software upgrades and support because the majority of these best practice processes are streamlined versions of the old ones, resulting in greater efficiency and reduced error rates.

Although the degrees of variation permitted will depend on the individual company's organization and politics, it is advantageous to minimize variation, as was true of customization (Chapter 18). The greatest benefits of packaged software implementation come from the use of standard software to automate common processes.

Will There Be One Project or Many?

Even if the company decides that there will be limited or even no variation among sites, it may choose to treat the overall implementation as a series of projects rather than one comprehensive project with a number of phases. This happens most often when a company has multiple divisions and has granted them a fair amount of autonomy. The differences are that multiple projects are:

- Scheduled independently of each other
- The responsibility of the individual division rather than a single corporate-level project team
- Normally financed by the individual divisions

In most cases, there is a single selection process with all divisions participating in it and agreeing on the product to be implemented.

As with most decisions, there are advantages and disadvantages to consider before organizing the overall implementation as multiple projects.

- *Advantages.* The primary advantage to multiple projects is that each division has the ability to choose the timing of its implementation. Some divisions may require more time to prepare, either because they have existing projects to complete or because they want to reengineer their processes. Because they have total control over the schedule, they can implement the software when it is most convenient for them.

■ *Disadvantages.* There are several disadvantages to the multiple-project strategy.
- *Simultaneous implementations may increase risk.* It is possible that more than one division may schedule its project at the same time. Not only may this mean competing for common resources (if there is a single data center or project team), but if these projects are occurring at the same time as the initial project, there will be no opportunity to learn from the problems that are encountered in the initial project. The risks of a big bang implementation (Chapter 10, Exhibit 10-2) apply to this scenario.
- *Funding may not be available when needed.* In most companies, funding for projects must be approved in the year that the project is to begin. If a division chooses to delay its implementation into future years, it is possible that economic conditions may have changed sufficiently that it will not be possible to obtain funding for the project and that its implementation may be delayed.
- *Priorities may change.* Priorities are similar to funding. Although the packaged software implementation project may be the highest priority for the corporation and even for each of the divisions when the project begins, it is possible that if individual projects are scheduled in subsequent years, the priorities for those divisions may change before the project is initiated, and the implementation may be delayed or may never occur.

If the implementation is to be run as multiple projects, risks are reduced if the champion can convince the various divisions to do the following:

■ Delay their implementation until the pilot sites are fully operational.
■ Coordinate their schedules to achieve staggered rather than simultaneous projects.
■ Attempt to obtain funding commitments, even if the project will occur in a future year.

Who Is In Charge?

This question applies only if the company decides that the overall implementation will be organized as multiple projects. In that case, it must also decide whether there will be a single project team responsible for all the projects or whether each implementation will have its own project team.

Exhibit 20-1   Comparison of Single versus Multiple Project Teams

Number of Project Teams	Advantages	Disadvantages
One for all projects	Lower training costs because fewer people will be involved Single learning curve and reduced repetition of mistakes	Potential scheduling conflicts if multiple divisions want to install simultaneously Higher travel costs because team will need to visit each division Divisions may not feel ownership of project if the team is not comprised exclusively of their staff
One per project	No scheduling conflicts Lower travel costs Greater ownership by division	Increased training costs Learning curve will be repeated for each project

The advantages and disadvantages of each approach are shown in Exhibit 20-1.

As is frequently the case, a hybrid organization can mitigate the risks of either approach.

Single-Project Team

If the company is going to have a single project team, it is advantageous to have members of each division serve as part of that team, not simply for the selection process but throughout the entire project. Not only does this increase the divisions' sense of ownership, but it also ensures that each division's perspective is considered when making decisions. The disadvantage to this approach is that the divisions may not want to release a key member of their staff for the length of the entire project.

Multiple-Project Teams

If the company decides to have multiple project teams, it is helpful to select the team leaders for each of the individual projects and have them participate in the initial project. Not only will they learn about the problems that are encountered and how to avoid them, but they will also have hands-on experience that should help reduce the length of their own projects.

This approach is not feasible if the divisions want to schedule their implementations concurrently with the initial project. It is also of less value if there will be substantial delays between the initial project and those of the divisions because the team leaders may either leave the company, be reassigned, or not retain the learning.

How Many Instances Will There Be?

The KISS (keep it simple, Stupid) principle applies to this question, with the ideal answer being a single instance of the software. This is the ultimate in simplicity and helps ensure that variation is kept to a minimum. It eliminates redundancy and helps promote sharing of best practices.

Although simplicity is desirable, there may be times when a company wants to have multiple instances. The primary reasons for choosing a multiple-instance strategy are:

■ *Reduced risk.* If the system is mission critical, the company may not want to have all its divisions dependent on a single instance.

■ *Improved performance.* Very large companies or those with unusually high transaction volumes may find that multiple instances improve their performance. This is particularly true when the sites are located around the globe and network speed has not been optimized.

■ *Highly diversified business processes.* In some companies, typically conglomerates, business processes vary greatly among the divisions, and there is little commonality of customers and suppliers. Although there are still advantages to a single instance, they are not be as great as for companies that can implement standard processes.

■ *Corporate politics.* Even though they have similar business processes and common customers and suppliers, some decentralized companies have a corporate culture that does not encourage common systems and shared databases. In these cases, although there are no performance issues to be resolved, it may be impossible to gain agreement for a single instance of the software.

Before choosing a multiple-instance strategy, the project team should consider the costs associated with it.

- *Licensing.* Depending on how the vendor prices its software, it is possible that the company will incur additional costs to license multiple instances. If this is the case, it is likely that there will also be increased costs for annual maintenance because that is frequently priced as a percentage of the initial licensing fee.
- *Ongoing support.* Each time that the vendor provides an update or release, it will be necessary to apply those changes to each instance. This translates into increased internal support costs for the corporation as a whole.
- *Interfaces.* If the company needs consolidated reporting, it will be necessary to provide a method to aggregate data from all instances. Even if the vendor provides this rollup capability, additional processing time is required to run it.

Will the Implementation Be Multicountry?

All the questions discussed above apply to multicountry implementations. The company may choose to have individual projects and separate instances for each country or geographic region. It may also allow customization by country. In addition, multinational companies face other challenges when implementing common software across country borders.

Multiple Languages

A key decision that the project team must make is whether to implement the project in multiple languages and, if so, which ones. There are three aspects to this question.

- The software and related documentation
- Training
- The help desk

Software and Documentation

The answer to this question is predicated on the vendor's offering the software in multiple languages. If English is the only language available, it is normally not feasible to attempt to translate screens and documentation.

Training

Even if training materials are available only in English, if the project team is offering instructor-led training, it is advisable to conduct that training in the end users' native languages. As discussed in Chapter 19, one of the objectives of training is to provide users with a favorable first experience with the system. Easily understood training is one way to achieve that goal.

Help Desk

There are few things in the software world more frustrating than having problems with a system and being unable to explain that problem to the help desk because of language barriers. Although the ultimate solution is to have multilingual staff at the help desk, this may not be feasible. Alternatives include:

■ Funneling all problems through a superuser who speaks the end users' language as well as English and who can translate problems for the help desk

■ Submitting problems in writing. Even if the end user's English is not perfect, it is often easier to communicate in writing than over the phone. The user has more time to compose the description of the problem, and confusion based on accents is eliminated.

The primary advantage of providing multilingual versions of the software is user acceptance. Even though many non–North Americans speak and read English in addition to their native language, having software, training, and support in local languages increases the likelihood of users truly accepting the project.

The disadvantage is increased cost. Even if the vendor provides a multilingual system and documentation in each language, providing training and help desk support in multiple languages requires specialized multilingual staff. There is normally a premium for these resources.

Local Laws

Before initiating a multinational project, the team needs to consider where data will be stored and how it will be used. (The answers to these questions may dictate the number of instances or require that database servers be located in specific countries.) It is possible that laws in countries outside the United States will not allow data to be transferred across national boundaries. This is particularly true in the European Union when employee data is involved because EU data privacy regulations restrict the type of data that can be taken outside a country. The project team should consult with an attorney who specializes in data privacy laws before developing the overall project plan.

Multisite and multinational projects can be complex and, as is true of all aspects of packaged software implementation, must be carefully planned.

POSTIMPLEMENTATION

Even when the software has been installed at the last site, the project is not complete. The longest phase of the software's life cycle is only beginning. Whether it is called support or maintenance, the postinstallation phase is an essential part of successful packaged software implementation. Chapter 21 discusses methods for ensuring that support meets end users' expectations and addresses the question of who should provide that support.

Postimplementation involves more than providing maintenance of the system. It also includes ensuring that the project has met its expected goals and is delivering the promised benefits. Chapter 22 outlines methods for assessing the project's value and addresses the final question: how to deal with possible mergers, acquisitions, and divestitures.

Chapter 21

Support

Although many project plans end when the software has been installed at the last site, the reality is that the project is not complete at that point. If the packaged software implementation is to be truly successful, the project team must ensure that the software is supported throughout its lifespan and that that support, as well as the system itself, continues to meet the end users' expectations. That is no easy task, particularly because the postinstallation phase is the longest one.

The cover of James Martin and Carma McClure's classic book *Software Maintenance*[1] represents a system's life as an iceberg with development being only the tip that appears above the surface. The largest part of the iceberg is the one that is hidden beneath the water: support. Continuing the iceberg analogy, ships (or, in this case, project teams) ignore the bulk at their peril. Support is critical. Project teams know that change is ongoing. The software will continue to evolve, being modified either to correct bugs or to add new functionality. Change is a constant and, to be successful, it must be managed. Even when the vendor is providing the actual coding modifications, providing adequate support is essential task for the company.

As with most tasks, this one is more manageable if divided into smaller initiatives.

Establishing End User Expectations

If support is to be successful, the project team must have a clear understanding of exactly what it is that end users expect. At the same time, end users' expectations must be realistic. This calibration of expectations is one of the most important aspects of support because unless it is performed, it is likely that there will be gaps between the end users' expectations of support and what the project team delivers. Those gaps can translate into unhappy users and frustrated project team members because the project team believes they are meeting expectations, whereas the users are disappointed and believe the team is either unresponsive or incompetent.

A four-step process will help ensure that both groups' expectations are aligned.

- Step 1: Create a steering committee.
- Step 2: Establish service-level agreements.
- Step 3: Implement a mechanism for capturing and reporting performance.
- Step 4: Communicate performance metrics.

Step 1: Create a Steering Committee

The steering committee is a specialized team, a group of end users with a vested interest in the system. Its role is not only to ensure that the system is operating at the desired level, but also to review and prioritize individual requests for changes to the system. Because the steering committee represents all end users, it is important to have the right individuals as members of the team.

The steering committee is typically convened by the chief information officer (CIO) or a program manager within the information technology (IT) department, and that individual may serve as the facilitator or leader. Although the leader normally invites end-user department heads to serve on the steering committee, in large organizations it is common for department heads to delegate their responsibility and for lower-ranking staff to be members of the steering committee. This is not a problem so long as the individuals chosen have the authority to speak for their departments.

As with all teams, it is important that the members of the steering committee have the right attributes. The characteristics shown in Chapter 2, Exhibit 2-4 are as important for the steering committee as they are for the software selection team. It is also important that the team members be knowledgeable about the system's functionality and its use within their departments.

One or More Committees?

If the company has multiple instances of the software, it needs to decide whether there will be one steering committee for the entire system or one per instance. This decision will be driven by a number of factors, including corporate politics. A single steering committee is most appropriate if both of the following are true:

- There is minimal variation among the instances.
- All support is being provided by a single organization.

If there are multiple steering committees, it is advisable to establish an executive steering committee comprised of key members of each of the individual steering committees. This group will be responsible for coordinating common efforts, including the timing of releases and upgrades, and may also serve as the official liaison with the vendor if problems need to be escalated to that level.

Charters and Agendas

When the steering committee is first convened, it is helpful to develop a team charter. Although this need not be as extensive as the typical project charter (Appendix B), a written document that outlines the team's commitments is an effective tool for ensuring a common understanding. Exhibit 21-1 shows the format of a steering committee charter.

Step 2: Establish Service-Level Agreements

When evaluating the support of a system, it is normal to have a series of metrics that report the level of support provided. Although this is an essential part of the evaluation process, the metrics are of little value unless there are clearly identified expectations for support. If, for example, the IT department reports that system availability for the month was 95 percent but there is no context, who can say whether this is a good or bad level of support? Was system availability 98 percent for the preceding six months? What level does the end user require? To avoid this problem and set the context, the IT department and the end user should establish

Exhibit 21-1   Steering Committee Charter

Summary	
System Name	
Team Leader	
Start Date	
Project Description	Review system support, prioritize outstanding requests for service, review and revise service levels as needed at monthly meetings.

Team Membership			
Name	Role	Department	% Time

Schedule				
Milestone/ Deliverable	Target Date	Owner	Estimated Cost	Comments
Initial Meeting				
Initial SLA Review				

Revision History		
Revision Number	Authors	Date

service-level agreements (SLAs). This process aligns expectations and helps avoid conflict between end users and the support organization.

If support is being provided by an outside firm, as discussed in Chapter 9, SLAs should be part of the contract with that firm. Even if support will be provided internally, it is important to establish — and meet — SLAs. The SLAs that are established should follow all the guidelines shown in Chapter 9.

Step 3: Implement a Mechanism for Capturing and Reporting Performance

Simply having agreed upon SLAs is of little value if performance is not measured and reported. The first step in measurement and reporting is to define the metrics that will be meaningful to the end users and the format in which they should be reported.

Before reports can be designed, it is necessary to develop the metrics themselves. This is a case where the KISS (keep it simple, Stupid) principle should be applied. Although there are dozens of metrics that could be generated, the likelihood is that only a few will be of value. One technique for determining which metrics are needed is to ask end users, "If you could have only three pieces of information to judge the system, what would they be?"

It is also important to understand the distinction between measurements and metrics. A measurement is a single dimension, capacity, or quantity, whereas a metric is a value calculated from multiple measurements. For example, consider the sample SLA report (Exhibit 21-2). Measurements include the number of requests received and the number completed within the SLA. The primary metric that is calculated is the percentage completed within the SLA. A secondary metric is the variance. Exhibit 21-3 provides a graphical representation of the performance metric.

SLAs should be SMART (specific, measurable, attainable, relevant, timebound); measurements should RAVE (be relevant, adequate, valid, and easy). Exhibit 21-4 uses the response to severity 1 calls to explain RAVE measurements.

As was true when drafting SLAs and creating metrics, it is important that the company design the reports and that end users evaluate and ratify the proposed formats and contents before they are given to the support organization. If support will be provided by the vendor or an outside firm, they may provide sample reports that they are currently producing for other customers. Although these can serve as a starting point, it is important that the reports be meaningful to the company.

Typically, reports are a combination of monthly statistics (as shown in Exhibit 21-2) and trending charts (Exhibit 21-3). The monthly statistics provide detailed information, including volumes, whereas the charts track performance against the SLA over time and can be used to determine whether performance is improving.

Once the reports have been designed, the team must ensure that they can collect the necessary data and generate the reports. If support will be provided by the vendor or an outside firm, it is likely that they will already have tracking systems that can be used to generate metrics; however, the team should make no assumptions. Instead, they should ask

Exhibit 21-2 Sample SLA Report

Service-Level Agreement Reporting
XYZ System
Month, Year

Service	No. Received (1)	No. To Be Completed per SLA (2)	No. Completed per SLA (3)	% Completed per SLA (4)	Variance (5)	Explanation (6)
Response to severity 1 calls						
Resolution of severity 1 calls						

(1) Count of all calls or other requests received for that service during the month.
(2) Calculation of number of requests that should have been completed by month's end. For example, if 100 calls were received, and the SLA is 95% response within three minutes, this column would show 95.
(3) The actual count of requests that were completed according to the SLA.
(4) A calculation of the percentage actually completed (# completed per SLA divided by # received).
(5) A count of the variance (either positive or negative) between # to be completed per SLA and # actually completed per SLA.
(6) An explanation of the reason an SLA was not met.

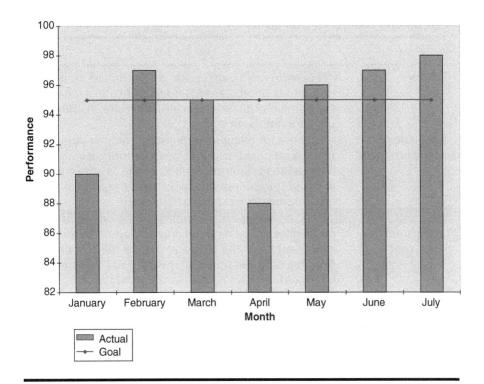

Exhibit 21-3   SLA Trend Chart

to see the system that will be used to record calls and their resolution so that they can be assured that all critical data is being captured. At a minimum, the vendor should provide written agreement that he will provide the reports that the company has specified.

If support will be provided in-house and if the company does not already have a call-tracking database for its existing help desk functions, it may be necessary to either develop or license a system. Selecting and installing that software should be done using the guidelines presented in earlier chapters.

Step 4: Communicate Performance Metrics

Although some companies simply publish the performance reports, a more effective method of communicating is through steering committee meetings because these allow a dialogue between end users and the support organization and help ensure that there are no credibility gaps. A basic

Exhibit 21-4   RAVE Measurements

Element	Explanation
Relevant	If 90 percent of all bug reports are submitted via e-mail rather than phone, there is no relevance to measuring the number of abandoned calls; therefore, abandoned calls are not measured.
Adequate to detect changes	If response time could be measured only in days but the SLA specified response times in hours, it would be impossible to determine whether the SLA was being met and if improvements were occurring. The measurement would not be adequate.
Valid and consistent over time	If the SLA specifies that support will be provided only on business days, a calculation of elapsed time that simply subtracts the date and time of the response from the date and time that the call was placed would be invalid because it makes no provision for nonworking days or hours.
Easy to capture	Although there might be value in measuring elapsed time in seconds rather than minutes, if the current tracking system records only minutes, the need to enhance the system to capture seconds would violate the "easy" requirement because recording in minutes will satisfy the end users.

precept in SLA reporting is that if the end users are surprised by the results that are reported, one of two things is true:

- The SLA is not relevant.
- The reporting is inaccurate.

It is helpful to have a standard agenda for the steering committee's meetings both to set expectations about what will be covered during the meeting and to establish responsibility for leading various portions of the meeting. Exhibit 21-5 outlines a typical agenda. Although the support organization makes the initial presentation, it is important that the end users' perspective also be expressed. To gauge satisfaction if end users are not vocal about their perceptions, the leader should ask each member of the steering committee to rate the support organization's performance on a scale of 1 to 5 and to explain any ratings of less than 3.

In addition to reviewing performance, one of the steering committee's responsibilities is the prioritization of requests for changes to the system. Although many of modifications that are needed may be the vendor's

Exhibit 21-5   Steering Committee Meeting Agenda

XYZ System Steering Committee Agenda
Date
Location

Time		Responsibility
10:00 – 10:10	Review of agenda	Steering committee leader
10:10 – 10:30	Review of monthly metrics and performance from support supplier's perspective	Support supplier (either in-house or outside vendor)
10:30 – 10:50	Review of project from end-user perspective	All end-user members
10:50 – 11:25	Review and prioritization of open requests	Leader
11:25 – 11:30	Scheduling of next meeting and other business	Leader

responsibility and will be provided in future releases to the base software, some of the requests for changes may apply to interfaces and other company customizations. In all cases, it is important for the steering committee to evaluate each request's importance. Development of a cost-time-impact ranking similar to that in Chapter 18, Exhibit 18-2 is helpful in this process.

Determining Who Will Provide Support

The previous step addressed the "what" component of support. Once that has been defined, the next step is to determine who will provide the agreed-upon levels of support. Although there are advantages to having all support provided by the same group, in the case of packaged software it is likely that at least two organizations, the company and the vendor, will be involved unless the company is using an application service provider (ASP). The vendor will provide updates and releases to the base software; the company will be responsible for applying those updates and making any changes to the configuration or reports, interfaces, conversions, extensions, i.e., RICE elements.

In a non-ASP environment, it is possible that any or all the company's components of support will be outsourced. The remainder of this discussion applies to non-ASP environments.

When establishing responsibility for support, it is important to evaluate each of the components and determine who would be the best provider. The primary components of support are the following:

- First-line response to problems and questions
- Second-line response to problems and questions
- Evaluation and application of vendor patches and upgrades
- Modifications to interfaces and other company-specific customizations
- Upgrades to user interfaces and other nonapplication-specific components

Although there are many similarities among these components, there are also several important distinctions.

First-Line Response to Problems and Questions

Because this is the end user's first point of contact, it can be argued that this is the single most important component of support. The user's satisfaction with the overall system will be influenced by how quickly and competently problems and questions are resolved. First-line support is typically referred to as the help desk.

Recognizing the importance of effective problem resolution, many companies have instituted the single point of contact (SPOC) concept in which users need call only one number, regardless of the type of problem they encounter. Both hardware and software are covered by the SPOC. There are both advantages and disadvantages to having an SPOC help desk.

Advantages

The primary advantage is that the help desk provides triage. The end user does not need to know whether the problem was caused by faulty hardware, an inoperative router, or the software. Problem diagnosis, resolution of simple problems, and forwarding of more complex ones to experts are all performed by the help desk. This simplification of reporting can increase end-user satisfaction.

A secondary advantage is that the help desk is normally available twenty-four hours a day, seven days a week, providing follow-the-sun (FTS) support to multiple time zones and employees who work nonstandard hours. Again, end-user satisfaction is increased by knowing that there will always be someone available to resolve a problem.

(It should be noted that although some proponents of FTS tout the benefits of one shift transferring its unresolved problem load to the next shift, there are distinct advantages to having the person who begins problem resolution complete it. Not only is there no need for a second person to familiarize himself or herself with the problem, but there is no risk of something being "lost in the translation" from one employee to another.)

Disadvantages

Because the SPOC typically responds to calls related to multiple systems, the technicians are normally generalists rather than specialists. This means that they are often unable to resolve an application-related problem or to provide guidance in the most effective way to use the system. If end-user expectations are for resolution on the initial call, it is likely that those expectations will not be met because the SPOC technician does not have the in-depth knowledge required to resolve the problem.

One technique for mitigating this risk is to have the SPOC technician transfer the call to the subject matter expert (SME) rather than simply placing the problem ticket in an e-mail bucket. This allows the end user to speak directly to someone who may be able to resolve the problem. There are, however, additional costs associated with this approach because SMEs do not typically work nonstandard shifts.

A different approach for first-line response is to establish separate responsibility for problem resolution and responses to questions about functionality. Although the former are sent to the SPOC, some companies have chosen to create superusers within the end-user departments. Their responsibilities include serving as mentors to others and responding to questions about the system's functionality as well as the most effective ways to use it.

- *Advantages.* There are several advantages to this division of responsibility. Not only does it free the help desk to work on actual bugs, but it also results in faster resolution of functionality-related questions. Additionally, because they are members of the department, superusers have a real-world understanding of the system and how it is used, adding to the credibility of their responses.
- *Disadvantages.* The primary disadvantage of superusers is that because they have other responsibilities, those other responsibilities may take precedence over responding to coworkers' questions. A secondary disadvantage is that unless questions and the corresponding answers are recorded in a database, knowledge may be lost. Although a formal help desk normally has a knowledge

information system that is used to determine whether a problem has occurred previously and, if so, what the resolution was, those tools may not be available to superusers.

Second-Line Response to Problems and Questions

Because the help desk may be unable to resolve all problems, it is important to establish an escalation procedure. As noted above, although problems can be forwarded through an e-mail queue, user satisfaction is typically higher if there is real-time call transferring, allowing the end user to speak directly to the person who will be working on the problem. The primary disadvantage of this approach is that it interrupts second-line responders and may increase the amount of time required for them to resolve problems. It may also be difficult for the first-line responder to determine the correct second-line contact, in which case there is little recourse other than forwarding the problem ticket to a general e-mail queue for the application.

Evaluation and Application of Vendor Patches and Upgrades

It is possible that some problems will require the vendor to create patches to the software. In addition, vendors typically provide periodic releases of their software that include new functionality as well as changes required by regulatory decrees. Part of the support function is to evaluate each of the patches and upgrades to determine whether or not they should be applied and, if so, when. When determining responsibility for this component of support, it is important that the group have a detailed understanding of the base system and any customizations that were made by the company so that they can determine the impact of applying updates and upgrades. The ideal candidates for this responsibility are members of the original project team.

Modifications to Interfaces and Other Company-Specific Customizations

Although problem resolution is a key component of support, changes and additions to functionality are also part of the support function. Either one may require modification to company-specific customizations as well as the base software. Although changes to the base software are provided by the vendor and are typically included in the maintenance agreement, company-specific software is not. It is important to establish responsibility for this work. As was true of the evaluation of vendor-supplied changes, it is key that the group responsible for company-specific customizations understand both the base system and the customizations.

Upgrades to User Interfaces and Other Nonapplication-Specific Components

Although most discussions of support focus on the application, it is also important to establish responsibility for other aspects of the end user's total experience. This includes changes to the user interface, such as Web browser upgrades and installation of new workstations. Because in most companies these functions are performed by a different group than the one that is responsible for application software, it is important that the two groups coordinate their projects to ensure that the user interface is upgraded only when the packaged software requires an upgrade or when both groups have determined that an upgrade will have no negative effect on the application software.

Although it is possible that a single group will have responsibility for each of the components of support, as noted above, that is unlikely. The reality of packaged software is that some problems cannot be resolved by first- or second-line support and must be referred to the vendor.

Whenever there is more than one group involved, it is possible to have communication gaps. To mitigate that risk, the company should establish common procedures and formal communication links. Each group should have a clear understanding of its responsibilities and boundaries. One method of establishing and communicating those responsibilities is to develop SLAs among the various organizations. Those should include the timeframe to respond to problems or questions as well as the timeframe for providing status reports. The same precepts that applied to SLAs with end users should be used when drafting intergroup SLAs.

It is also key to establish overall accountability. Rather than handing off responsibility to a different group, it is preferable to have the person who was the end user's initial contact retain responsibility for the problem until it is resolved. Although this person may not be the one who will actually provide resolution, he or she will be the one who provides updates to the end user and who marks the problem closed when the end user is satisfied. The advantages of this approach are that the end user has a single person who is accountable for the problem resolution and that second-line responders are not interrupted by calls or messages asking for status. The disadvantage is that the user is distanced from the person who is actually resolving the problem.

The Legacy System Dilemma

When providing for support, it is important to consider not simply the new commercial off-the-shelf (COTS) package that will be installed, but also legacy systems. For the purpose of this book, legacy systems are defined as any existing systems that will eventually be replaced by the new application.

The fundamental problem with legacy systems is that although they are scheduled to be replaced, the date of that replacement may be years in the future. In the interim, there are end users who depend on those systems to do their jobs and who expect the systems to be maintained during that period.

As was true for support of the new packaged software, it is important to establish realistic end-user expectations and to determine who will provide the support.

When establishing expectations, all the points listed above are applicable. In addition, it is essential to define the work that will be provided during the interim "lame duck" period. Even if the company had previously established SLAs, they should be reviewed and potentially amended. Although it is to be expected that certain services that were provided in the past, notably fixing bugs, will continue, others may not.

Maintenance of software can be divided into three categories:

- *Corrective.* Fixes to bugs and other program errors. Corrective changes are designed to restore the system to its originally designed functionality.
- *Adaptive.* Work required by regulatory changes or changes in the business. These changes may add functionality but are nondiscretionary.
- *Perfective.* Modifications that add functionality but are not mandated. This includes enhancements.

For most companies, the first two categories of changes are nonnegotiable. They must be made, even while the system is in lame duck mode. The third, however, presents challenges. It is necessary to weigh the importance of customer satisfaction, which would be improved if all requests were satisfied, with the cost of enhancing a system that will be retired. The most effective method of dealing with this dilemma is to establish a steering committee to review all requests for perfective changes and to approve only those that have a compelling cost-benefit.

In addition to determining what work will be done, the company also needs to decide who will do that work. If support is already being provided by an outside firm, the answer is simple: have that firm continue to support the system, even though it may be at lower levels than in the past. In this case, it will be necessary to revise SLAs and monthly fees. Even though the per-user cost of support may increase as the system is retired from one or more locations, the overall costs should be reduced.

If, however, support is provided by in-house staff, the question is more complex. Support of legacy systems during their lame duck period can either be provided by the existing staff or be outsourced to another firm. There are advantages and disadvantages to each approach.

- Existing staff
  - *Advantages.* The primary advantage to retaining existing staff is continuity. The staff understands the systems and their idiosyncrasies, and the end-user community has an ongoing relationship with them.
  - *Disadvantages.* If, as is often the case, the existing staff's positions will be eliminated when the systems are retired, there is little or no motivation for them to perform their jobs well. They may also obtain new positions, leaving the legacy system without adequate support.
- Outsourced
  - *Advantages.* There are several advantages to outsourcing support of legacy systems. The first is that the outsourcer has a clear motivation to provide good service. (They will not be paid unless they do.) The second is that at least some members of the existing in-house staff can be freed up to work on the implementation of the new system. Their knowledge of the legacy systems can be invaluable in designing interfaces and in configuring the COTS solution.
  - *Disadvantages.* The primary disadvantage to outsourcing is the learning curve associated with new people assuming responsibility for the legacy systems. Even though the outsourcer's staff is trained to learn new systems quickly, there is still a transition period when SLAs may suffer. There is also an additional cost during the transition period because the company is paying existing staff to train the outsourcer as well as paying the outsourcer to learn. Other disadvantages are that if the in-house staff will be laid off, they have little incentive to help the outsourcer learn the system. This may lengthen the transition period and increase the associated costs. Furthermore, end users, who were comfortable with the in-house staff, may resist the change.

The success of a packaged software implementation is measured not only by how quickly and effectively it was installed, but also by how well it runs once it is installed. Because the postimplementation period is the majority of the software's life span, it is critical to plan for ongoing support and to staff that support adequately.

Reference

1. Martin, James and McClure, Carma. *Software Maintenance.* Englewood Cliffs, NJ: Prentice Hall, 1983.

Chapter 22

The Future

In addition to providing for ongoing support of the system, there are four more tasks to be accomplished before the project team can be disbanded.

- Conduct a postmortem.
- Implement a control plan.
- Develop a plan for decommissioning legacy systems.
- Establish a process for handling acquisitions and divestitures.

The Postmortem

Not all projects are successful, and even those that are might have been improved if the project team had had the advantage of other teams' experience and advice. The purpose of a postmortem is to document this team's experiences and provide written advice for future projects.

When the final site has been installed, the team should take an honest look at the overall project, identifying successes and failures and, in the case of the latter, suggestions for preventing them or at least reducing their impact. Although there are a variety of ways to obtain this information, two that have proven effective for some companies are brainstorming and sticky notes.

Brainstorming

All project team members participate in a round-robin with each one presenting successes while a designated scribe lists them on a flip chart. There is no discussion of any of the points until everyone's ideas are exhausted. At that time, the team begins to eliminate redundancies and group similar items. The same process is followed for failures. Once the redundancies are eliminated and grouping is complete, the team repeats the process, trying to identify ways in which each of the successes could have been made even more successful and how each of the failures could have been prevented or their severity lessened.

Brainstorming works well with teams that have established a high level of trust and where no member feels intimidated by another.

Sticky Notes

Less trusting or vocal groups may prefer the sticky notes approach. In this, each team member is given two different colored packs of sticky notes. Each person is asked to record successes, one per note, on the first color and failures, again one per note, on the second. The notes are then placed on a flip chart for consolidation and grouping. Mitigating actions can be identified either by using sticky notes in a third color or, depending on the team's comfort level, through an open discussion.

No matter which method is used to capture the points, the facilitator should stress that the activity is not designed to assign blame but rather that the purpose of the postmortem is to provide future teams with guidance and to increase the likelihood of future projects being successful. And, because teams may be reluctant to admit that there were any failures, the facilitator may choose to refer to failures as opportunities for improvement.

Like all key information throughout the project's life, these "lessons learned" should be documented. Exhibit 22-1 shows a sample postmortem report.

The Control Plan

Chapter 13 points out that sustainability is a hallmark of successful change and that measurements and controls are needed to create that sustainability. One method of implementing those measurements and controls is to create a formal control plan. A control plan, or as some companies call it, a value achievement assessment (VAA), has two portions. The first provides a mechanism for determining whether the benefits that were

Exhibit 22-1 Postmortem Report

Project name:	
Project start date:	
Project completion date:	
Team leader:	
Champion:	
Postmortem date:	

Project Phase	What Went Well?	How Could the Success Be Increased?	What Areas Needed Improvement?	How Could They Be Improved?

projected in the business case have been achieved. The second outlines the corrective action plan that should be implemented if the benefits are not achieved. Exhibit 22-2 illustrates a VAA.

Some companies, particularly those with Six Sigma training, address the second portion before the project is implemented. They conduct a brainstorming session to identify possible reasons why a benefit might not be achieved and ways to get the project back on track (the corrective action).

The advantage of identifying potential problems and remedies in advance is that the corrective actions can be implemented at the first sign of a problem, rather than having to determine the cause and possible corrective action. The drawback is the time required to identify and analyze problems that may never occur.

In either case, whether the corrective action plan is developed in advance or when a problem is first identified, it is important that the plan be implemented along with another measurement of benefits to verify that the corrective plan achieved its desired results.

Whereas the postmortem is a one-time event, the VAA is not. Even if no problems occur, the assessment should be repeated on a regular basis, ideally quarterly, to ensure that benefits continue to accrue. The project charter (Chapter 2, Exhibit 2-1) should also be updated with the actual results achieved.

Because of the ongoing nature of the VAA, the project's champion should assign responsibility to one individual and should ensure that the assessment is performed.

Exhibit 22-2   Value Achievement Assessment

Project name:							
Champion:							
Assessment date:							
Primary assessor:							
Benefit Category (1)	Expected Benefit (2)	Actual Benefit (3)	Variance (4)	Causes of Variance (5)	Plan to Correct (6)	Primary Responsibility (7)	Target Completion Date (8)

(1) The benefit categories that were established in the business case; e.g., cost reduction, cost avoidance, cycle-time reduction, error reduction.

(2) The projected benefit as shown in the business case.

(3) The actual benefit achieved as of the assessment date.

(4) The difference between expected and actual benefits. Positive variances indicate that benefits exceeded the original projection.

(5) Used only for negative variances. The assessor should convene a team to help determine the reasons why benefits were not achieved.

(6) Used only for negative variances. Should include a detailed plan, often referenced as a separate document.

(7) Used only for negative variances. The name of the individual responsible for implementing the corrective action plan.

(8) Used only for negative variances. The date when the corrective action plan will be implemented. A subsequent VAA should be scheduled to ensure that the corrective action plan achieved the desired results.

In addition to the VAA, some companies publish periodic scorecards, presenting a graphical representation of the benefits that have been achieved. Exhibit 22-3 shows a sample scorecard. Like project status communicated throughout the implementation, the purpose of the scorecard is to provide an easily understood explanation of the progress the project team has made in reaching their goals.

Scorecards are frequently posted on project Web sites, included in newsletters, or converted into posters to reach the maximum audience. Responsibility for creating them is often assigned to the person who will perform the VAA.

Legacy System Decommissioning

The third step is to ensure that legacy systems are run only as long as necessary. This is important because at least some of the expected project benefits will accrue only when all legacy systems are retired.

Many companies admit that legacy systems continue to run long after their expected retirement date, either because all the legacy data was not converted to the new system or because of end users' greater comfort level with the old system and reluctance to change. To avoid this problem, the company should develop a schedule for decommissioning legacy systems and assign responsibility for monitoring and reporting the progress of the systems' retirement.

Exhibit 17-2 in Chapter 17 can be used as the starting point for developing the plan. The team should review all interfaces listed on the inventory, revalidate the retirement dates, and then work with end users and the operations department to cease running of both the legacy system and the interface on the retirement date. At the same time that they are reviewing the interface inventory, the team should also determine whether there are other systems that will be replaced by the new system and when they should be retired.

Because system retirement is normally viewed as an IT function, the CIO is often the person who assigns responsibility for the monitoring once the retirement schedule has been established.

Acquisitions and Divestitures

Change is a fact of corporate life, and for many companies that change includes mergers, acquisitions, and divestitures (MADs). One of the challenges associated with those changes is bringing new locations, divisions, or entire companies onto an existing system or, in the case of divestitures,

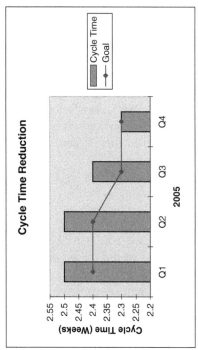

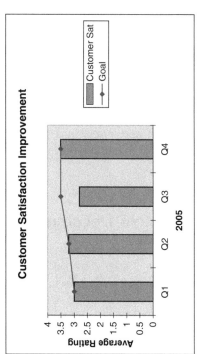

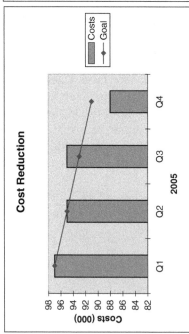

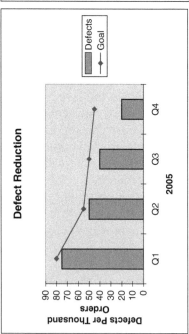

Exhibit 22-3   Project Scorecard

providing needed data to the acquiring company before removing the divested locations or divisions' information from the system.

When MADs are being evaluated, the IT department is often asked to provide a time and cost estimate for the associated system changes. Rather than having to guess and perhaps be wrong by orders of magnitude, it is helpful to establish an MAD plan as part of the initial project.

The project team has a better understanding of the problems associated with implementing the software than anyone and are the logical group to develop a guidebook for both acquisitions and divestitures. At a minimum, the document should include a basic project plan, showing all the key steps as well as notes about any idiosyncrasies the team discovered. Even if the company has never acquired or divested locations or divisions, the time invested in preparing an MAD guidebook is minimal compared with the effort that could be expended in the future.

With the project evaluated and the future planned, the packaged software implementation is complete. The team can now celebrate their success.

APPENDICES

Appendix A

List of Acronyms

ASP   Application Service Provider; a vendor who provides and runs packaged software on its own machines

CBT   Computer-Based Training

CIO   Chief Information Officer

COTS   Commercial Off-The-Shelf; a synonym for "packaged software"

CRM   Customer Relationship Management

CSFs   Critical Success Factors; those elements of a project that must go right if the overall project is to succeed

DBA   Database Administrator

DBMS   Database Management System

DLL   Dynamic Load Library

EDI   Electronic Data Interchange; the protocol for transmitting data from one company to another

ERP   Enterprise Resource Planning; the comprehensive suites of software that encompass most aspects of manufacturing and the supporting back office operations

FAQs   Frequently Asked Questions; normally a document that is part of the project's formal communications

Five Ps Prior Planning Prevents Poor Performance

Five Ws Who, What, Where, When, and Why; the basic elements that should be included in a project charter and many other documents

Four Ps Purpose, Picture, Plan, and Part; characteristics of successful change

FTS	Follow the Sun; typically used to describe 24/7 help-desk support
GIGO	Garbage In, Garbage Out
GPS	Global Positioning System
IP	Intellectual Property; proprietary knowledge including trade secrets, patents, trademarks, and copyrights
IPO	Input, Process, Output; the three components of the overall process
IRR	Internal Rate of Return; the interest rate that the company uses to calculate Net Present Value
KISS	Keep it simple, Stupid; the basic principle for successful implementations
MAD	Mergers, Acquisitions, and Divestitures
MSA	Master Services Agreement; the primary contract specifying terms and conditions as well as rates; may or may not include specific work to be performed
NDA	Nondisclosure Agreement; a document that vendors or individual consultants sign that prohibits them from disclosing any company confidential information; may also include noncompete clauses and assignment of intellectual property rights for anything developed while working on the company's account
NPV	Net Present Value; a calculation used to determine the value over time of the money invested in a project
OF	Outside Firm; a Systems Integrator, boutique firm, or general-purpose staffing firm that the company engages to assist with the project
PMO	Program Management Office; the team responsible for the success of a large project or program
RAVE	Characteristics of measurements and metrics; Relevant, Adequate to detect changes, Valid, and consistent over time, Easy to capture
RCS	Rumor Control Session; an informal communication method designed to help employees cope with impending change
RFI	Request for Information; a document requesting that a vendor respond to a series of questions related to his ability to provide the company with services or software; typically does not require firm price quotations
RFP	Request for Proposal; a document requesting that a vendor respond to a series of questions related to his ability to provide the company with services or software; normally includes pricing

RICE	Reports, Interfaces, Conversions, Extensions; the custom programming typically associated with packaged software
RIF	Reduction in Force; layoff
ROI	Return on Investment
SARAH	Shock, Anger, Resistance, Acceptance, Hope; the stages associated with major change
SCM	Supply Chain Management
SDLC	System Development Life Cycle; the formal process of creating and implementing software
SI	Systems Integrator; a firm with expertise implementing a specific COTS package
SLA	Service Level Agreement; defines the quality and quantity of work that a vendor will provide in a service-based contract; typically refers to support-type agreements
SMART	Specific, Measurable, Attainable, Relevant, Timebound; characteristics of good problem statements and service levels
SME	Subject Matter Expert; a company employee with expertise in a specific function, either a member of an end user department or IT department
SOW	Statement of Work; normally an amendment to an MSA, identifying the specific work to be performed but not the overall Ts and Cs
SPOC	Single Point of Contact; typically refers to help desks
T&M	Time and Materials; a method of paying for services based on the actual number of hours expended whether or not deliverables are produced
TCO	Total Cost of Ownership; an assessment of the cost of software or hardware over its expected lifespan; includes ongoing as well as initial costs
Three Cs	Clarity, Commitment and Conciseness; used to describe the characteristics of an effective project charter
Ts and Cs	Terms and Conditions; normally applies to contracts and refers to the nonpricing elements of contracts and license agreements
TSO	Time-Sharing Option
VAA	Value Achievement Assessment; the mechanism for determining whether the project's overall goals were met

Appendix B

The Project Charter

It can be argued that the charter is the most important document in a project because it is used to establish the project and provides a summary of key information. Although optional, its value as a single document that summarizes the project cannot be underestimated. Exhibit B-1 shows a sample charter. The remainder of this appendix outlines the use of the charter and explains how to complete each field.

Who creates it?

Although the project's champion provides information for some of the fields including the first draft of the project description and the list of team members and their time commitment, it is normally the team leader or a designated recorder or scribe who is responsible for creating the charter.

When is it created?

Key fields are completed during the team's first meeting. Others are added at later stages in the project.

Exhibit B-1 Project Charter

Summary				
Project description (problem to be solved)				
Start date		Target completion date		
Departments impacted		Processes impacted		
Estimated cost		Estimated ROI		
Team leader		Champion		
Benefits				
	Units	Current	Goal	Projected date for achievement/ actual achievement date	Actual achieved
Cost reduction					
Cost avoidance					
Improved customer satisfaction					
Other end-user benefits					
Team Membership				
Name		Role	Department	% Time
Schedule				
Milestone/ deliverable	Target date/ actual completion date	Owner	Estimated cost	Comments

Exhibit B-1 (continued)   Project Charter

Support Required		
Training required		
Other support required		
Critical Success Factors and Risks		
Critical success factors		
Risks		
Approvals		
Role/title	Name	Date
Revision History		
Revision number	Authors	Date

Who is responsible for updating the form?

The champion, recorder, or scribe has continuing responsibility for the accuracy and completeness of the charter.

How often is it updated?

Whenever information shown on the form changes, the charter should be updated.

Who can view the data?

At a minimum, the charter should be available to all team members and affected end users (although some companies may insist that financial information be removed before distributing it to external customers). Ideally, the charter should be available to anyone within the organization.

Field	How to Complete It
Summary section	This section serves to document key descriptive information about the project.
Project description	Enter a brief description of the project, including a summary of anticipated benefits. Once the formal problem and goal statements are developed, they should be added to this field.
Start date	Enter the date that the project was initiated. Depending on the company's preference, this can be either the date that the team was chartered or the date of the first team meeting. The start date should be entered at the first team meeting.
Target completion date	Enter the date that the total project is expected to be completed. Although this field is subject to revision as the project progresses through the various phases, it should be entered as soon as it is estimated.
Departments impacted	Enter the names of all departments that will use the new system or be affected by the project.
Processes impacted	If only specific processes within a department will be affected, list them.
Estimated cost	Enter the total estimated cost of the project. This should include internal costs and fees for any outside assistance as well as the software license costs.
Estimated ROI	Enter the estimated financial benefit, that is, the return on investment that is projected.
Team leader	Enter the name of the person who has been designated the team leader. Like the description of the project, this information should be available and entered at the first team meeting.
Champion	Enter the name of the project champion. This information should be available and entered at the first team meeting.
Benefits section	The purpose of this section is to quantify the projected benefits of the project. Although four potential benefit categories have been listed, it is likely that a project will have other benefits. These should be described and quantified on separate lines. When "Other End User Benefits" are quantified, it is important to replace the words "Other End User Benefits" with the specific benefit to be achieved.

(continued)

Field	*How to Complete It*
Benefits—Units	All entries in the benefits section should have the unit of measure specified in this field. Cost reduction and avoidance might be specified in percentages or in thousands of dollars, whereas customer satisfaction units might be "scale of 1 to 5."
Benefits—Current	Enter the current or baseline level of this item.
Benefits—Goal	Enter the projected level for this item once the project is complete.
Benefits—Projected date for achieve-ment/actual achievement date	Enter the date at which the benefits are anticipated to have been realized. When the benefits are actually achieved, enter that date, preceded with an "A."
Benefits—Actual achieved	Enter the level that was actually achieved once the project is complete.
Team membership section	This section identifies the people who will serve on the team, their roles, and the percentage of time they are expected to devote to the project.
Name	Enter the team member's name.
Role	Enter his or her role on the team. At a minimum, Team Leader should be identified, with all other participants being listed as Team Members.
Department	Enter the team member's department or, if he or she is an external customer, his or her company affiliation.
Percent time	Enter the percentage of time the team member is expected to spend on the project. It should be noted that this is an average, and that at certain phases of the project, participation may be at a higher or lower level.
Schedule section	This section serves as a high-level project plan, showing the dates on which various phases are targeted to be completed. Longer projects may divide phases into smaller milestones and may document the schedule for completion of specific deliverables such as process maps or benchmarking results.
Milestone/ deliverable	Enter the name of the milestone or deliverable.
Target date/actual completion date	Enter the date on which the milestone or deliverable is expected to be completed. When the milestone or deliverable is complete, enter that date, preceded with an "A."
Owner	Enter the name of the person with overall responsibility for the milestone or deliverable. This may not always be the team leader.

(continued)

Field	How to Complete It
Estimated cost	If there will be costs in addition to team members' time, enter them here. Costs may include travel expenses. Items listed in the "Support Required" section should not be repeated here.
Comments	This field can be used to indicate the completion of a milestone or to document the reasons for a changed target date.
Support required section	The purpose of this section is to identify any training or other types of support that are necessary for the project's success.
Training required	List any training that team members will need. End user training should *not* be included here.
Other support required	List any other items that are not currently available but that the team will need. This could include additional laptops or servers, a dedicated project room, administrative support, etc.
Critical success factor and risk section	The purpose of this section is to identify the CSFs and risks that the project faces.
Critical success factors	Enter the events that must occur if the project is to be successful.
Risks	Enter the potential reasons that the project may not be successful.
Approval section	The approval section serves to document the review and approval of the project charter. Approvals of other project documents are recorded on the individual deliverables.
Role/title	If the approver is the project champion or sponsor, enter the role; otherwise, enter the individual's title.
Name	Enter the reviewer's name.
Date	Enter the date on which the reviewer approved the project charter.
Revision history section	The purpose of this section is to document when changes were made to the project charter and by whom.
Revision number	Enter the revision number. Normally revisions are given sequential whole numbers.
Authors	Enter the name of the persons who actually revised the document. This may or may not be the persons who instigated the change to the document.
Date	Enter the date on which the revision was made.

Appendix C

Suggested Reading

1. Chorafas, Dimitris N., *Integrating ERP, CRM, Supply Chain Management and Smart Materials*. Boca Raton, FL: Auerbach Publications, 2001.
2. Conner, Daryl R., *Managing at the Speed of Change*. New York: Villard, 1992.
3. Eason, Ken, *Information Technology and Organisational Change*. Philadelphia: Taylor & Francis, 1988.
4. Johnson, Spencer, M.D., *Who Moved My Cheese?* New York: G.P. Putnam's Sons, 1998.
5. Kanter, Rosabeth Moss, *The Change Masters*. New York: Simon & Schuster, 1983.
6. Lewis, William E., *Software Testing and Continuous Quality Improvement*. Boca Raton, FL: Auerbach Publications, 2000.
7. Martin, James and Carma McClure, *Software Maintenance*. Englewood Cliffs, NJ: Prentice Hall, 1983.
8. Sikka, Vijay, *Maximizing ROI on Software Development*. Boca Raton, FL: Auerbach Publications, 2005.
9. Tayntor, Christine B., "The Outsourcing Contract, Part 1: The Process," *Information Management: Strategy, Systems and Technologies*. Boca Raton, FL: Auerbach Publications, 2003.
10. Tayntor, Christine B., "The Outsourcing Contract, Part 2: Terms and Conditions," *Information Management: Strategy, Systems and Technologies*. Boca Raton, FL: Auerbach Publications, 2003.
11. Tayntor, Christine B., "A Practical Guide to Staff Augmentation and Outsourcing," *Information Management: Strategy, Systems and Technologies*. Boca Raton, FL: Auerbach Publications, 2000.

12. Tayntor, Christine B., "Software Testing Basics and Guidelines," *Information Management: Strategy, Systems, and Technologies.* Boca Raton, FL: Auerbach Publications, 1998.

Index

C

Champion role, the
  change management, 202–203
  implementation of COTS software,
    160–161
  selection process for COTS software, 9,
    13
Change, dealing with; *see also under*
    Ground rules for
    implementation
  basics of change, 178–179
  communication, effective
    clarity, 183
    conflict, coping with, 189–190
    consistency, 184
    formal communication, 185–188
    informal communications, 189
    ongoing message delivery, 184
    rumor mill and grapevine, 184–185
    targeted audience, 184
  impact of change, 180–181
  negotiation process, 95
  overview, 177
  phased implementation, 144
  professional services agreements,
    117–119
  roles associated with change, 179–180,
    182
  scope, changes in
    overview, 202
    professional services agreements,
      117–119
    request for proposal, 59–60
    service contracts, 125–126
  successful change, components of,
    182–184
Charter, project
  clarity required for, 14–15, 18–19
  commitment, writing/focusing as steps
    toward, 15
  conciseness required, 20
  example of a, 16–17
  explaining how to use the, 292, 295–298
  overview, 14
  sample, 294
  SMART criteria, 15, 18–19
  team members, 19–20
Chief information officer (CIO), 264
Chorafas, Dimitris, 219

Clarity
  change, communicating, 183
  charter, project, 14–15, 18–19
Classroom training, instructor-led, 243, 244
Coding
  change management, 201–202
  configuration, 221
  customizations, extensions and, 240
  data conversions, 230–232
  installation, software, 208–209
  interfaces, 227
  reports, 235
  standards for COTS software
    implementation, 196–197
Commercial off the shelf (COTS) software,
    1, 3; *see also individual subject
    headings*
Commitment
  change, successful, 182
  charter, project, 15
  phased implementation, 147
Communication skills; *see also under*
    Change, dealing with
  ground rules for implementation,
    203–204
  leader, team, 23–24
  plan (formal) showing major steps, 148
  support/maintenance, software/system,
    269–271, 275
Company ownership with assistance from
    outside firms, 154–156
Composite ranking spreadsheet and
    vendor/product evaluation, 67,
    70–73
Computer-based training (CBT), 243, 244
Conciseness and project charter, 20
Conferences and identifying
    requirements/potential
    products, 46
Confidentiality and software licenses, 107
Configuration
  coding, 221
  defining the term, 217
  requirements, defining the, 218–220
  simple or complex procedure, 217–218
  testing, 221
Conflict
  change, communicating, 189–190
  company ownership with assistance
    from outside firms, 156
Conformance and software licenses, 108

CPSIA information can be obtained
at www.ICGtesting.com
Printed in the USA
BVHW04*0309030918
525858BV00010BB/45/P

9 780849 334108